Writing Between
Cultures

Writing Between Cultures

A Study of Hybrid Narratives in Ethnic Literature of the United States

HOLLY E. MARTIN

McFarland & Company, Inc., Publishers
Jefferson, North Carolina, and London

LIBRARY OF CONGRESS CATALOGUING-IN-PUBLICATION DATA

Martin, Holly E., 1952–
 Writing between cultures : a study of hybrid narratives in ethnic literature of the United States / Holly E. Martin.
   p.   cm.
 Includes bibliographical references and index.

 ISBN 978-0-7864-6660-3
 softcover : 50# alkaline paper ∞

 1. United States — Literatures — History and criticism.
 2. American literature — Minority authors — History and critism.
 3. Narration (Rhetoric) 4. Ethnicity in literature. I. Title.
 PN843.M145 2011
 810.9'920693 — dc23   2011035430

BRITISH LIBRARY CATALOGUING DATA ARE AVAILABLE

© 2011 Holly E. Martin. All rights reserved

No part of this book may be reproduced or transmitted in any form or by any means, electronic or mechanical, including photocopying or recording, or by any information storage and retrieval system, without permission in writing from the publisher.

Front cover design by David K. Landis (Shake It Loose Graphics)

Manufactured in the United States of America

McFarland & Company, Inc., Publishers
 Box 611, Jefferson, North Carolina 28640
 www.mcfarlandpub.com

For my family —
Rich and Nia

Acknowledgments

Parts of chapters two and five were previously published in earlier forms. Part of chapter two appeared in an earlier version in "Hybrid Landscapes as Catalysts for Cultural Reconciliation in Leslie Marmon Silko's *Ceremony* and Rudolfo Anaya's *Bless Me, Ultima*" in "Humans and the Environment," a special issue of *Atenea*: *A Bilingual Journal of the Humanities and Social Sciences* (*Revista Atenea*, ISSN 0885-6079) 26.1 (2006): 131–150. A section of chapter five dealing with Chinese American works written in Chinese was first presented as a conference paper titled "The Rewards and Perils of Multiple Subjectivity in Three Chinese-language American Novels" given at Fudan University, Shanghai, China, in 2005. The conference was "Querying the Genealogy: An International Conference on Chinese American Literature and Chinese Language Literature in the United States." This paper was later expanded and published as "Mental Illness as Metaphor in Hua-ling Nieh's and Li-hua Yu's Chinese-language American Novels" in *Comparative American Studies: An International Journal* 4.3 (2006): 347–367. This journal can be found online at www.maney.co.uk/journals/cas and www.ingentaconnect.com/content/maney/cas. Another section of chapter five, discussing code-switching, appeared in an earlier version as "Code-switching in U.S. Ethnic Literature: Multiple Perspectives through Multiple Languages" in *Changing English* 12.3 (2005): 403–415.

I would like to thank my husband, Rich, for reading and responding to early drafts of the manuscript, and my daughter, Nia, who never doubted I would finish this book.

Table of Contents

Acknowledgments	vi
Introduction: Ethnicity, Ethnic Literature and Hybrid Narratives	1
ONE • Magical Realism: Blurring the Boundaries Between the Magical and the Ordinary	21
TWO • Surveying the Land: Hybridity in Landscapes and Sites of U.S. Ethnic Literature	45
THREE • Mythical and Legendary Figures: Forming Fictional Multicultural Identities	80
FOUR • Comedy and Tragedy: The Ironic Double Spaces of Ethnic Humor	114
FIVE • Multilingual Expression: Hybrid Perspectives Through Language	146
Conclusion: Hybrid Perspectives and the Demarginalization of Ethnic Literature in the United States	184
Works Cited	195
Index	203

Introduction: Ethnicity, Ethnic Literature and Hybrid Narratives

"I learned to make my mind large, as the universe is large, so that there is room for paradoxes," writes Maxine Hong Kingston in *The Woman Warrior* (29). What exactly does this statement mean, and what is its implication for the study of ethnic literature? The paradoxes Kingston writes of generate from her growing up Chinese American — a participant in two different and often conflicting cultures. Through her writing, Kingston shows how she came to accept both cultures within her identity, not through privileging one over the other or through glossing over the discord, but by accepting both as part of her identity in spite of conflicting beliefs and views. As she says, she made her "mind large." Her expansive means of self-reconciliation should not be mistaken for assimilation, a process through which she would have gradually abandoned her Chinese heritage in order to be fully accepted by the dominant U.S. culture. To the contrary, Kingston creates a hybrid sensibility that recognizes and values both aspects of her identity, and even more importantly, goes beyond the two worldviews to a third alternative — one that allows her not only to accept both cultures and their interactions, but also to perceive what it is to live beyond the limitations of any one particular cultural view. Kingston is not alone in portraying a multicultural identity in this manner. Many ethnic authors, in order to express their characters' multicultural experiences, have incorporated a hybrid perspective into their works by using narrative strategies that simultaneously present two cultural viewpoints within one narrative space. The variety of ways in which authors create these double narratives, which I call hybrid narratives, to add multiple perspectives to their works and the ways in which hybrid narratives have helped to move ethnic literature away from its minority status within U.S. literature are the subjects of this book.

Literature written by authors who are members of minority ethnic groups was once located on the margins of U.S. culture, but recent developments in ethnic literature, connected to a growing political awareness of minority rights, are moving it to a position more central to the core of U.S. American literature.* Oddly, this is not because it is becoming more mainstream U.S. American, but because it is becoming more ethnic. Ethnic U.S. American writers are creating a center for their literature by reclaiming aspects of their heritage languages and cultures and incorporating them into their work. Often they convey aspects of being both American and a member of their ethnic group by using hybrid narrative techniques. The English language and U.S. mainstream culture hold primary places in U.S. American ethnic literature, but they have slipped from being the defining center and now must share the stage with other cultural traditions and tongues. Ethnic literature in the United States is a culturally hybrid literature, and as such, it presents a multiple view illustrating how two or more cultures can co-exist and how the ethnic writer in a multicultural context manages to tread the spaces in the betwixt and between.

Beginning with the Civil Rights movement of the 1960s and the signing of the new Immigration and Nationality Act by Lyndon Johnson in 1965 (abolishing racial discrimination in immigrant law), a period of unprecedented growth in ethnic minority population, awareness and pride followed. Along with the changes in social demographics, ethnic literature in the United States increasingly became a significant force within U.S. American literature. Ethnic literature, of course, was present before the 1960s, but from that decade on it has virtually mushroomed within the U.S. literary scene. As the voices of ethnic groups have strengthened in the political realm, so also in the literary sphere, as Native Americans, Asian Americans, African Americans, Mexican Americans and others have put their words to paper, transforming U.S. literature by introducing non–Anglo views expressed in voices that often speak languages other than English.

Before discussing ethnic literature specifically, it may be helpful to look at the concept of ethnicity or the word ethnic itself, especially as they are perceived in the United States. Going back to the 1977 edition of *Webster's New Collegiate Dictionary*, the following definitions are given for "ethnic" as an adjective: "1: HEATHEN 2: of or relating to races or large groups of people

---

*I use the term "U.S. American" instead of the more common "American" to specify the literature, culture and people of the United States, because the term American applies to a much broader region — all of North, Central and South America — and I do not want to usurp the term to apply only to the United States. However, the term "United States" does not lend itself to a pronounceable adjectival form, and so I have chosen to use "U.S. American." For an interesting discussion of the term American and its hegemonic overtones, see Janice Radway, "What's in a Name? Presidential Address to the American Studies Association, 20 November, 1998," *American Quarterly* 51.1 (March 1999): 1–32.

classed according to common traits and customs." "Ethnic" as a noun is defined as "a member of an ethnic group; *esp*: a member of a minority group who retains the customs, language, or social views of his group." The noun "ethnicity," simply, is defined as "ethnic quality or affiliation" (393). The first definition of ethnic as an adjective, "HEATHEN" (*Webster's* capitalization, not mine), seems startling in the present time; it has a negative connotation, meaning someone strange, uncivilized and irreligious. Although by the 1997 edition of *Webster's College Dictionary* it has moved farther down on the list of definitions for ethnic, it is interesting to note its primary position in the 1977 edition. Ethnic, at least as recently as 1977, had significant negative connotations, perhaps arising from the general population's fears of people who were different, or other. The fears have not necessarily gone away, but in regards to the term "ethnic," the connotations have become more positive in popular usage — ethnic restaurants, ethnic art, ethnic neighborhoods, are all terms that are now used to indicate something different, other, but different in an interesting, perhaps even adventurous, way. The definition in the 1997 *Random House Webster's College Dictionary* (which, incidentally, is the same as more recent editions) is quite different, and the change in definition from 1977 to 1997 reveals a growing emphasis on ethnic difference as a positive characteristic versus ethnic difference as a problem that needs to be assimilated away. The 1997 edition of the *Random House Webster's College Dictionary* defines "ethnic" as

> 1. pertaining to or characteristic of a people, esp. a group ... sharing a common and distinctive culture, religion, language, etc. 2. being a member of an ethnic group, esp. a group that is a minority within a larger society.... 3. belonging to or deriving from the cultural traditions of a people or country.... 4. *Obs.* pagan; heathen. 5. a member of an ethnic group [449].

And the term "ethnicity" is defined as "1. ethnic traits, background, allegiance, or association. 2. an ethnic group" (449).

Both the older and the more recent definitions of ethnic, either as an adjective or as a noun, deal with the term in regards to a person's origins, including race, appearance and whatever customs, languages and social views have been brought from the country of origin. It is evident, however, that the newer definitions emphasize culture more than origin as the shared characteristic of the group. The synonym "heathen" appears (along with "pagan") in the 1997 edition, but it has been moved from the number one definition to number four, and it is preceded by *Obs.* for obsolete. At least one definition in both the older and the newer editions specifies that in order to be considered ethnic, the person must also be part of a minority group. This might explain why people of English origin in the United States are rarely classified as ethnic — they are too big a group. Nevertheless, other groups from the British

Isles sometimes qualify as ethnic — the Irish, the Scotch and the Welsh, as do some groups from Western Europe such as the Germans, the Polish and the Scandinavians. What is clear from these definitions is that to be considered ethnic, a person must resemble the ethnic group to the extent that he or she manifests some of the group's characteristics, whether they be physical, cultural or social.*

As important as what the definitions do include is what they leave out. Missing is any explanation of the political ramifications of belonging to an identifiably ethnic group, and how much, if any, leeway or choice there is as to whether or not a person is considered a member of a particular ethnic group. Only the definition of ethnicity in the more recent editions indicates that being part of an ethnic group could be at least partly voluntary by using the words "allegiance" and "association" rather than limiting membership strictly to origins. This recognition that ethnicity could be at least partially a matter of choice gives a clue as to the possible future trend for defining ethnicity in the United States.

In *Beyond Ethnicity: Consent and Descent in American Culture*, Werner Sollors traces the development of the concept of ethnicity in the United States. From the confusion that generally surrounds the use of the terms "ethnic" and "ethnicity," Sollors has isolated two trends that have guided the U.S. American view of ethnicity from the times of the Puritan immigration to New England: descent and consent. Sollors defines these terms and their relation to ethnicity as follows:

> Consent and descent are terms which allow me to approach and question the whole maze of American ethnicity and culture. They are relatively neutral though by no means natural terms. Descent relations are those defined by anthropologists as relations of "substance" (by blood or nature); consent relations describe those of "law" or "marriage." Descent language emphasizes our positions as heirs, our hereditary qualities, liabilities and entitlements; consent language stresses our abilities as mature free agents and "architects of our fates" to choose our spouses, our destinies, and our political systems [6].

Although descent in the form of one's biological inheritance has obviously played a major role in considerations of ethnicity, the possibility of consent, one's action as a free agent in determining one's own destiny, has always been a viable factor as well. The theory commonly known as "the melting pot" proposed that while immigrants came to the U.S. with their own inherited ancestry (descent), they chose to become U.S. Americans (consent) and thereby agreed to transform their views and behavior in order to fall in line with the perceived U.S. American norm. In the 1960s, however, an influential book

---

*The discussion of dictionary definitions is not meant to be an exhaustive study, but merely to indicate trends.

entitled *Beyond the Melting Pot* (1963) by Nathan Glazer and Daniel Patrick Moynihan appeared, it recognized the fallacies of the melting pot theory and led the way for the revival of ethnic identification that has characterized ethnicity since the 1960s. It appears people did not want to melt away their ethnic backgrounds to become one, united U.S. American group, but on the contrary wanted to emphasize their ethnicity. Identifying strongly as part of one's ethnic group as well as identifying oneself as U.S. American became a choice. Metaphors for the United States turned away from the "melting pot" and instead became the "salad bowl" or the "mosaic," allowing individuals to retain their ethnic differences yet still operate together to form a cooperative whole. At the same time, the movement for civil rights in the 1960s sought to ensure that the rights of ethnic minorities were recognized by the dominant group so that according to law, one need not blend into the dominant group in order to preserve one's rights.

Although one may acquire an ethnic group by descent, through heredity, an emphasis on one's own ethnicity as a point of pride is also a matter of consent. But what about the choice of one's ethnic group? Can one choose one's ethnic group as a matter of consent? One need look no further than to ethnic and racial violence in the United States to realize that at times, there are significant political consequences to belonging to an identifiable ethnic group. Although in the past there have been acts of violence and discrimination committed against white ethnic groups, such as the Irish, the violence both in the past and in more recent times has primarily centered on groups of color — African Americans, Latinos, Asian Americans and Native Americans. And although not people of color under U.S. census definitions, the Jewish population and the Arab American community (especially since September 11, 2001) have felt the brunt of ethnic violence in the U.S. as well.

At times, people categorized as being members of a particular ethnic group that is a target of discrimination have chosen to improve their lots in life by "passing" as a member of another ethnic group that is not so much out of favor. Laura Browder's book, *Slippery Characters: Ethnic Impersonators and American Identities*, recounts the lives of a variety of ethnic border crossers, people who in order to gain some advantage or to escape some disadvantage chose to represent themselves as belonging to a different ethnic group than that of their origins. Browder looks at a unique genre of literature, autobiographies by ethnic impersonators, and finds that these ethnic impersonators escaped their unwanted identities by plunging themselves wholeheartedly into the stereotypes of their newly chosen ethnicities. Sylvester Long, a black janitor in the 1920s, for example, became the Native American Chief Buffalo Child Long Lance. Browder writes of him, "He not only authored a best-selling autobiography but became a movie star and had his own line of running shoes. He embraced his 'Indian' identity in every aspect of his life" (7). In more recent times, there is the example of Forrest Carter, the former Ku Klux Klan member who reinvented himself as a new-age Cherokee Indian. Carter attained national fame with his best-selling book *The Education of Little Tree*—a false autobiography about his nature-centered, Indian upbringing. Before Carter was exposed by the historian Dan T. Carter (same last name, but no relation) of Emory University as an imposter, according to Browder, Forrest Carter had sold a half-million copies of his book, Little Tree fan clubs had sprouted up around the U.S., and a Hollywood film of his life was being planned (Browder 1).

Whereas Browder presents some notorious characters who through exploiting racial stereotypes were able to shift identities and ethnically reconfigure themselves, such people are no longer so extraordinary in the United States. Traditionally in the United States, race has been looked upon as the most essential of the aspects of identity, being identified with biological inheritance and appearance, whereas ethnicity has been associated with culture — a more fluid aspect of one's identity. Furthermore, race in the United States is often limited to two categories — black and white. Of the white category, Ruth Frankenberg writes in her introduction to *Displacing Whiteness*, it is the "unmarked marker" and "whiteness remains unexamined — unqualified, essential, homogeneous, seemingly self-fashioned, and apparently unmarked by history or practice (e.g., the notion of 'racial-ethnic communities' as synonym for 'communities of color')" (Frankenberg 1). Equally nebulous, the black category sometimes means everyone who is "not white," and sometimes is only restricted to African Americans. As Browder points out, both race and ethnicity are "slippery" categories and are themselves subject to change (Browder 8).

Slowly, ethnicity in the United States seems to be becoming more a matter of consent. Although the options available for ethnic choices may be curtailed by one's race, this is not always the case. One can sometimes cross the border between racial categories by using the vehicle of ethnicity. For example, someone claiming to be Middle Eastern in the United States would be considered white, even if their skin color were dark. Native Americans, Latinos and Asian Americans, while certainly considered to be ethnic groups, often escape the categorization of race, falling somewhere through the cracks between the black-white polarity of racial thinking in the United States. Race and ethnicity have many interconnections, and the boundaries between the two are often blurry; sometimes the terms are used interchangeably, and for this reason they can be confusing. For the purposes of this work, ethnicity will be viewed as the broader category. Following Werner Sollors' suggestion as stated in *Beyond Ethnicity*, "it is most helpful not to be confused by the heavily charged term 'race' and to keep looking at race as one aspect of ethnicity" (39).

Concepts of ethnicity have undergone major revisions in recent years. In "Re-Thinking Cultural Identity," which introduces *Beyond the Binary: Reconstructing Cultural Identity in a Multicultural Context,* Timothy Powell provides a historical perspective on the development of Cultural Studies.

> For the past twenty years, the central project of Cultural Studies has been to deconstruct the epistemological structures of Eurocentrism and to recover historical voices that were overlooked because of an entrenched ethnocentrism that privileged the elite, white, heterosexual, abled, male, European perspective [1].

One outcome of this deconstructing process has been the formation of an analytical set of binaries such as "Self/Other, Center/Margin, Colonizer/Colonized" that have helped scholars of cultural systems work out the interactions of oppression (Powell 1). Powell traces the origins of binary analysis in these terms back to the writings of Frantz Fanon in the 1950s and 1960s. This first stage of binary analysis was necessary, argues Powell, because it brought into the open marginal voices that made evident the diversity of U.S. American identity. However, such binary analysis was and remains overly simplistic. It eventually led to the formation of new cultural centers, based on race and/or ethnicity, which led to the rise of identity politics and its preoccupation with determining authenticity. Describing the dilemma inherent in identity politics and the search for authenticity, Powell writes:

> Like Eurocentrism, the singular focus on trying to identify new ethnic centers tended to collapse and oversimplify the historical complexities of black, white, Native American, Chicano, Asian American, gay and lesbian, Puerto Rican, and women's cultures and the many points at which these cultures intersected, overlapped, or else came sharply into conflict [Powell 2].

Ethnicity is not a neat and tidy set of categories into which people can be categorized according to essential definitions. One need only apply for a job that requires the filling out of an Equal Opportunity Program (Affirmative Action) form to see the problems with trying to strictly define discrete ethnic categories. First, like many others, the creators of the Equal Opportunity Program forms do not try to distinguish race from ethnicity. The heading for the categories from which the job applicant must choose for self-identifying (based on an informal survey I conducted by looking at some fifty sample forms) most often simply reads "Race/Ethnic Group."* These definitions follow:

WHITE: Not of Hispanic Origin: *Persons having origins in any of the original peoples of Europe, North Africa, or Middle East.*
BLACK: Not of Hispanic Origin: *Persons having origins in any of the black-racial groups of Africa.*

---

*Although there are variations in Equal Opportunity Program forms, they are basically the same and almost all use the U.S. Census Bureau definitions for race/ethnicity included here.

HISPANIC: *Persons of Mexican, Puerto Rican, Cuban, Central or South American, or other Spanish culture or origin, regardless of race.*
ASIAN or PACIFIC ISLANDER: *Persons having origins in any of the original peoples of the Far East, Southeast Asia, the Indian Subcontinent, or the Pacific Islands. This includes, for example China, Japan, Korea, the Philippine Islands, and Samoa.*
AMERICAN INDIAN or ALASKAN NATIVE: *Persons having origins in any of the original peoples of North America and who maintain cultural identification through tribal affiliation or community recognition.*

Each definition is preceded by a place to checkmark the group with which the applicant chooses to self-identify, but the decision is not always easy or clear cut. The U.S. Census Bureau in the past used the definitions for race and ethnicity cited above, but used them somewhat differently from most Equal Opportunity Program forms.* When surveying and counting people for the 2000 census, the Census Bureau for the first time allowed respondents to check more than one category to indicate if they were of mixed race or ethnicity. On the 2010 census form the racial categories were increased, allowing respondents to check, for example, Korean or Japanese instead of Asian, or to write in their race. But most Equal Opportunity Program forms, and other similar forms, restrict the respondent to checking only one category. This creates an obvious dilemma for people of mixed ancestry, and for others as well. Egypt, for example, is in North Africa. An Egyptian who might be Nubian in origin, and therefore black in appearance, would be instructed to check white. Someone who has his or her origins in an indigenous people of Mexico might not know whether to check Hispanic or Native American. Would a black Cuban living in the United States want to identify as black or, as instructed, as Hispanic? Are people from China and India really enough alike to be lumped into the same Asian category? And what about the many people who are of mixed race or ethnicity? Even though respondents to these forms are allowed to self-identify, the complications are many and come from the mistaken notion that the boundaries between the categories can be made rigid and exclusive. The categories are too neatly divided to deal with the messiness of real life. As long as people migrate, intermarry and learn new languages

---

*These revised definitions, as used by the U.S. Census Bureau in Census 2000, were based on the 1997 revised standards on race and ethnicity of the Office of Management and Budget. Contrary to the popular tendency to think of race in the United States as either black or white and to consider ethnic groups to be numerous, the 1997 revisions established five racial categories: American Indian or Alaska Native, Asian, Black or African American, Native Hawaiian or Other Pacific Islander, and White. A sixth racial category, Some Other Race, was also added. The 1997 standards only allowed for two possible ethnicities: Hispanic or Latino and Not Hispanic or Latino, and this distinction has carried on through the 2010 census, even though the categories for race in 2010 have been expanded. I include this information to show that even when racial and ethnic categories are strictly defined, there are obvious overlappings and differences in interpretation. (See website information for the United States Census Bureau in Works Cited.)

and cultural customs, they will be hard to characterize in such a simplistic manner.

The aim of this discussion, however, is not to denigrate the purpose of Equal Opportunity Program forms nor of the U.S. Census which seek, respectively, to notify as many segments of the population as possible of job openings and to determine needs of specific communities based on population demographics. The purpose is only to show the mercurial nature of ethnic categories and the pitfalls of attempting to categorize people into specific groups. What the cultural study of ethnicity needs now, getting back to Timothy Powell, is theoretical paradigms that allow for the study of ethnicity within a multicultural context. Paradigms that allow for the fluidity of changing concepts of ethnicity and that take into account the interactions between groups as well as within, even if the interactions are antagonistic.

This call for recognizing the complexities and differences of cultures within a multicultural context is also the focus of an interview with Homi Bhabha, conducted by Jonathan Rutherford. The interview appears with the title "The Third Space: Interview with Homi Bhabha" in Rutherford's edited volume, *Identity: Community, Culture, Difference*. In the interview, Bhabha expresses what he means by cultural difference as opposed to cultural diversity. Cultural diversity, he states, is based on an ethnocentric view as to what is the norm, i.e., the dominant culture, with other cultures seen as variations upon this norm:

> Although there is always an entertainment and encouragement of cultural diversity, there is always also a corresponding containment of it. A transparent norm is constituted, a norm given by the host society or dominant culture, which says, "These other cultures are fine, but we must be able to locate them within our own grid." This is what I mean by a *creation* of cultural diversity and a *containment* of cultural difference [208].

The distinction Bhabha makes here is between *diversity* (which can be absorbed, assimilated, made "one" with the dominant norm) and *difference* (which retains its plurality). Bhabha goes on to say, "We really do need the notion of a politics which is based on unequal, uneven, multiple and *potentially antagonistic*, political identities" (208).

Yet for Bhabha, there is hope for communication between cultures not because of a shared or familiar content that comes from all members of all cultures being human, but from the shared predilection of all cultures for forming symbols (signifiers). The formation of signifiers by all cultures allows for the possibility of translation from one culture to another, both of language and of culture, and therefore, because of the predisposition for translation, no signifier can claim originality or essentialism. Each signifier exists in conjunction with its translated forms and may itself be a translation. For this reason, according to Bhabha, there exists within each culture an aspect of otherness because each has the tendency to form symbols and to translate them across cultures. This is what Bhabha refers to when he states that because of this element of otherness contained within each culture, all cultures are hybrids. But hybridity is not merely the existence of another culture within a given culture, but the synergy of the two that create what Bhabha calls the "third space":

> But for me the importance of hybridity is not to be able to trace two original moments from which the third emerges, rather hybridity to me is the "third space" which enables other positions to emerge. This third space displaces the histories that constitute it, and sets up new structures of authority, new political initiatives, which are inadequately understood through received wisdom [211].

The focus of this work on the creation of multiple perspectives through hybrid narratives within ethnic literature attempts to take this next step of examining ethnic works of literature within their multicultural contexts in a manner that relates the interaction of the ethnic culture with the dominant culture and, where relevant, with other ethnic minority groups. The intent is not just to examine aspects of the two composite cultures, but to see the "third space," the betwixt and between — where the combination of cultures presents new possibilities and provides the unique perspectives of ethnic literature in the United States. By using techniques that allow for the simultaneous representation of aspects of U.S. American culture and aspects of the author's native or heritage culture within a work of literature, these works cease to be marginalized and become a representation of the multicultural social and cultural makeup of the United States itself. They exemplify the concepts of cultural difference and cultural translation, as opposed to cultural diversity, because they do not assume the dominant culture to be the norm.

Although each of the chapters of this work could, conceivably, be a monograph topic unto itself, the purpose is to lay out an approach to studying ethnic literature through examining hybrid narrative strategies that can serve as the basis for a comparison for all ethnic works. In the past, the study of ethnic literature has often been restricted to that of one particular ethnic group, or a few related groups, such as Latino/a literature, Asian American literature, African American literature, etc. And although there is much to be gained through an in-depth study of one particular ethnic tradition, a comparative approach which looks at characteristics of ethnic literature in general may also have much to contribute to the understanding of literature in a multicultural context. Some authors, such as Jeanne Rosier Smith in her book *Writing Tricksters: Mythic Gambols in American Ethnic Literature* and Krista Comer in *Landscapes of the New West*, do consider more than one ethnic literature, but in these cases the category for comparison is limited to only one characteristic of comparison, the use of trickster figures in the first instance and landscapes in the second. The purpose of this work is to prepare the ground for further inquiry into and comparison of the individual, hybrid narrative strategies that ethnic authors employ to create multiple perspectives within their works. It is an approach that demonstrates that ethnic U.S. American literature is indeed reclaiming its ethnic character, and that through this reclaiming, it is commanding a central role in the literature of an increasingly multicultural United States.

With some exceptions, this study looks at works written since 1960 by U.S. American authors who self-identify as members of a particular ethnic group and who write about their own or their characters' multicultural experiences within the United States.* It includes authors who have immigrated to the United States as well as authors who are second or even later generation U.S. Americans. For those whose first language was not English and who learned their first language in a country outside of the United States where that language is commonly spoken, their first language and also their first culture will be referred to as native. For those born in the United States whose native language is English and whose first culture is U.S. American, their non–English language and their non–U.S. American culture will be referred to as their heritage language and culture. The aim of this work is not so much to focus on particular authors, but to examine strategies of narrative used for multicultural representation as illustrated by particular authors. Hybrid narratives used to depict multicultural experience include techniques such as magical realism, multilingualism, humor, and the use of figures from myth and legend such as saints, folk heroes and tricksters that create a multiple perspective affect within the works in which they occur.

The works selected for examples of these hybrid narrative strategies are primarily by Chinese American, Mexican American, and Native American authors, although some others are included. These three groups have been chosen for two reasons. One, there are a significant number of works being written in the United States in Chinese and in Spanish, and in combinations of Spanish and English. I include some works written in native language by Mexican and Chinese Americans who choose not to write in English. Although other groups of Latino Americans also write in Spanish, I concentrate on Mexican Americans because the borderland culture of the southwestern United States lends itself to a hybrid portrayal. Two, Native American works are emphasized because of the nature of reservations, which, like Chinatowns, barrios and the borderland spaces, are simultaneously separate yet also inextricably entwined with the geography of the United States.

*Multicultural here, as the word would suggest, refers to a character of a minority ethnic background in relation to his or her interactions with the white U.S. American culture and/or with other ethnic groups.

In order to clarify what is meant by a minority literature, it is helpful to examine the three characteristics of a minor literature as they are defined by Gilles Deleuze and Félix Guattari in *Kafka: Toward a Minor Literature*. These three characteristics are (1) the deterritorialization of language, (2) the connection of the individual to a political immediacy, and (3) the collective assemblage of enunciation (18). The deterritorialization of language refers to the language used by minority authors who write in a language that is not connected with the area in which they live, who cannot communicate through writing in their native language with readers of the dominant culture, and who, therefore, have a sense of inferiority about the language in which they write. The connection of the individual to a political immediacy refers to the tendency of minority writers to subordinate personal, domestic concerns on a small, individual scale to broader, national concerns that affect the political status of the group as a whole. And finally, the collective assemblage of enunciation regards the obligation that many minority writers feel to speak not for themselves as individuals, but for their ethnic group as a whole—to be a representative voice for their group.

According to Deleuze and Guattari, these are the characteristics that indicate a minority literature located on the margin of society. However, since the 1960s, ethnic literature has been moving away from these characteristics, and thus away from the marginal minority spaces it has occupied in U.S. American literature. Through presenting a multiple perspective by the use of hybrid narratives, ethnic minority writers reclaim their languages and cultures within their literature while still retaining the American context as the locus of their work. Each hybrid strategy used by ethnic authors portrays the multiple perspectives of ethnic life in a multicultural context. As will be shown in the body of this work, these particular strategies—elements of magical realism, the symbolization of place, mythical figures and tricksters, humor, and multilingualism—are especially effective as devices through which an author may present a multiple perspective within a piece of writing. Summaries of each chapter follow below.

Magical realism, the subject of chapter one, is a mode of writing that is especially well suited to multicultural works. The seamless, commonplace blending of the dichotomies of magic and the ordinary in magical realism and the characteristic blurring of other boundaries such as those between life and death, fact and fiction, dominant and subdominant echo two worlds that intermingle within a multicultural character when dealing with the sometimes conflicting dualities of living within and between two cultures. Magical realism provides a method for those who find themselves on the margins of society — marked for reasons of race, ethnicity, language, gender (or for any other reason)—to subvert the assumption of a center to U.S. American culture that is based solely on the unmarked norm (white, Anglo, English-speaking). In magical realism the boundaries blur and opposites can be reconciled. Writers can invert the concepts of center and margin and can remake the center, if desired, as their own.

The chapter on magical realism gives a brief background of the nature and development of magical realism beginning with Franz Roh's essay on Post-Expressionist painting, the first instance of the use of the term "magical realism."* Also mentioned are Alejo Carpentier's essay "On the Marvelous Real in America" and the development of Magical Realism as a literary movement in Spanish American literature with brief examples from Jorge Luis Borges and Gabriel García Márquez. The chapter, however, stresses that magical realism can be found in other regional literatures outside of Latin America and focuses on examples of ethnic literature in the United States that exhibit the characteristics of magical realism.

Wendy Faris' article "Scheherazade's Children: Magical Realism and Postmodern Fiction" provides the basis for a discussion of the characteristics of magical realism and for examining the relationship of magical realism to the postmodern. Although the characteristics of magical realism do fit in theoretically with postmodern thought, the ties to traditional ethnic culture are of central importance in magical realism. Magical realist, ethnic writers in the United States are concerned with preserving their traditions and communities from the possibility of usurpation by the dominant culture. Postmodernism is part of that dominant culture, and although magical realist writers partake of some of the characteristics of postmodernism, on the whole, these writers resist the mainstream and create a literature that represents their own views of reality by incorporating their traditional languages, histories, stories, and landscapes in an attempt to ensure the cultural survival of their own communities.

Just as the worldview of a novel can be doubly inscribed with both the magical and the ordinary, within the same space a place can also contain more than one historical or cultural significance. In U.S. American ethnic literature, landscapes and other spaces, both natural and manmade, have an integral role to play. The use of places that contain the histories of two or more cultures and the use of contrasting places as symbolic of cultural conflict are both means to create a hybrid perspective. These types of places, including both landscapes and manmade spaces, that contain a double significance are the topics of discussion in chapter two. The presence of two cultures on one mountain in Leslie Marmon Silko's *Ceremony* and the contrast of the south-

---

*To avoid confusion, the technique of combining realism and magic in a work will be referred to as magical realism with a lower case "m" and a lower case "r." In specific reference to the literary movement in Spanish American literature, Magical Realism will be capitalized.

western desert and the city of Los Angeles in N. Scott Momaday's *The House Made of Dawn* graphically portray the cultural conflict within the main characters of each novel. In *Ceremony*, the mountain is a doubly inscribed landscape containing both Native American and Anglo histories. In *The House Made of Dawn*, the southwest Native American view of traditional, ritual links with the desert landscape stands in stark contrast to the images of urban life and commercialized Native American traditions found in Los Angeles.

The landscape in Leslie Marmon Silko's "Yellow Woman," down to and including the type of road Yellow Woman walks on, accurately depicts the main character's inner feelings and her movement in and out of the legendary versus the ordinary world. The riverside plays a prominent role as the place where one goes to seek adventure, and the river itself serves as the transitional element, providing a crossing between the legendary landscapes of the Yellow Woman tale and the domestic spaces of ordinary life.

The dichotomies of Rudolfo Anaya's *Bless Me, Ultima* find their symbolism in the contrast of place. The plains represent the cowboy spirit, indigenous religion, restlessness and the sea, while the valley represents the farmers, Catholicism, patience and the river. Negotiating his way between the geographic symbols representing two ways of life, the plains connected with his father and the valley with his mother, six-year-old Antonio must reconcile not only where he will reside, but what type of person he will be.

The geographical contrasts of places which represent the ethnic minority character's struggle between two cultures need not always be natural landscapes. Urban landscapes can take on particular significance, such as Maxine Hong Kingston's portrayals of San Francisco and of Chinatown, an area which serves to preserve Chinese culture and yet only exists outside of China. Kingston also uses individual buildings such as schools and theaters to represent cultural spaces. U.S. American ethnic works make clear that where one lives is part of who one is, and to understand the place, or the changes in places, is to understand the character.

Whereas chapter two uses the vehicle of landscapes and other spaces as keys into the subjectivity of fictional characters, chapter three looks at ethnic group identities, a multiple-subject model for exploring individual identities, and at how mythical and legendary figures might provide an alternative subjectivity for characters by allowing them to imagine another point of view (that of the mythical character) in assessing their situations within their multicultural environments. The possible sources for a character's alternative subject, or alter-ego, include mythological, religious and cultural personages as well as tricksters. For example, the goddess Coatlique from Aztec mythology, who simultaneously represents opposites of male/female and birth/death, appears in Gloria Anzaldúa's writing as a model for overcoming duality. Fa

Mu-lan, the Chinese legendary heroine who took her father's place in war, shows up in Maxine Hong Kingston's *The Woman Warrior*, embodying both masculine and feminine ideals. Religious figures also have a role to play in providing alternative perspectives. The Virgin of Guadalupe, who symbolically unites the Native Americans of Mexico with the Catholic religion of Spain — thereby blurring the borders between the two cultures — figures prominently in the writing of Richard Rodriguez and other Chicano writers.

A special kind of mythical figure, the trickster, is important enough to warrant a section of its own. Found in the mythology and folklore of many cultures, the trickster has maintained a place in modern literature. The trickster's ability to change shape, size and specie make it an apt character for ethnic literature as a model for adaptation and change. Through transformations, the trickster survives and often triumphs, no matter what dilemmas cross his or her path. Two specific tricksters are discussed in both their traditional roles and in the roles they play in modern novels. The Monkey King, as he appears in the classic Chinese novel *Journey to the West* and in Maxine Hong Kingston's contemporary novel *Tripmaster Monkey*, proves himself to be a master of trickery. He uses his transformational skills to bring Buddhist texts to China in the classic novel and to build a community through theater in Kingston's novel. Nanabozho, the woodland trickster of the Chippewa tribe, is also famed for his adaptability. Like all tricksters, in his transformations he represents the many individuals of his culture, yet his mythological origins also represent the cultural unity that holds the community together.

Although traditional tricksters are often animals, in novels people can also take on the characteristics and functions of a trickster, showing through their adaptability to change and their quick wits the way to survive cultural transformation and upheaval. Whittman Ah Sing, the prankster of Maxine Hong Kingston's *Tripmaster Monkey*, through the medium of the theater, transforms from one traditional Chinese hero to another and from one figure in U.S. culture to another in rapid succession as he attempts to dramatize the entire breadth of Chinese and U.S. American culture in one very long play. The primary characters in Louise Erdrich's *Love Medicine* each carry a characteristic of the trickster Nanabozho as part of their individual identities. Together they form a trickster community that adapts to change and hardship in creative ways in order to ensure the continued survival of their culture.

Traditional tricksters and their modern counterparts show characters in the process of change, confronting conflicting situations that an ethnic, minority character must negotiate to form his or her own identity. The tradition of the trickster, therefore, is a natural addition for ethnic stories set in modern times. They portray the sometimes difficult process of adapting to change and do so with great playfulness and good humor.

Expanding on the discussion of the role of humor and community begun in chapter three, chapter four looks at instances of humor that contribute to inverting ethnic hierarchies in U.S. society. Notions of the dominant and the subdominant group are often flipped in ethnic humor, putting the oppressed group in a superior position. Since humor receives a special dispensation to transgress the social boundaries of propriety, it has been an effective means for changing how people in the United States view ethnicity and social hierarchies. Humor leads to more tolerant attitudes toward minority groups as it provides a lighthearted, indirect way of transversing cultural difference. The subjects ethnic writers choose for humor include not only the obviously funny aspects of life, but also darker situations which in reality may be a source of pain or anxiety, such as instances of ironic humor based on discrimination, language miscommunication, conflicting cultural differences and other misunderstandings experienced between ethnic groups. In these cases, humor serves to mitigate pain and lightens a situation that otherwise could only be tragic.

The subject of cultural differences is a natural one for those living between two cultures who need to reconcile in some way the conflicts of a multicultural life. Humor gives a means to highlight and to work through the dualities of the two cultural systems in a manner that downplays the potential seriousness of the situation. Such humor may serve a political end by distinguishing the "us" from "them," and thereby contributing to feelings of group solidarity. Or, on the contrary, a character may want to divide him- or herself from his or her ethnic group, as in Gish Jen's humorous portrayal of a Chinese American girl's conversion to Judaism in *Mona in the Promised Land*.

Chapter five focuses on the multilingual uses of language in ethnic literature. Multilingual narratives are one of the key factors in the movement of ethnic works from the margins of U.S. American literature toward the center, as the strategy of writing in multiple languages, often without translation, is a reclaiming of the writer's native language within the U.S. American context. The chapter, therefore, begins with a discussion of the first characteristic of a minority literature as described by Gilles Deleuze and Félix Guattari in *Kafka: Toward a Minor Literature*: the deterritorialization of language. Speaking of the German-speaking Jews in Prague as an example, the authors show how a minor literature is at least partially the result of authors not being able to speak or write fluently the language of the country in which they live, and when they write in their native language, they can only reach a limited, minority audience who also speaks that language. The minority language itself is deemed to have a lower status than the language of the area, even by those who speak and write in the minority language. The result is what Deleuze and Guattari termed a minor literature. In contrast to the notion of a deterritorialized language as the hallmark of a minor literature, ethnic writers in the U.S. have reasserted their native or heritage languages into their works in a manner that intermingles the non–English language with English. By this means, the writers have inserted their works into the center of U.S. American literature without having to write exclusively in English.

Mikhail Bakhtin's notion of heteroglossia as described in *The Dialogic Imagination* claims that the novel contains a variety of language forms and registers, and that "the novel can be defined as a diversity of social speech types (sometimes even diversity of languages) and a diversity of individual voices, artistically organized" (262). The interactions of these languages and their varieties, the dialogic of them, argues Bakhtin, are essential to the genre of the novel which contains many more languages than just that of the author or the narrator. Each language element contributes to the overall meaning of the work, and it is how the languages work together that creates the style and texture of the novel, not any particular language functioning alone. Thus the use of multilingualism by ethnic authors in the U.S. exemplifies the multi-languaged and multi-voiced qualities that Bakhtin describes as instances of heteroglossia.

The writing of a U.S. American work wholly in a language other than English may not seem to be a multilingual technique at first appearance, but when the author uses this language to express uniquely U.S. American ideas and experiences, a hybrid perspective is created through the opposition of the non–English language describing situations that are set in an English-speaking context. The works written in Chinese by Chinese American author Nieh Hua-ling, such as *Sang ching yu tau hong* (*Mulberry and Peach*), provide an example. This novel follows a young Chinese woman's journey to the United States and relates her experiences with U.S. American culture. The tension created between the use of the Chinese language to describe places, situations and customs within the United States portrays the cultural "betweenness" the young woman feels. For example, the woman applies a Chinese concept of eating people, used in modern Chinese literature as a symbol of the inhumaneness with which people treated each other under the traditional Confucian bureaucracy, to the story of Donner Pass, an instance of a nineteenth-century wagon train traveling west that becomes stranded in the snowbound mountains between Nevada and California. For the sake of survival, the stranded people resort to cannibalism, eating the dead members of their party. Instead of interpreting the story of Donner Pass as a willingness on the part of people to do anything to survive in the winter wilderness, the woman views the legend as characteristic of U.S. American cruelty.

Code-switching is a bilingual use of language that involves writing the work in two languages. The author switches between the two to create desired effects, sometimes aesthetic and sometimes political, and the switching gives a hybrid perspective to the work. Code-switching can emphasize the bilingual person's experiences of multiplicity, can show authenticity through the vehicle of language, and can point out aspects of multicultural experience not easily accessible through the use of English alone. The rules and occasions for code-switching follow specific patterns, and the language used can add meaning beyond the words themselves. Gloria Anzaldúa's *Borderlands/La Frontera* provides an example of a work which creatively incorporates code-switching to enhance its meaning.

When the author cannot assume that words from her non–English language will be understood by most readers, she may insert translations as does Pat Mora in her novel *House of Houses*. Another author might insert mini language lessons within the text to explain a term or concept. Gish Jen, for example, explains in *Typical American* the resultative verb forms of the Chinese "to see" and "to hear" which indicate whether or not the object perceived by the subject was indeed seen or heard.

Henry Louis Gates' explanation of "Signifying," a way of talking which alters the normal meaning of the English word, is an example of a double-voiced, hybrid type of speech originating in the African American community. Signifying uses the English language, but still manages to create a multilingual effect. The alteration in the meanings and implications of the words gives the language a multiple perspective since the altered word not only carries its new meaning, but also retains vestiges of the old. The meaning of an expression, often ironic, relies on the gap between the accustomed meaning of the word and the new meaning it receives from Signifying.

Metalanguage, instances when characters or narrators discuss language itself, adds a multilingual effect to a narrative text. In *Hunger of Memory*, Richard Rodriguez vividly describes the sounds of the Spanish language. Although he uses very little actual Spanish in the text, the reader senses the presence of the Spanish language throughout the book as it is integrally connected with Rodriguez's topic regarding the loss of cultural roots. Other examples of characters discussing language come from Louise Erdrich's *Love Medicine* in which the characters occasionally reflect on the significance of the use of the old language in different contexts and by different people.

Finally, the use of silence in a text can be a form of multilingualism when it is used in a manner specific to an ethnic minority culture. King-Kok Cheung's notion of articulate silence is particularly common in the works of Asian-American women. When using articulate silence, the author indirectly tells the narrative and allows dreams, myths and legends to express the intended meanings of a work. Maxine Hong Kingston's *The Woman Warrior* exemplifies the use of silence and its many causes, forms and meanings. Silence also plays a significant role in Sigrid Nunez's autobiographical novel, *A Feather on the Breath of God*, as the key characteristic she remembers about her father.

The conclusion looks again at the characteristics of a minor literature as defined by Deleuze and Guattari and examines them in relation to what has been stated in the earlier chapters of the text. The conclusion emphasizes that the use of hybrid narratives, which give voice to the viewpoints and languages of the ethnic author's native or heritage culture, are moving ethnic literature away from the margins of U.S. American literature and away from its minority status. Ethnic literature, with its incorporation of multicultural aspects, does not merely enrich U.S. American literature, it is already a crucial part of the literary culture of the United States. To fully appreciate the contributions of ethnic writing to U.S. literature, there is a need for further investigation into the characteristics of this literature and the literary techniques employed to bring hybrid perspectives into the texts themselves. Multiculturalism reflects the reality of the United States today, and an understanding of the hybridity presented in ethnic literature can only lead to a fuller appreciation of what ethnic writers bring to the literary culture of the United States.

Chapter One

Magical Realism: Blurring the Boundaries Between the Magical and the Ordinary

A man curses the rain in the Philippines and causes a drought in New Mexico; a saint appears in a woman's greasy oven window to tell her where to look for her deceased daughter; a dead three-year-old rises from her coffin and flies to the top of a church — unusual happenings? Normally, yes, but not so in the literature of magical realism. The works of literature discussed in this chapter interweave elements of magic and the ordinary to create a complex worldview in which the appearance of a spirit is as expected as a neighbor coming by for coffee.

One conclusion to be drawn from the introduction might be that the boundaries between ethnicities are not rigidly fixed, that the *choosing* of one's ethnic identification, to some extent, depends not only on one's inherited origin, but to some extent *is* a matter of choice or self-identification. The boundaries between ethnic groups, however, are not the only divisions that blur within the pages of ethnic literature. In the genre of magical realism (an intentional oxymoron), the very worldview presented consists of a melding of the magical and the ordinary. Magical realism lends itself well as a form of expression to ethnic works in a multicultural environment because it embodies a hybrid blending of opposites. Commonplace binary configurations — magic and reality, life and death, body and spirit, fact and fiction, self and other, center and margin — commingle and coexist on an equal footing. Neither aspect is more important nor more characteristic of reality, and consequently, the coexistence of these opposites destabilizes or displaces the usually accepted hierarchies normally found within binary relations. This commingling of opposites resembles the complexity of two or more worldviews that ethnic writers, their narrators, and their characters must contend with as part of being a minority culture within a multicultural setting. However, a reader should keep in mind that magical real literature *is* literature, and is meant to be read as literature, intentionally crafted to create a particular affect, and not as a literal depiction of the authors' ethnic beliefs or as a means of exoticizing so-called "primitive" ways of viewing the world. Frederick Luis Aldama reinforces this view in *Postethnic Narrative Criticism*, stating that "the most basic property of a literary text is that it performs within society ... as a literary text. That is, a text is a piece of literature when and only when the community of readers does not regard it primarily as a source of information or as a conveyor of truth or falsity, but, instead, reads it as a narrative with its own kind of rationale" (7).

Although there exists some disagreement on the exact definition of magical realism* and controversy over whether the term can be applied to any works other than the literature of Latin America, this work follows the view of Lois Parkinson Zamora and Wendy B. Faris as expressed in their introduction to *Magical Realism: Theory, History, Community*.† Zamora and Faris refute the idea that the term "magical realism" can only apply to a specific movement within Latin American literature and argue that magical realism occurs in literatures throughout the world:

> It is true that Latin Americanists have been prime movers in developing the critical concept of magical realism and are still primary voices in its discussion, but this collection considers magical realism an international commodity. Almost as a return on capitalism's hegemonic investment in its colonies, magical realism is especially alive and well in postcolonial contexts and is now achieving a compensatory extension of its market worldwide [2].

Of key importance to this study, magical realism also finds fertile ground within ethnic literature in the United States. Magical realism has an appeal for many ethnic writers in the U.S. not only because of its tendency to subvert hierarchical relations, thus challenging the status quo of all binary relationships, but also because it reverts back to the traditional, heritage world views of some U.S. American ethnic groups. These traditional world views still have

---

*To avoid confusion, I remind the reader that the technique of combining realism and magic in a work will be referred to as magical realism with a lower case "m" and a lower case "r." In specific reference to the literary movement in Spanish American literature, Magical Realism will be capitalized.

†To understand the strong association between magical realism and Latin American literature, see Alejo Carpentier, "On the Marvelous Real in America" (1949); Angel Flores, "Magical Realism in Spanish American Fiction" (1955); Luis Leal, "Magical Realism in Spanish American Literature" (1967); and Amaryll Chanady, "The Territorialization of the Imaginary in Latin America: Self-Affirmation and Resistance to Metropolitan Paradigms." All three are collected in Lois Parkinson Zamora and Wendy B. Faris, eds., *Magical Realism: Theory, History, Community* (Durham: Duke University Press, 1995).

some credence among contemporary members of ethnic society. Indeed, often these shared views, along with traditional customs and practices of the people, provide a cohesive factor for the ethnic community and attract those members who wish to maintain a traditional sense of their ethnic identity. In her article "Past-On Stories: History and the Magically Real, Morrison and Allende on Call," P. Gabrielle Foreman emphasizes that the appeal of magical realism, as opposed to fantasy or surrealism, is that it harkens back to historical, ethnic traditions and through these traditions relates the individual to the community:

> It is in the revelation of family histories that the worlds of *The House of the Spirits* and *Song of Solomon* are constituted: worlds full of walking, talking ghosts, women with green hair and no navels, marvelous worlds. Magic realism, unlike the fantastic or the surreal, presumes that the individual requires a bond with the traditions and faith of the community, that s/he is historically constructed and connected [286].

Magical realism does not separate the magic and the ordinary worlds from each other. In fact, the magic often seems to be an extension of the ordinary. Unlike in fantasy where the character must often cross over (through a looking glass, trap door, secret tunnel, etc.) into the fantasy realm and expects, at some point, to return to the ordinary, in magical realism, both worlds coexist within the same space and both are integral to reality. Characters who hold a magical real view of the world accept the intermixing of magic as part of their everyday lives. They do not acknowledge divisions between what is ordinary and what is magical, but accept both as the vital components of reality. Rawdon Wilson describes the coexistence of the two realms within one reality in his chapter "Metamorphoses of Fictional Space: Magical Realism":

> Try to imagine it as if two distinct geometries had been inscribed onto the same space. Think of it as copresence, as duality and mutual tolerance, as different geometries at work constructing a double space. Magical realism focuses the problem of fictional space. It does this by suggesting a model of how different geometries, inscribing boundaries that fold and refold like quicksilver, can superimpose themselves upon one another [Wilson 210].

And later in the same chapter, Wilson writes:

> The hybrid nature of this space becomes evident when you observe the ease, the purely natural way in which abnormal, experientially impossible (and empirically unverifiable) events take place. It is as if they had always already been there; their abnormality normalized from the moment that their magical realist worlds were imagined. The narrative voice bridges the gap between ordinary and bizarre, smoothing the discrepancies, making everything seem normal [Wilson 220].

This acceptance of the magical within the ordinary routines of daily living, without searching for a logical explanation or cause, forms the keystone of magical realism and distinguishes it from fantasy.*

A Brief History of Magical Realism: From Art to Literature

Franz Roh, a German art critic, was the first to use the term "magic realism" in his work, *Post-Expressionism, Magical Realism*† that appeared in Germany in 1925, describing the paintings of Post-Expressionism. Roh saw a return to Realism in the figural style of the Post-Expressionists after the Expressionists' preoccupation with abstract, fantastic and exotic art. But although the Post-Expressionists returned to painting identifiable, real objects, there was a significant difference in the manner of presenting the objects that differed from the earlier Realism:

> But consider carefully, this new world of objects is still alien to the current idea of Realism. How it stupefies the rearguard and seems to them almost as inappropriate as Expressionism itself! How it employs various techniques inherited from the previous period, techniques that endow all things with a deeper meaning and reveal mysteries that always threaten the secure tranquility of simple ingenuous things: excessively large bodies, lying with the weight of blocks on a skimpy lawn; objects that don't imitate the least movement but that end surprisingly real, strange mysterious designs that are nevertheless visible down to their smallest details! [Roh 18].

---

*One type of fantasy, however, does bear some resemblance to magical realism. This is the type of fantasy Tzvetan Todorov termed the "marvelous" in *The Fantastic: A Structural Approach to a Literary Genre*, trans. Richard Howard (Cleveland: Case Western Reserve University Press, 1973). In the genre of the marvelous, supernatural events are accepted and provoke no surprise in the characters. However, unlike magical realism, the events are still subject to laws even though "new laws of nature must be entertained to account for the phenomena" (41).

†The original title was *Nach-Expressionismus, Magischer Realismus: Probleme der neuesten Europäischen Malerei* (Leipzig: Klinkhardt and Biermann, 1925).

Most critics and theorists of magical realism use either the term "magic" or "magical" realism, with the meaning of both being interchangeable. Maggie Ann Bowers, however, has distinguished between the two terms, reserving magic realism to mean "a term introduced in 1925 referring to [visual] art that attempts to produce a clear depiction of reality that includes a presentation of the mysterious elements of everyday life." This definition accords most closely with Roh's sense of the term "magic(al) realism," although his works have been discussed and translated with both "magic" and "magical" being used. Bowers defines magical realism as "a term introduced in the 1940s referring to narrative art that presents extraordinary occurrences as an ordinary part of everyday reality." When using a term to encompass both magic realism and magical realism, Bowers uses "magic(al)" (131). Distinguishing between magic(al) realism in the visual arts and in literature is useful, but since so many theorists use the terms interchangeably, it is difficult to be consistent. I have chosen to use "magic realism" in my own writing when specifically discussing the visual arts and to otherwise use "magical realism" except when directly quoting an author who uses the term "magic realism."

What Roh sees in the new art is a depiction of ordinary objects, but the realistic objects have an aura of mystery, of magic, that emanates from them. In describing why he uses the term "magic" in his book to describe the objects, Roh claims in the preface that if he used the word mystic, it would seem as though the mystery descended from another realm, but with the objects of magic realism, he writes, "I wish to indicate that the mystery does not descend to the represented world, but rather hides and palpitates behind it" (Roh 16). With these words Roh establishes the foremost characteristic of magic realism, that the magic must seem to be an integral part of the real world. Whereas the old Realists merely painted the exteriors of objects, and the Expressionists only the inner essences and spirits of the objects, magic realism shows the object from its inner essence, or spirit, to its outer surface. As Roland Walter explains in his book *Magical Realism in Contemporary Chicano Fiction*, Roh conceived of magic realism as an aesthetic category, a way of representing the mystery of reality through painting (13).

As Irene Guenther discusses in "Magic Realism, New Objectivity, and the Arts during the Weimar Republic," Roh eventually paid a high price for his support of the Post-Expressionist art movement, which he referred to as magic realism. As the Nazi party rose in power, they denounced the movement and prevented many of its artists from painting. The works were held up as objects for ridicule in satiric displays known as degenerate art shows or abomination exhibitions. Artists such as Max Beckmann, Max Ernst, Otto Dix and George Grosz were declared bolshevists, and Roh himself in 1933 was taken to the Dachau concentration camp. He was eventually released through the efforts of a noted art historian, Wilhelm Pinder. In 1962, Roh wrote a book about the atrocities of the Nazi cultural cleansings entitled *"Entartete" Kunst ("Degenerate" Art)* (Guenther 55).

Before Roh coined the term "magic realism" in his 1925 essay, magical realism had an important precursor in Austria that eventually brought about the application of the term to both art and literature. An Austrian writer and artist, Alfred Kubin, published an illustrated novel titled *Die andere seite (The Other Side)* in 1909. Describing this novel in 1995, Irene Guenther writes:

> In it, Kubin set out to explore the "other side" of the visible world — the corruption, the evil, the rot, as well as the power and mystery. The border between reality and dream remains consistently nebulous; *Unheimlichkeit* (uncanniness) prevades the novel, which takes place in the capital city of Dreamland in Asia. Kubin also illuminated "the other side" in "this side of things" in his disquieting illustrations in order to render the duality of existence and, thereby, achieve a unified double vision, a conjunction of the invisible essence of reality [Guenther 57].

An admirer of Kubin's, the writer Ernst Jünger corresponded with Kubin in the 1920s. "He was particularly interested in Kubin's binary concept — the invisible and the visible, the interior and the exterior in the existence of things, and the fusion of the two" (Guenther 58). Influenced by Roh's work describing magic realism in painting, Jünger began in 1927 to use the term "magical realism" to describe works, both artistic and literary, that had the qualities he sensed in Kubin's work. Jünger is considered the first to use the term in relation to literature.

Also in 1927, Massimo Bontempelli, an Italian writer and critic, extended the term "magical realism" (*realismo magico*) to literature in an article in the journal *900*. Although it is not certain whether Bontempelli had a connection with Franz Roh or not, Irene Guenther, in tracing the extension of the term magical realism from art to literature, provides evidence that suggests that Bontempelli and Roh might have had some connection through the German art and literary journal *Der Querschnitt*. Bontempelli contributed to the journal and would likely have read its articles on developments in modern art in Germany. Also, the German artist Georg Kaiser, considered by Roh to be a magic realist, assisted Bontempelli with the editing of some issues of Bontempelli's journal, *900* (Guenther 60).

Again in 1927, a pivotal year for the spread of the term "magical realism," Roh's book *Post-Expressionism, Magical Realism* was translated into Spanish and appeared first partially and then in its entirety in José Ortega y Gasset's *Revista de Occidente*, published in Madrid. Available and circulated in Spanish, Roh's work reached Latin America and had an impact on the field of literary criticism there. Once the term began to appear in widely circulated journals, it spread rapidly throughout Europe and Latin America, but it was in Latin America that the characteristics of magical realism were eventually transformed into the major literary movement now known specifically as Magical Realism.

Magical Realism in the Americas

Alejo Carpentier, in a 1949 essay, "On the Marvelous Real in America," develops a concept of magical realism that is uniquely American, *lo real maravilloso americano* (the American marvelous real) (Carpentier 88n). Carpentier's use of the term "marvelous" to describe the overwhelming effect of the uniqueness and beauty of America, however, has earlier roots. "Marvelous" was a common expression among the earliest Spanish explorers in writings describing their first encounters with the American landscape and its inhabitants. In the diaries of Christopher Columbus (who although Italian by nationality wrote about his voyages in Spanish), the word "marvelous" frequently appears to express his feelings of awe over what he observed, particularly in his observations of nature and of the original inhabitants of the Americas. In the following example from his entry of Sunday, October 21, 1492, Columbus describes the lush vegetation and bird life of one of the islands:

> Aquí es unas grandes lagunas, y sobre ellas y a la rueda es el arboledo en maravilla, y aquí y en toda la isla son todos verdes y las yervas como en el Abril en el Andaluzía y el cantar de los paxaritos que pareçe qu'el hombre nunca se querría partir de aquí, y las manadas de los papagayos que ascureçen el sol, y aves y paxaritos de tantas maneras y tan diversas de las nuestras que es maravilla [Colón 121].
>
> [Here there are some large lakes, and around and overhanging them is the marvelous forest. Here and throughout the island everything is green, and the vegetation is like in April in Andalusia. And the singing of the birds, it seems a man would never want to leave here. And the flocks of parrots that block out the sun, and birds of so many kinds and so different from ours that it is a marvel.*]

Nature, however, is not the only marvel of the islands, and in some entries, such as that of Sunday, November 4, Columbus crosses over from describing the merely marvelous into expressing belief in the fantastic in his description of what he anticipates he will find in his travels:

> Entendió también que lexos de allí avía hombres de un ojo y otros con hoçicos de perros que comían los hombres, y que en tomando uno lo degollavan y le bevían la sangre y le cortavan su natura [Colón 131].
>
> [I understood also that far from here there were some men with one eye and some with dog noses that ate men, and that as soon as they took one, they cut his throat, drank his blood and cut off his genitals.†]

In *Marvelous Possessions: The Wonder of the New World*, Stephen Greenblatt suggests that Columbus uses the term "marvelous" to such a great extent in his diaries because "the marvelous is closely linked in classical and Christian rhetoric to heroic enterprise" (74). He places Columbus' use of the term in the context of philosophical and aesthetic discussions, known in Columbus' time, regarding the voyages of Odysseus and the connection of heroism to the ability to present marvels that arouse wonder. Greenblatt also proposes that Columbus may have wished to associate his discoveries with a Christian sense of the marvelous, recounting marvels as a means of presenting the evidence of a spiritual presence. Thus, Greenblatt argues, accounts of the marvelous were an expected part of any telling of a voyage to the Indies, a place of fabled wealth, spices and other exotic products; and therefore, the term marvelous became essential vocabulary in the accounts of American explorations.

*My translation.
†My translation.

The term "real maravilloso" was actually first used in relation to Latin American literature by the Chilean writer Francisco Contreras in 1927 (Walter 15). But Carpentier, later in his 1949 essay, takes this word "marvelous" and extends its meaning to include all of the magical qualities that couple with reality in the concept of magical realism. In addition, he emphasizes the awe-inspiring quality of the American environment to create his concept of the American marvelous real. In Carpentier's view, Latin America embodies the magical in its landscape and its people, and because of its unique culture, geography and mixtures of people, unusual minglings and juxtapositions of objects just naturally occur. In the conclusion of his essay, Carpentier writes:

> Because of the virginity of the land, our upbringing, our ontology, the Faustian presence of the Indian and the black man, the revelation constituted by its recent discovery, its fecund racial mixing [*mestizaje*], America is far from using up its wealth of mythologies. After all, what is the entire history of America if not a chronicle of the marvelous real? [Carpentier 88].

Carpentier's notion of the marvelous real continues to undergo transformation. In a 1955 essay, "Magical Realism in Spanish American Fiction," the literary critic Angel Flores criticizes the then current approaches to the study of Spanish American literature, claiming that it had only been studied from thematic or biographical approaches. Neither of these approaches, he complains, paid any attention to the aesthetic value of Spanish American works, nor did they shed any light on structural or stylistic characteristics. Flores comments in the essay on the observations of the literary critic Dudley Fitts, and he agrees with Fitts' assessment that the overall state of Latin American literature was somewhat lackluster, lacking in literary giants. However, Fitts makes an exception (and Flores agrees) for the Argentinean writers Jorge Luis Borges and Eduardo Mallea. But Fitts, Flores asserts, does not go beyond singling out Borges and Mallea. He does not offer any reasons as to why these authors are exceptional. Flores claims that they and other exceptional writers of the time are noteworthy because their works adhere to a particular trend: "This trend I term 'magical realism'" (Flores 111). Flores traces the trend back to Marcel Proust, Franz Kafka and the artist Giorgio de Chirico. "Kafka," Flores writes, "had mastered from his earliest short stories ... the difficult art of mingling his drab reality with the phantasmal world of his nightmares" (Flores 111–12). Flores then goes on to explain how the combination of realism and the fantastic have characterized Latin American literature since the Colonial period, and he cites the writings of Columbus and of the explorer Cabeza de Vaca as early examples of writing that incorporate the magical along with the real.

In answer to Angel Flores, another Latin American critic, Luis Leal, challenges Flores' notion that Magical Realism derived from Kafka's work and disagrees with Flores over other authors that Flores considers to be Magical Realists. Leal defines Magical Realism in his article of 1967, "Magical Realism in Spanish American Literature," as follows:

> Magical realism is, more than anything else, an attitude toward reality that can be expressed in popular or cultured forms, in elaborate or rustic styles, in closed or open structures. What is the attitude of the magical realist toward reality? I have already said that he doesn't create imaginary worlds in which we can hide from everyday reality. In magical realism the writer confronts reality and tries to untangle it, to discover what is mysterious in things, in life, in human acts [Leal 121].

Leal agrees with Flores that in Kafka's *Metamorphosis* the characters acknowledge the man's transformation into a cockroach without great surprise or astonishment, almost as if it were a natural event, but the characters lack what Leal sees as an integral part of Magical Realism: "Their attitude toward reality is not magic; they find the situation intolerable and they don't accept it" (121).

Leal concludes his essay with an explanation of a key distinction between fantasy and magical realism. In fantasy, the character seeks to understand the logical reason behind the occurrence of a magical event because the world of the fantastic novel is still ruled by reason, despite the eruption of the fantastic. There are logical rules to be discovered in fantasy which may differ from the rules of ordinary life, but which nevertheless govern the fantastic occurrences. In magical realism, no such rules of logic exist. The characters merely accept that the illogical sometimes happens. "In order to seize reality's mysteries the magical realist writer heightens his senses until he reaches an extreme state ... that allows him to intuit the imperceptible subtleties of the external world, the multifarious world in which we live" (Leal 123).

Although some critics, such as Leal, claim that the literature of Jorge Luis Borges is too aligned with fantasy to be considered Magical Realism, many others view Borges to be an important early influence on Magical Realism in South American literature. In an article entitled "Sources of Magic Realism/ Supplements to Realism in Contemporary Latin American Literature," Scott Simpkins suggests that the inadequacy of language to fully convey reality is the motivation for magical realist authors. By incorporating the magical, the illogical, and the irrational, magical realist writers attempt to bridge the gap between language and the reality it attempts but fails to fully describe. One technique authors use to extend language into the realms of the magical is the technique of defamiliarization, a term coined by the Russian Formalists (literary theorists). When an ordinary object is presented with undue emphasis, with great attention to its details, or in an unfamiliar setting, it becomes something worthy of more attention than it usually commands in its ordinary mode of existence. An Andy Warhol painting of a Campbell's soup can, for example, draws the viewer to pay such extraordinary attention to the can that it may become transformed into art simply by the viewer's attitude towards it and its location in an art museum. This process is what is referred to as defamiliarization.

Borges, in his short story "The Garden of Forking Paths," proves himself to be a master of defamiliarization. The story is based on the reader's mistaken but normal assumptions that a book (in this case, a novel) is a piece of writing that follows a certain logical development of a story line, and that a labyrinth, in the context of the story, is a maze constructed, life-sized, outdoors. The main character of the story is Yu Tsun, a Chinese man who happens to be a German spy operating in England, who also happens to have had a famous great-grandfather, Ts'ui Pên, who announced that he would retire to write a book and to construct a labyrinth. Upon Ts'ui Pên's death, his relatives, including Yu Tsun, are unhappy to discover the novel is completely unintelligible with the same characters monotonously appearing over and over in different events and in different roles. It is only when Yu Tsun visits a renowned Sinologist, Stephen Albert, that he learns that the book is actually both a book and a labyrinth combined. In explanation, Stephen Albert tells Yu Tsun:

> After more than a hundred years, the details are irretrievable; but it is not hard to conjecture what happened. Ts'ui Pên must have said once: *I am withdrawing to write a book.* And another time: *I am withdrawing to construct a labyrinth.* Every one imagined two works; to no one did it occur that the book and the maze were one and the same thing [Borges 25].

Following a clue that Ts'ui Pên left in a letter, stating that he wanted to construct a labyrinth that would be infinite, Albert realizes that the book is meant to fork in time rather than in space:

> Almost instantly, I understood: "the garden of forking paths" was the chaotic novel; the phrase "the various futures (not to all)" suggested to me the forking in time, not in space. A broad rereading of the work confirmed the theory. In all fictional works, each time a man is confronted with several alternatives, he chooses one and eliminates the others; in the fiction of Ts'ui Pên, he chooses — simultaneously — all of them. *He creates*, in this way, diverse futures, diverse times which themselves also proliferate and fork. (Borges 26)

Thus Borges in this short story defamiliarizes both the normal concepts of book and of labyrinth to create on the one hand, a suspenseful spy story, and on the other, a complex statement on the nature of time and the infinite possibilities it holds for the future. Although most of Borges' work would not be considered Magical Realism, in this respect, extending language to create a fuller vision of reality, Borges resembles the Magical Realists.

Although the purpose of this chapter is to discuss magical realism in ethnic literature in the United States, there is another figure from Latin American Magical Realism without whom no discussion of magical realism can be complete. This figure is the Colombian author Gabriel García Márquez, Nobel Prize winner in 1982, and the quintessential writer of Latin American Magical Realism. Gabriel García Márquez displays his most famous and influential Magical Realism style of writing in *One Hundred Years of Solitude*, a novel permeated by the presence of magic to such an extent that the reader becomes accustomed to all manner of magical happenings, such as flying carpets and telekinesis, and accepts them with the same unquestioning attitude as is displayed by the characters in the novel. The novel covers a century in the history of one family, beginning with the couple José Arcadio Buendía and Ursula Iguarán, who encounter both the ordinary and the magical in the total reality of their lives. José Arcadio is an inventor, and the worlds of magic and scientific invention exist for him side by side. The family lives in the tropics, an area seemingly imbued with magic because of its strong sunlight, bright colors and exotic plant and animal life. Their village, Macondo, exists as a timeless, isolated realm. The subsequent generations of Buendías all carry the same, or very similar, names, a naming practice that integrates the living and the dead, the past and the present. The story itself is supposedly, within the context of the novel, written by a ghost named Melquíades who returns to Macondo after dying of a fever. At the end of the novel, another character descended from the Buendías, Aureliano, deciphers the text (it is written in Sanskrit as well as being encoded in a complicated manner) and realizes that the text contains the history of his family — written one hundred years ahead of time. As Aureliano reads about the history of his family, eventually reaching the accounts of his present life, a strong whirlwind begins blowing outside the house:

> He began to decipher the instant that he was living, deciphering it as he lived it, prophesying himself in the act of deciphering the last page of the parchments, as if he were looking into a speaking mirror. Then he skipped [ahead in the text] again to anticipate the predictions and ascertain the date and circumstances of his death. Before reaching the final line, however, he had already understood that he would never leave that room, for it was foreseen that the city of mirrors (or mirages) would be wiped out by the wind and exiled from the memory of men at the precise moment when Aureliano Babilonia would finish deciphering the parchments, and that everything written on them was unrepeatable since time immemorial and forever more, because races condemned to one hundred years of solitude did not have a second opportunity on earth [García Márquez 447–48].

If magical realism is an attempt to supplement language, as Simpkins proposes, to close the gap between the words and their referents and bring the text closer to reality by incorporating elements of magic, the writer must also be concerned with the limitation that is necessarily inherent in a book — that it comes to an end on the last page, and therefore, cannot be real. Borges attempts to circumvent this limitation of the text in his short story "The Garden of Forking Paths" by creating within the story a labyrinth of a book that contains a multitude of possibilities and that could, conceivably, go on infinitely. In this way, Borges avoids the artificial restriction of only one conclusion and brings his story more in line with the myriad possibilities for the future that are contained in life. In *One Hundred Years of Solitude*, García Márquez also attempts to circumvent the conclusion of the book by having the book destroyed by a magical whirlwind before the conclusion is reached. In a sense, the book never comes to an end. Scott Simpkins comments on the never-ending conclusion of *One Hundred Years of Solitude* as follows:

> By doing this, he manages to go beyond the bounds of realistic texts ... as his text ends both literally and magically within itself. The text virtually supplements itself out of its textual plane through a magical dodge which appears to prevent its conclusion (i.e., the physical end of the book). Yet, within the drive behind the magical supplement, a maneuver constantly out-maneuvering itself like a dog chasing its tail, the text always disappears into itself, an envelope of infinite beginnings forever grounded by the medium it employs to escape the textual dead end [Simpkins 157].

For Gabriel García Márquez, magical happenings in his works bring the representation of reality that a novel attempts to create a step closer to that reality. Part of merging the novel with reality, of erasing the border between reality and fiction, consists of attempting to break out of the textual limitations of the novel. In this respect and others, magical realism shares some characteristics with postmodernism.

Magical Realism and Postmodernism

Literary critics such as Wendy Faris and Theo L. D'Haen have written articles comparing magical realism to postmodernism, generally situating magical realism within the broader movement of postmodernism. Postmodernism itself is a term that, while first used in the 1930s by the Latin American critic Frederico de Onís, has only gained prominence since the 1960s. According to D'Haen in his essay "Magical Realism and Postmodernism: Decentering Privileged Centers," postmodern works exhibit the following characteristics: "self-reflexiveness, metafiction, eclecticism, redundancy, multiplicity, discontinuity, intertextuality, parody, the dissolution of character and narrative instance, the erasure of boundaries, and the destabilization of the reader" (D'Haen 192).

Although these characteristics of postmodernism can be found in works that could carry a double classification as being both postmodern and magical real, there are two related characteristics in particular which distinguish magical realism and which keep the two categories from being synonymous. Magical real writing, generally, comes from outside the economically, politically and socially privileged centers of culture. D'Haen writes, "It is precisely the notion of the ex-centric, in the sense of speaking from the margin, from a place 'other' than 'the' or 'a' center, that seems to me an essential feature of that strain of postmodernism we call magic realism" (194). But magical realism does not stop at merely presenting voices speaking out from the margins of society; magical real works actually attempt to displace the discourse of the central literary movements. D'Haen explains the strategy behind this usurpation:

> My argument is that magic realist writing achieves this end by first appropriating the techniques of the "centr"-al line and then using these, not as in the case of these central movements, "realistically," that is, to duplicate existing reality as perceived by the theoretical or philosophical tenets underlying said movements, but rather to create an alternative world *correcting* so-called existing reality, and thus to right the wrongs this "reality" depends upon. Magic realism thus reveals itself as a *ruse* to invade and take over dominant discourse(s) [195].

Magical realism is a way for those who for reasons of class, race, ethnicity, language, gender, or disability (or any other reason) find themselves on the margins of society, to subvert the assumptions of the center and to remake the center as their own. It is also a means of writing by which those who are part of the privileged center of society can reject the status quo by questioning the underlying assumptions of that privileged center, and thereby can present an alternative, more inclusive, view of reality.

Minority magical realist writers seek to preserve their traditions, histories and communities from the hegemonic force of a dominant culture. By incorporating into their works their traditional languages, histories, stories, and landscapes, these writers resist mimicking the mainstream and create a literature that represents their own views of reality. In this manner, they not only ensure the cultural survival of their own communities, but as their works continue to gain acceptance, these writers also bring into question the entire notion of a dominant culture.

Magical Realism in U.S. Ethnic Literature

As mentioned earlier in this chapter, Lois Parkinson Zamora and Wendy B. Faris in their edited volume *Magical Realism: Theory, History, Community* express the opinion that magical realism exists in the literatures of many countries, and their edited volume contains articles by literary critics discussing magical realism in the literatures of Germany, the United States, India, Africa and Japan as well as Latin America.

Recently, the strains of magical realism emerging from their countries of origin have found prominent places in ethnic literature of the United States. To provide a framework for examining the magical real characteristics of ethnic literature in the U.S., and also to provide an organization for the characteristics of magical realism which have been discussed so far, examples of works of ethnic literature which contain magical realism will be discussed in relation to the five characteristics of magical realism as delineated by Wendy Faris in her article "Scheherazade's Children: Magical Realism and Postmodern Fiction." This article not only provides a basis for an explication of the characteristics of magical realism, but also for examining further the relationship of magical realism to the postmodern. The five characteristics in brief are:

1. The text contains an "irreducible element" of magic....
2. Descriptions detail a strong presence of the phenomenal world....
3. The reader may hesitate ... between two contradictory understandings of events — one ordinary and one magical....
4. We experience the closeness or near-merging of two realms, two worlds....
5. These fictions question received ideas about time, space and identity (Faris 167–173).

The characteristic appearing first in Faris' delineation of the primary characteristics of magical realism is, not surprisingly, "The text contains an 'irreducible element' of magic, something we cannot explain according to the laws of the universe as we know them" (167). The magical events in magical real novels are events that within the context of the book, actually occur within the reality that has been created by that book. The events do not occur because the character is imagining them, hallucinating them, or simply making them up. The character does not awaken later to discover that the magic was all a dream, like Alice in *Alice in Wonderland*, nor does the character prove to be mentally ill or on drugs later in the book. The magic happens, and often more than one character witnesses the event.

In Ana Castillo's *So Far from God*, a three-year-old girl dies at the opening of the novel. At her funeral several days later, the dead child rises from her coffin and magically flies to the roof of the church. Although some possible explanations occur later in the novel as to why the child became alive again (perhaps she had an epileptic fit and only appeared to be dead), no explanation is offered or expected as to how the resurrected girl flew to the top of the church. Many people witness this occurrence, yet no one seems unduly disturbed by the phenomenon, except perhaps for the priest who suspects that her flight might be the work of the devil — as equally implausible as the child simply having the ability to fly. The witnesses accept the event and declare the girl to be a saint, but she is not considered to be especially unique in her sainthood as others have performed miraculous feats before her and were also bestowed with sainthood. In fact, when the girl, who becomes known as La Loca Santa (The Crazy Saint), refuses to heal people or to perform miracles for others to observe, "Santa" is dropped from her name, and she simply becomes La Loca. No one forgets that she died, came back to life, and flew to the top of the church, but in a world that is occasioned with many miraculous happenings, these events are not so extraordinary.

> Epilepsy notwithstanding, there was much left unexplained and for this reason Sofi's baby grew up at home, away from strangers who might be witnesses to her astonishing behavior, and she eventually earned the name around the Rio Abajo region and beyond, of La Loca Santa.
> For a brief period after her resurrection, people came from all over the state in hopes of receiving her blessing or of her performing of some miracle for them. But because she was so averse to being close to anyone, the best that strangers could expect was to get a glimpse of her from outside the gate. So "Santa" was dropped from her name and she was soon forgotten by strangers [Castillo 25].

La Loca continues to accomplish miraculous feats, such as curing her sister from horrible disfigurations that she suffered in an assault. For the most part, her miracles are done for her family within her home. It is not until the end of the book that La Loca develops a social conscience and a concern for others, primarily because of the tragedies she sees her sisters endure in their interactions with the world. In spite of her extreme isolation, La Loca develops AIDS, and there is absolutely no way, even in the mind of the most suspicious reader, that she could have contracted the disease in any of the known, possible ways. The reader must conclude that La Loca magically gives the disease to herself as an act of compassion for those who are suffering from AIDS. Because her isolated way of life is well known by the people of the village, their awareness of the disease is heightened and La Loca, like a well-known actor or singer, lends her celebrity to call attention to the disease: "Many still believed in her. A great wave of sadness, like a dry ocean tide, went over the whole region when the news spread that La Loquita Santa was dying again" (Castillo 231).

Often the magic in magical realism serves as social criticism, and the magic performed by La Loca in *So Far from God* makes a strong statement against the uncaring, discriminatory practices of the dominant society against Chicanos and of men against women. After her resurrection as a three-year-old, for example, La Loca avoids people because of their smell. Their odor, she claims, reminds her of the smell of the places she went while she was dead. And later, she senses the smell especially strong within her father, an alcoholic and a gambler who abandoned his wife and daughters. Both the medical profession and the clergy, members of the dominant culture, receive stabs of satire as well in the account of La Loca's resurrection. The doctor who misdiagnoses her as dead serves as an example of incompetence in the profession and as an indictment against doctors who do not treat minority people with the care they should receive. And of all the people who witness La Loca's flight to the top of the church, the priest is the one who most lacks faith:

> "Come down, come down," the priest called to the child. "We'll all go in and pray for you. Yes, yes, maybe all this is really true. Maybe you did die, maybe you did see our Lord in His heaven, maybe He did send you back to give us guidance. Let's just go in together, we'll all pray for you."
>
> With the delicate and effortless motion of a monarch butterfly the child brought herself back to the ground, landing gently on her bare feet, her ruffled chiffon nightdress, bought for the occasion of her burial, fluttering softly in the air. "No, Padre," she corrected him. "Remember, it is *I* who am here to pray for *you*." With that stated, she went into the church and those with faith followed [Castillo 24].

In *Esperanza's Box of Saints* by María Amparo Escandón, it is again a priest and Eperanza's best friend, Soledad, who have the most doubt about Esperanza's visions. When the novel begins, Esperanza, a young widow who has just lost her twelve-year-old daughter to a mysterious illness, confesses to her priest that she has had a vision of San Judas Tadeo — the saint for desperate cases. The saint appears to Esperanza while she prepares food for the guests who have come to her daughter's funeral:

> I hadn't cleaned the oven in months. And now I realize it hasn't been procrastination. A heavenly reason was causing my untidiness. San Judas Tadeo needed the grime to appear to me. I looked at the glass at an angle so as not to confuse the reflection of my face with his image. I saw his green velvet robe and his sparkling gold medallion. The image came and went until it settled on the murky glass, like when the moon, sort of insecure, reflects itself on the Papaloapan River [Escandón 15].

Although not a bad man, the priest in *Esperanza's Box of Saints*, Father Salvador, has his faults. For one, he lusts after Esperanza because she reminds him of the nanny he had as a boy. He lusted after the nanny as well, and one night, after story time, the nanny crawled into bed beside him and introduced him to manhood. With this memory still very much alive for him, Father Salvador struggles with his conscience over his attraction to Esperanza. Much worse, however, he fails to recognize the spiritual power of Esperanza's simple, traditional faith, and he doubts her vision. After Esperanza's visit, Father Salvador prays:

Why is San Judas Tadeo appearing to Mrs. Díaz in such a private way? Is she telling the truth? What do his words mean? I told her to keep the apparition to herself. I didn't know what else to say. I wanted to consult with you before giving her more advice. This is not an easy story to believe. People may think she's just overwhelmed by her daughter's death. And it might be precisely that [Escandón 23].

Soledad, Esperanza's lifelong friend whom she has lived with since both of their husbands died together in a bus accident twelve years ago, also lacks Esperanza's faith and doubts her vision. When Esperanza insists that her daughter Blanca is not dead because the saint told her so, Soledad wonders about Esperanza's sanity:

> This was the first of many times when Soledad would question Esperanza's mental health. To her, the girl's death was a fact as clear and tangible as the funeral itself. She had signed the death certificate as a witness, she had seen the casket being covered with dirt at the cemetery, and she had prayed for Blanca's soul along with sixty or so other people who attended the service. Clearly, the next step was to mourn her, accept the fact with resignation, and move on [Escandón 31].

With both Father Salvador and Soledad doubting Esperanza's vision of San Judas Tadeo, it would seem that the requirement that the characters in a magical real novel accept the magic would be violated. At first it is, but the reader does not doubt the "reality" of Esperanza's vision within the context of the novel, and eventually, both Father Salvador and Soledad decide that it is a lack within themselves that keeps them from believing in the vision and that Esperanza is the one who sees the true reality. In a prayer in which he asks for guidance in advising Esperanza, Father Salvador laments the fact that he himself has never had a vision, because, he feels, he lacks the faith to accept one: "She must learn to interpret San Judas Tadeo's messages. The problem is that I can't teach her. I have never seen an apparition. You must have a reason for depriving me of that privilege. As much as I've wished for it to happen in all my years of service to You, I still haven't experienced the slightest sign from Heaven" (Escandón 56). Soledad also comes to the conclusion that Esperanza possesses a special faith, and that her visions are not the hallucinations of mental illness, but a gift:

> Esperanza, I believe that you believe. And I hope that's enough for you because that's as far as my faith goes. I understand you now. I've thought about it a lot. Please forgive me. I don't have the power that you have. Not all of God's children have your capacity for faith. I'm handicapped in that respect. You are lucky. Faith is the most powerful shield against the worst, and you have it. But you cannot force someone to believe. Please don't ask so much from me. And I promise I won't make it all more difficult on you [Escandón 240].

So although not all the characters immediately accept the magical vision in *Esperanza's Box of Saints*, the magical turns out to be an essential part of reality that all of the characters eventually accept, but only some are fortunate enough to experience.

The second characteristic of magical realism in Faris' list focuses on the real: "(2) Descriptions detail a strong presence of the phenomenal world — this is the realism in magical realism, distinguishing it from much fantasy and allegory, and it appears in several ways. Realistic descriptions create a fictional world that resembles the one we live in, in many instances by extensive use of detail" (169). This description of the realism in magical realism could fit any realistic text, but the difference in this realism is its juxtaposition alongside the magical. Even in the details of the realistic passages, there exists a sense that something exists behind the details, and that it is through an intense observance of the details of reality that the magic may be discerned. Esperanza's oven window is an example of a mundane, realistic detail, but through concentrating on the glass, drizzling with grease, Esperanza sees her saint. The effect is similar to a "Magic Eye" picture — the viewer stares with intensity at the surface of the picture, only to have it "pop" into a three-dimensional image of an entirely different, and seemingly otherworldly, scene.

In *House of Houses* by Pat Mora, characters both living and dead share the same realistic spaces. In one scene, the narrator, Patricia, takes a walk with her father who has just died four days previously. Although one character is living and the other dead, they experience the same sensual pleasures while exploring an outdoor market:

> As I approach the vendors calling out their morning greetings to one another, I think of the baskets of multicolored potatoes in Peru, of the gleaming candied fruits and vegetables in Mexico — green figs stuffed with coconut, rich brown sweet potatoes, oranges crusty with dried syrup. And I begin to hear my father's voice enjoying this meandering from stall to stall with me.
>
> "*Mira todos los chinitos!*" he says, as he studies the faces of Asian merchants busy bringing out their white, green and purple vegetables. Like many Mexicans, my father is fond of the diminutive, -*ito*, an ending he uses when observing any ethnic group including Whites. "*Pobres güeritos,*" he might say, "poor Anglos, they're doing the best they can," watching some awkward attempts to dance *salsa* or unwillingness to display emotions [Mora 115].

Although the details of the fruits, vegetables and other sights of the market are realistic, described in vivid detail, and create the image of a realistic scene, the presence and participation of Patricia's deceased father reminds the reader in magical realism, the magical also has an equal role to play within the world that is ordinary.

Faris' third characteristic of magical realism acknowledges that some magical real events leave open the possibility of two explanations — one ordinary and one magical: "(3) The reader may hesitate (at one point or another) between two contradictory understandings of events — and hence experiences some unsettling doubts" (171). Faris uses the example of Beloved, the ghost or ghost-like character in Toni Morrison's novel of the same name. It is never crystal clear whether or not Beloved is an actual person or a ghost of Sethe's daughter, murdered by Sethe in infancy in Sethe's desperate attempt to save the baby from being returned to slavery. Sethe believes Beloved is her child, and Sethe delights in her belief that her child has returned from the dead, but there is an evil intent within Beloved, and she slowly begins to suck the life out of Sethe. Near the end of the novel, the women of the town come to help Sethe and to drive Beloved away with their prayers, but Sethe sees a white man approaching, mistakes him for her former slave owner, and attempts to attack the man with an ice pick. In the confusion that follows, Beloved disappears. Later Paul D., Sethe's friend and lover, tries to make sense of what those who witnessed Beloved's disappearance have to tell about what happened. And above all, he wonders if Beloved was a real woman or an evil apparition:

> He wanted to talk more, make sense out of the stories he had been hearing: whiteman came to take Denver to work and Sethe cut him. Baby ghost came back evil and sent Sethe out to get the man who kept her from hanging. One point of agreement is: first they saw it [Beloved] and then they didn't. When they got Sethe down on the ground and the ice pick out of her hands and looked back to the house, it was gone. Later, a little boy put it out how he had been looking for bait back of 124, down by the stream, and saw, cutting through the woods, a naked woman with fish for hair [Morrison, *Beloved* 267].

In the end, the ambiguity of Beloved makes little difference. Whether she is ghost or real, she is unsettling, part of a past too painful to be remembered, and therefore, "it was not a story to pass on" (275). Gradually the characters of the novel forget the details about Beloved and decide some things are best not remembered, "So they forgot her. Like an unpleasant dream during a troubling sleep" (275). Morrison leaves it to the reader to decide Beloved's true nature, or to simply accept the ambiguity and to realize that some things are too troubling to try and figure out.

In Amy Tan's novel *The Hundred Secret Senses*, the ordinary and the magical possibilities for interpreting an event are expressed through two half-sisters' viewpoints. Olivia, the narrator, born in the United States, is half Chinese and half Anglo. Her older sister Kwan, with whom Olivia shares a father, was born in China to their father's first wife. Kwan does not come to the United States until she is eighteen, and she brings with her strong traditional beliefs in ghosts and superstitions. When Olivia's apartment develops strange noises, they each have their own ideas as to what could be causing the noises:

> A structural engineer suggested that the racket might be coming from the useless radiator pipes. A seismic safety consultant told me that the problem might be simply the natural settling of a wood-frame building.... My mother said it was rats, possibly even raccoons....
>
> When my sister heard the thumps and hisses, she came up with her own diagnosis: "The problem not some*thing* but some*body*. Mm-hm." ...Kwan walked around my office, her nose upraised, scenting like a dog in search of its favorite bush. "Sometime ghost, they get lost," she said. "You want, I try catch for you." She held out one hand like a divining rod [Tan 134].

In this scene, Kwan decides, after some checking, that the problem is not a ghost but an angry person stuck inside the walls. Although to Olivia the explanation sounds ludicrous, the truth turns out to be close to what Kwan has predicted — an angry and deranged neighbor has stuck electronic sound equipment inside the walls to harass and frighten them. Although sometimes Kwan's predictions and the actual events that occur can be explained as coincidences, she is never completely wrong, and the possibility of her having clairvoyant powers always remains plausible within the context of the book.

So Far from God, Ana Castillo's novel discussed above, also generates this sense of hesitancy in the reader as to what is real and what is magical. In *Postethnic Narrative Criticism*, Frederick Luis Aldama comments on *So Far from God*: "Though the net effect of the novel is that the narrator does not distinguish between the real and the magical, there is at times an element of playful hesitation. The reader is never completely sure if an event — magical or real — has taken place or not" (89). The hesitancy is caused, in part, by what Aldama terms the "metacritical effect" of Castillo's narrator, who acts as a "signpost to direct readers within the fictional world of the characters and their experiences with the racist and sexist ideological structures that make up the society of the spectacle" (89). The narrator is far from all knowing, and often herself questions the factuality of what she has described, emphasizing the subjectivity involved in reporting an event. For example, the character Caridad can see into the future. When describing Caridad's last prophecy, the narrator adds, "Especially since this last one foretold Caridad's own departure from home and therefore it is quite a matter of individual opinion whether one wants to consider it a prediction or simply an announcement. In any case, Caridad, like the other times, fell into a trance beforehand" (Castillo 50). The narrator's metacritical comments, in this case as to whether Caridad's pronouncement is a prophecy or not, add not only a playful ambiguity to some of the magical events, but also create an informal, comic affect in the novel.

Most of the examples that have been discussed above in relation to the first three characteristics of magical realism also exemplify the fourth: "(4) We experience the closeness or near-merging of two realms, two worlds" (Faris

172). Specifically, in Pat Mora's novel *House of Houses*, we see how the border between the realms of the living and the dead are blurred as characters, whether deceased or not, take an active part in the occurrences and in the conversations of the novel. The line between the living and the dead is also ill defined in the character of Beloved whose ambiguous nature keeps the reader guessing; is she real or is she a ghost? In *Esperanza's Box of Saints*, Esperanza sees the spiritual within ordinary, everyday objects. She on several occasions sees a saint in her oven window, and once, while looking at a mural of the Virgin of Guadalupe spray painted on a highway underpass, she smells the Virgin's roses.

Lipsha Morrissey, a Chippewa Indian in Louise Erdrich's novel *Love Medicine*, merges the magical and the real when he attempts to prepare a magical potion that will cause his grandfather, Nector, to once again love his grandmother, Marie. Although knowing the dangers of concocting a love medicine, Lipsha decides to proceed and puts his thoughts to imagining what kind of love medicine will work. One day while sitting under a tree, he looks up and sees two Canada geese. Realizing that Canada geese mate for life, Lipsha decides that if he can get two geese hearts and have his grandparents eat them, perhaps they, too, will love each other for life. Canada geese hearts prove difficult to obtain, however, and taking the easy way out, Lipsha eventually gives up hunting geese and goes to the grocery store and buys two frozen turkeys.

> I told myself love medicine was simple. I told myself the old superstitions was just that—strange beliefs. I told myself to take the ten dollars Mary MacDonald had paid me for putting the touch on her arthritis joint, and the other five I hadn't spent yet from winning bingo last Thursday. I told myself to go down to the Red Owl store.
> And here is what I did that made the medicine backfire. I took an evil shortcut. I looked at birds that was dead and froze [245].

Next Lipsha tries to get the turkey hearts blessed, but when both a priest and a nun refuse to bless them, he sticks his fingers in the holy water himself and blesses the hearts. In *Love Medicine*, however, actions in the real world have impact in the magical world, and vice versa. When Lipsha tries to feed the turkey heart to his grandfather, Nector chokes on the heart and dies.

The fifth and final characteristic of magical realism Faris mentions reads as follows: "(5) These fictions question received ideas about time, space and identity" (173). In Leslie Marmon Silko's novel *Ceremony*, conceptions of time, space and identity merge and scramble throughout. The book opens with the following verses about Ts'its'tsi'nako, the Thought-Woman, also known as the Spider-Woman, who creates reality simply by thinking it. She is the creator of stories, but reality *is* the stories. Because of the connections of the webs of her thought, all things in reality are connected through her, so that the events happening in one time or place have repercussions in all others.

> Ts'its'tsi'nako, Thought-Woman,
> is sitting in her room
> and whatever she thinks about
> appears.
>
> She thought of her sisters,
> Nau'ts'ity'i and I'tcts'ity'i,
> and together they created the Universe
> this world
> and the four worlds below.
>
> Thought-Woman, the spider,
> named things and
> as she named them
> they appeared.
>
> She is sitting in her room
> thinking of a story now
>
> I'm telling you the story
> she is thinking [1].

The interconnectedness of times, places and events forms the basis for understanding Leslie Marmon Silko's *Ceremony*. At the beginning of the book, Tayo, a young Native American of the Laguna tribe, returns from fighting in the Pacific during World War II. He suffers from shell shock, and in his feverish dreaming, he struggles with memories that seem to tangle and twist together so that one leads to another in an endless web, moving back and forth from past to present. Through the memories, the reader learns about Tayo's experiences in the war and about his tradition-laden childhood spent on the reservation with his aunt, his uncles Robert and Josiah, and his cousin Rocky, who is with him during the war. Uncle Josiah, in particular, represents to Tayo the traditional life of ritual and ceremony that he leads on the reservation, and Tayo's affection for Uncle Josiah runs deep. During the trauma of war, Tayo begins to confuse identities, and one day when he has orders to shoot some Japanese soldiers, one of the soldiers becomes Tayo's uncle:

> That was when Tayo started screaming because it wasn't a Jap, it was Josiah, eyes shrinking back into the skull and all their shining black light glazed over by death [7–8].

The other soldiers provide explanations for Tayo's confusion of his uncle with a Japanese soldier — battle fatigue, hallucinations from his fever — but when Tayo returns to the Laguna reservation, Uncle Josiah is dead.

Rocky also is wounded. While Tayo and another soldier try to carry Rocky in a blanket stretched between them, they slip and slide in the mud because of the torrential rains. Tayo curses the rain in the jungle, and prays for the downpours to stop. His curses and prayers have power, but the effects occur not in the jungle, but on the Laguna reservation in New Mexico:

> So he had prayed the rain away, and for the sixth year it was dry; the grass turned yellow and it did not grow. Wherever he looked, Tayo could see the consequences of his praying; the gray mule grew gaunt, and the goat and kid had to wander farther and farther each day to find weeds or dry shrubs to eat. In the evenings they waited for him, chewing their cuds by the shed door, and the mule stood by the gate with blind marble eyes ... and he cried for all of them, and for what he had done [14].

Tayo blames himself for Uncle Josiah's death and for the drought that brings such suffering to the animals and to the people on the reservation. At first the reader feels that all these mishaps are not Tayo's fault, but the interconnections continue to happen. Tayo passes out at a train station and when some Japanese Americans try to help him, he thinks he is back in the prisoner of war camp in the Pacific. When one of the Japanese Americans, a small boy, looks back at him, Tayo sees Rocky's face as he looked as a young boy. People, time and places keep shifting, nothing seeming to stay where it belongs:

> So he cried at how the world had come undone, how thousands of miles, high ocean waves and green jungles could not hold people in their place. Years and months had become weak, and people could push against them and wander back and forth in time. Maybe it had always been this way and he was only seeing it for the first time [18].

As the novel progresses, the reader realizes that Tayo deserves some of the blame for what has happened because of his participation and contact with an evil much greater than himself— an evil that for Tayo's time is epitomized as the war. Other friends of Tayo's were in the war and also have problems adjusting when they return to the reservation. They go through traditional ceremonies believed to purify a warrior of his wrongdoings, but the old ceremonies do not seem to help. The evilness has grown too large, too powerful, and new ceremonies must be created. Tayo eventually seeks the help of a powerful medicine man, Betonie, and is given a series of tasks to do. Although at first glance the tasks appear to have nothing to do with Tayo regaining his sanity and peace, each task becomes part of an overall ceremony that helps Tayo put his world back in focus. He finds his Uncle Josiah's lost cattle, a special pattern of stars, a mountain and a woman; and through the finding of these things, Tayo begins to heal and to realize that the people and the things he thought he had lost are not really lost to him at all, as long as he remembers them.

But the evil, set into motion in an ancient time, and destined to be carried out by white people operating as the tools of the ancient destroyers, makes a final play for Tayo. Since Tayo is rumored to be crazy, his former friends kidnap him in hopes of gaining some reward for his capture. Tayo senses their intent and escapes, but then the group turns on Tayo's former best friend, Harley, and tortures him. Knowing that Tayo probably is in hiding and witnessing the scene, the group's leader, Emo, hopes to capture Tayo when he comes to Harley's rescue. This is the final test for Tayo, and he almost fails it in his desire to rescue Harley. But again identities have transformed, and although Tayo remembers that they were once his friends, he sees the transformation in the men and realizes that even Harley contains little of his former identity. The men have become tools of the ancient evil, and for Tayo to participate in any way, even to stop Emo from torturing Harley to death, would be to once again be sucked into a pattern of events and consequences that would allow the evil to continue. So Tayo resists the urge to take part in the violence, and for the time being, the evil is defeated.

These examples of magical realism as they appear in ethnic literature in the U.S. show how the genre reacts against the notion of a purely scientific reality governed by laws of logic and rationality. Unlike fantasy which devises new laws according to which strange and unexpected events may be explained, magical realism rejects the notion of a rule-governed reality altogether. Even things which seem to be so clearly opposite, such as a living person and a dead person, can change places with ease and can even share the same spaces. It is easy to see why this genre has its appeal, particularly among people who have been disillusioned with laws, have found that the law enforcers who are meant to protect them sometimes end up abusing them, and who have been told that their traditional beliefs and stories are simply nonsense. Magical realism is a means by which to make all things possible — a way to make those who feel they have been on the bottom rise to the top. It is also a way to present a reality that those who are too rule- and evidence-bound cannot perceive and, therefore, it allows those who see the magic palpitating behind the real to have a sense that they possess a more complete, a more vivid sense of reality. Magical realism provides a way to foreground tradition in a world that, in its haste for progress, has left many people out of the bright promises of modernity. Magical realism appears in the literatures of many different times and places, and although it is often a genre existing on the margin of society, in magical realism, the border between the margin and the center disappears.

Chapter Two

Surveying the Land: Hybridity in Landscapes and Sites of U.S. Ethnic Literature

From the beginnings of literature in what is now the U.S., going back to the oral traditions of Native American literature and to the writings of the early Spanish explorers, physical spaces have played a key and often symbolic role in the literary representations of America. In contemporary ethnic literature of the U.S., landscapes often function as the symbolic holders of tradition, either as designated sacred spaces or simply as reminders of the histories enacted within them. In *Multicultural American Literature*, A. Robert Lee writes, "Terms like location, locale, or the local, offer no fixed schematic, ... But they do point up how, within ethnic fiction, 'site' becomes always as much time as place, an accumulation of memory" (189).

The works discussed in this chapter demonstrate how authors can symbolically use landscapes, or other physical sites, to represent the cultural conflicts experienced by minority individuals who are striving to maintain their heritage within the majority culture. The depiction of two variant landscapes may represent the dual aspects of the individual's cultural environment, each landscape representing one particular culture. In some cases, when the land itself embodies hybrid characteristics containing the histories of conflicting cultural groups, a site can actually serve as a catalyst that jolts the character into a heightened state of awareness of his or her own cultural hybridity. Such realization may occur when the character contemplates a hybrid site (or sites) and an anxiety arises within him or her that leads to a moment of crisis. To resolve the crisis, the character *usually* works out a reconciliation of the two disparate sites, a reconciliation that also may lead to an integration of the disparate parts of his or her own identity. In such cases, the landscapes or other physical places take an active role, actually leading the characters into an awareness and a reconciliation of the opposing cultural pulls warring within them. In *Place and Vision: The Function of Landscape in Native American Fiction*, Robert Nelson acknowledges the agency of landscape, pointing out the tendency of critics to overlook the possibility of an active landscape: "Generally speaking, literary criticism resists the notion that the land has a life of its own and tends instead to proceed as though vitality were a quality imposed on the land by human imagination but not vice-versa" (8). Nelson here refers to landscape in Native American novels particularly, but, as will be shown in this chapter, the occurrence of landscape as an active participant applies to other ethnic works as well.

Landscapes may be presented as real, actual places, or one may be real in the sense of ordinary, and another magical. In the previous chapter, the phenomenon of magical realism was described in one instance as the coexistence of the realms of the magical and the ordinary within one reality, occupying the same geometric space. A passage from Rawdon Wilson's chapter "Metamorphoses of Fictional Space: Magical Realism," quoted previously, bears repeating here:

> Try to imagine it [magical realism] as if two distinct geometries had been inscribed onto the same space. Think of it as copresence, as duality and mutual tolerance, as different geometries at work constructing a double space. Magical realism focuses the problem of fictional space. It does this by suggesting a model of how different geometries, inscribing boundaries that fold and refold like quicksilver, can superimpose themselves upon one another [210].

I repeat this quotation in order to use this same image of doubly-inscribed space as a model of how two conceptions of a landscape can exist within only one topographical area, creating a hybrid landscape or space. In the context of a U.S. ethnic work of literature, the rendering of landscapes imbued with a double history, or a double significance, mirrors the state of the ethnic minority character, attempting to resolve the dualities of two cultures, two languages, two ways of being a U.S. American.

If Dorothee E. Kocks is correct in *Dream a Little: Land and Social Justice in Modern America* when she states that "[U.S.] Americans tend to hold on to land, even to cling to it, as a last certainty in an uncertain world," a tendency she refers to as "the geographic embrace," then U.S. Americans who encounter other ethnic views regarding land within the U.S. should be prepared to have the earth, at least figuratively, slip out of their grasp (31). The earth's landscape is less certain than one might think. As rock-solid as it may seem, land is no less slippery a category than we previously have seen to be true of ethnicity and of reality and magic. "The content of nature's lesson," Kocks writes, "depends in large part on the content of the viewer" (xiii).

For the white, non-minority culture in the U.S., landscape stands as a national symbol for the rich natural abundance and the inherent goodness of the United States of America and its peoples. One need only look at the lyrics of songs such as "America the Beautiful" to see the connection popularly believed to exist between beautiful nature, God, and the people believed to be blessed by God by virtue of living in such a beautiful place. Landscapes in many works of ethnic literature of the U.S., however, more deeply underscore the crucial importance of land to culture and identity. For ethnic American authors, landscapes present alternative histories to the mainstream culture and question accepted notions about the meanings of places by exposing lingering traces upon the land of violence, oppression, forced labor and ecological damage. These more unpleasant aspects of landscape also contribute to the formation of the identity of the people who live within the land, and the land bears the scars of the struggles for political power that have been enacted upon it. In *Landscapes of the New West*, Krista Comer writes about the "new regionalists"— those writing about the U.S. American West in the postmodern age, including women and members of minority groups formerly excluded from the scope of western literature: "Many of the new regionalists are as invested in rewriting history, and in reimagining the spatial terrain on which particular histories play out their various power struggles, as they are in producing something like Art or a Great American Novel" (10).

In works written by ethnic authors of the new West, landscapes are reconceived, respatialized, and given added or alternative meanings. In her introduction, Comer mentions Gloria Anzaldúa as an author who destabilizes notions of geopolitical space, particularly in the area we refer to as the borderlands: "In the process of respatializing that borderlands area — reconnecting it to the nexus of the Mexican, colonial Spanish, and indigenous histories from which it arises — an alternative geographic imaginary as well as history and sensibility come into being" (9–10). To expand on Comer's comments, the following passage on the Battle of the Alamo from *Borderlands/La Frontera: The New Mestiza* exemplifies how Anzaldúa presents an alternative, historical view:

> In the 1800s, Anglos migrated illegally into Texas, which was then part of Mexico, in greater and greater numbers and gradually drove the *tejanos* (native Texans of Mexican descent) from their lands, committing all manner of atrocities against them. Their illegal invasion forced Mexico to fight a war to keep its Texas territory. The Battle of the Alamo, in which the Mexican forces vanquished the whites, became, for the whites, the symbol for the cowardly and villainous character of the Mexicans. It became (and still is) a symbol that legitimized the white imperialist takeover. With the capture of Santa Anna later in 1836, Texas became a republic. *Tejanos* lost their land and, overnight, became the foreigners [6].

So the Alamo, for the whites, provided a symbol of an injustice perpetrated against them by the Mexicans. "Remember the Alamo" became a rallying cry for instigating the Mexican American War after which Texas, New Mexico, Arizona, Colorado and California became U.S. territories. On the other hand, for the Mexicans, the Alamo represented an act of self-defense against the imperialist incursions of the whites into Mexican territory. Thus one territory came to possess two conflicting historical interpretations, and this conflict continues to exist, stretching along the entire borderlands region between the U.S. and Mexico. With the fixing of the political border between the U.S. and Mexico by the 1848 Treaty of Guadalupe-Hidalgo, citizens of Mexico, without moving from their lands, suddenly found themselves to be citizens of the United States, living in a space with two conflicting cultures. The borderlands area itself, with its dual and conflicted history, appears ill-defined and arbitrary. Anzaldúa writes:

> The U.S.–Mexican border *es una herida abierta* where the Third World grates against the first and bleeds. And before a scab forms it hemorrhages again, the lifeblood of two worlds merging to form a third country — a border culture. Borders are set up to define the places that are safe and unsafe, to distinguish *us* from *them*. A border is a dividing line, a narrow strip along a steep edge. A borderland is a vague and undetermined place created by the emotional residue of an unnatural boundary. It is in a constant state of transition [3].

Although borderlands present an obvious case where two or more conflicting views of the same landscape may simultaneously exist, other areas can be equally superimposed with different, culturally-linked meanings. A landscape may seem to be a stable, fixed category, a topographical reality that everyone can agree upon and that can be observed objectively as being a mountain, a valley, a lake, a forest, etc.; but landscape can be used to present a variety of cultural and political meanings. Krista Comer explains that "landscape is not 'real' but is rather a particular type of social discourse around which various cultural questions get discussed — especially ... questions of national identity" (12).

Ceremony

In the previous chapter on magical realism, the character Tayo from Leslie Marmon Silko's book *Ceremony* was discussed. Silko's novel *Ceremony* centers on the relationship of land to culture and its crucial role in Native American identity. Tayo, the main character of Silko's novel, is not a full-blood Indian: he is half white and half Laguna. Culturally, he was raised as a Laguna Indian and was taught traditional ways of life by his Uncle Josiah. Tayo must, nevertheless, learn how to control and integrate his white heritage before he can be healed from his war trauma and take his place as a member of the tribe. Much of the evil doings in the book seem to come from whites, but Silko did not make Tayo half Laguna and half white for nothing. Whites are presented in the novel not as evil in and of themselves, but as tools brought into existence by evil witchery set into motion in primordial time. An evil witch, in order to win a contest as the most evil of all witches, set loose in the world a craving for killing and destroying, hoping humankind would eventually destroy itself. The evil witch conceived of, and thereby created, the destroyers through thought: "The destroyers: they work to see how much can be lost, how much can be forgotten. They destroy the feeling people have for each other.... Their highest ambition is to gut human beings while they are still breathing, to hold the heart still beating so the victim will never feel anything again. When they finish, you watch yourself from a distance and you can't even cry — not even for yourself" (229). The destroyers invented the whites and found them to be easy to manipulate into carrying out their destructive acts. Tayo has white in him, and as part of his healing ceremony — the most important part — he needs to reconcile the two conflicting halves of his identity as part of learning to resist the manipulations of the destroyers. Traveling the Laguna land, the land of his cultural identity, helps him accomplish this reconciliation. As Gayle Ruth Siebert notes in "Frontiering Tayo's *Interior Landscapes*," the exterior landscape has a direct connection with the interior spaces of Tayo's mind. She observes Tayo's confining mental illness at the beginning of the book, describing the physical barriers that similarly restrict him: "Tayo discovers his fragmented self embodied in metaphors of boundaries — hospital walls and fences — which signify his exploration of the frontier within himself" (198).

Early in the novel, Tayo joins the army along with his cousin Rocky to fight in the Pacific during World War II. While in the war, Tayo suffers from confusions of people and places. For Tayo, the Philippines, where he is stationed, and the Laguna reservation converge at one moment into one hybrid place, and he sees his Uncle Josiah, as mentioned in the previous chapter, as one of the Japanese soldiers he has been ordered to shoot:

> When the sergeant told them to kill all the Japanese soldiers lined up in front of the cave with their hands on their heads, Tayo could not pull the trigger.... In that instant he saw Josiah standing there; the face was dark from the sun, and the eyes were squinting as though he were about to smile at Tayo. So Tayo stood there, stiff with nausea, while they fired at the soldiers, and he watched his uncle fall, and he *knew* it was Josiah.... Rocky had reasoned it out with him; it was impossible for the dead man to be Josiah, because Josiah was an old Laguna man, thousands of miles from the Philippine jungles and Japanese armies [7–8].

In spite of Rocky's assurances, Tayo cannot escape the feeling that his uncle has been killed, and sure enough, when he returns to Laguna, Josiah had died during the time Tayo was fighting the Japanese.

In another incident from the war, the Philippines and the Laguna Pueblo again interconnect. Rocky is severely wounded and he and Tayo are prisoners of the Japanese. They are forced to travel, and Tayo and a corporal carry Rocky between them on a blanket. The rain pours down unceasingly, making it difficult to walk, difficult to carry Rocky, and causing Rocky's wounds to fester.

> The sound of the rain got louder, pounding on the leaves, splashing into the ruts; it splattered on his head, and the sound echoed inside his skull. It streamed down his face and neck like jungle flies with crawling feet.... The corporal fell, jerking the ends of the blanket from his hands, ... and he started repeating "God-damn, goddamn!"; it flooded out of the last warm core in his chest and echoed inside his head. He damned the rain until the words were a chant, and he sang it while he crawled through the mud to find the corporal and get him up before the Japanese saw them [12].

Although Tayo has good reason to curse the rain, when he returns to Laguna, he finds the pueblo caught up in a severe drought. The drought and Josiah's death in relation to Tayo's actions in the Philippines may seem to be coincidences, but Tayo, through not stopping the killing of Japanese soldiers and through cursing the rain, has become a participant in the overall plan of the destroyers. He has failed to see the interconnections of his actions in one place with the consequences that appear in another. As such, his actions have fed the network of destruction and he has indeed, unintentionally, contributed to Josiah's death and the drought. As Jeff Karem argues in "Keeping the Native on the Reservation," what Tayo did not realize was that "all natural forces are 'part of life,' and that you ought not to 'swear at them,' because disaster can result from upsetting those forces" (26). The white doctors who treat Tayo for battle fatigue try to convince him that the convergences of person and place he experienced were only the results of his illness, but Tayo, correctly, feels responsible.

Tayo returns home from the war, but the medical profession has not cured him. Nor do traditional healing ceremonies work for Tayo, or for the other Laguna veterans returning from the war. The traditional ceremonies for warriors, such as the Scalp Ceremony which Tayo's friends have undergone, prove to be ineffective against modern realities. The scalp ceremony does not work because it fails to integrate opposite compulsions of attraction and repulsion that Tayo and his friends have felt in their encounters with the white world. The power of the scalp ceremony is no match for the modern power of destruction that with the discovery of nuclear energy has reached a level that did not exist in traditional times:

> The Scalp Ceremony laid to rest the Japanese souls in the green humid jungles, and it satisfied the female giant who fed on the dreams of warriors. But there was

something else now, as Betonie [a medicine man] said: it was everything they had seen — the cities, the tall buildings, the noise and the lights, the power of their weapons and machines. They were never the same after that: they had seen what the white people had made from the stolen land.... Every day they had to look at the land, from horizon to horizon, and every day the loss was with them; it was the dead unburied, and the mourning of the lost going on forever [169].

Tayo's mental illness results not only from his direct experiences in the war, but also from the full realization of what he and his people have lost: their culture, their family members, and particularly, their land. He faces the immense power, even within himself, of the unleashed compulsion to destroy. To heal himself, as Patricia Clarkson Smith and Paula Gunn Allen suggest in "Earthly Relations, Carnal Knowledge," Tayo "must 'close the gap between isolate human beings and lonely landscape' brought about through old witchery that has led not only to Tayo's illness but also to World War II, strip-mining, nuclear weapons, racism, and a drought-plagued land" (191).

In *The Sacred Hoop*, Paula Gunn Allen confirms that Tayo must reestablish his connection with the land through ceremony. As she observes, "Tayo's illness is a result of separation from the ancient unity of person, ceremony, and land, and his healing is a result of his recognition of this unity" (119). To become well again, Tayo must reintegrate himself back into his traditional life and place in the world, but he also must understand the part of him, symbolically represented by his white blood, that seeks to follow the pattern set by the destroyers. Such a healing requires an encounter with the landscape of the Laguna Pueblo and its surrounding area, not just as Indian land, but as land containing both Indian heritage and white destruction.

To right himself after having encountered the overwhelming evil of the war, Tayo visits the medicine man, Betonie, who lives on the edge of Gallup, New Mexico, and the open desert. Silko depicts Gallup as an absolute hellhole of a town where Indians suffer from exploitation by whites. Betonie's position on the land bordering Gallup indicates that he himself has found a way to live both between and among whites and Indians, and he knows Tayo must learn the same. As part of his healing ceremony, Betonie gives Tayo several tasks to perform. Tayo must find four things: a woman, a particular pattern of stars, his uncle Josiah's lost cattle, and a particular mountain. As Tayo goes about his quest for these items, he encounters Ts'eh, a woman who on the one hand is a helping mountain spirit, and on the other is a physical, tangible woman who teaches Tayo how to love again. With the guidance of Ts'eh, Tayo travels to certain specific sites that circumscribe the physical boundaries and the spiritual places of the pueblo.*

---

*Robert Nelson in his book *Place and Vision: The Function of Landscape in Native American Fiction* carefully traces the path Tayo takes in the novel as it relates to the actual geographic spaces

As Robert Nelson has noted in *Place and Vision*, Tayo must visit particular places, "these helpers/healers must be visited at *certain places*— which is to say Tayo must re-visit the land itself in order to reestablish contact with the power of healing that he may find there" (14).

In *Landscapes of the New West*, Krista Comer argues that Tayo becomes well again as a result of his reconnection with the earth, and she criticizes Silko for maintaining and perpetuating a stereotypical myth that nature has the ability to "rejuvenate, redeem, restore sanity and right relation to self, to local community, and to global community" (133). However, Comer oversimplifies Tayo's healing ceremony. James Tarter in "Locating the Uranium Mine" explains that "Laguna culture has developed intricate meanings tied to specific plants, animals, and geographical features like water holes, knobs of rock, or *Tse'pi'na*, Mount Taylor, the Old Woman in the clouds, around which Tayo's quest revolves" (100). And Paula Gunn Allen spells out the intricacy of the relationship of land and identity in "Iyani: It Goes This Way," observing that "this relationship [is not] one of mere 'affinity' for the Earth. It is not a matter of being 'close to nature.' The relationship is more one of identity, in the mathematical sense, than of affinity. The Earth is, in a very real sense, the same as ourself (or selves)" (191). Tayo's recovery entails much more than just a simple reinvolvement with nature. Tayo does become well again as a result of his wilderness journey, but he has to resolve conflicting histories that he sees have taken place on the land. Comer herself claims that Betonie is a modern medicine man who "works his magic as much through telephone books, old newspapers, and Coca Cola-advertising train calendars as he does through the expected items in a medicine man's bag" (132). Betonie's eclecticism and integration of the old with the new make it clear that the remedy for Tayo's illness is not simply a traditional reintegration with nature in a pure, untouched state. Although Tayo does need to reestablish himself with his former rituals and traditions, including a relationship to the natural world, he must also learn to live with change, change which sometimes causes a destruction of the natural world. The destruction of mining and fencing is visible in the landscapes that Tayo visits, and the double significance these lands hold creates an incongruity and an anxiety in Tayo that he must resolve. The incongruity is the same disjunction he feels within himself as a member of both the white and the Indian world and as both a destroyer and a person who hates destruction.

As mentioned above, Tayo receives guidance from Ts'eh during his ceremony. Lorelei Cederstrom in "Myth and Ceremony in Contemporary North

---

[continued] of the Four Corners area, where New Mexico, Arizona, Nevada and Colorado meet (see Nelson, Chapter 1).

American Native Fiction" identifies Ts'eh as Corn Woman from Pueblo mythology (295). But Ts'eh herself is a hybrid character. Robert Nelson in *Place and Vision* connects all of the female spirits who appear in the novel (Night Swan, Spider Grandmother, and Ts'eh) as different avatars of the same "life-giving spirit" (20). As one of these avatars, Ts'eh also clearly is the manifestation in human form of the spirit of Tse-pi'na, the Indian name for Mount Taylor. Nelson explains her connection with the mountain:

> ...This lady, who stands figuratively at both the entrance and the exit to the spirit mountain Tse-pi'na, is clearly at home here where she is ... and the suggestion of Ka't'sina [Kachina, mountain spirit] identity in the description we're given of her ... both imply that she functions, here in the evolving ceremony, as a spirit belonging to this place in ways that Tayo does not yet belong. Because she is encountered where she is, and because she seems so "at home" in this place, she should probably be taken as the mountain avatar of the genetrix spirit — a version of Tse-pi'na, "the woman veiled in clouds," as well as a more youthful version of both Spider Grandmother and the Night Swan. Further, since she is assigned no name in this episode, and since physiognomically she appears ... to be identical with the one who calls herself "Ts'eh" later in the novel, and since "Ts'eh" as a nickname could be taken to be a shortened form of either "Ts'its'tsi'nako" *or* "Tse-pi'na," we can hear at this stage of the ceremony of the novel a significant coming-together of heretofore uncomfortably separated aspects or avatars of the regenerative force Tayo seeks — and seeks to integrate into his own vision and experience [20–21].

Paula Gunn Allen in *The Sacred Hoop* further discusses the life-giving spirit of Ts'eh: "Ts'eh is the matrix, the creative and life-restoring power, and those who cooperate with her designs serve her and, through her, serve life" (118). However, Ts'eh is also a woman in the physical sense, and what is most important, as argued by Lisa Orr in her article "Theorizing the Earth," Ts'eh "is someone Tayo learns from, not worships" (155).

While on his wilderness quest, Tayo travels to the mountain that Betonie has asked him to find. The mountain scenery simultaneously contains two histories — one Laguna and one white. First, the Laguna history:

> The white ranchers called this place North Top, but he remembered it by the story Josiah had told him about a hunter who walked into a grassy meadow up here and found a mountain-lion cub chasing butterflies; as long as the hunter sang a song to the cub, it continued to play. But when the hunter thought of the cub's mother and was afraid, the mountain-lion cub was startled and ran away. The Laguna people had always hunted up there.

And the white history:

> All but a small part of the mountain had been taken. The reservation boundary included only a canyon above Encinal and a few miles of timber on the plateau. The rest of the land was taken by the National Forest and by the state which later sold it to white ranchers who came from Texas in the early 1900s. In the twenties

and thirties the loggers had come, and they stripped the canyons below the rim and cut great clearings on the plateau slopes.... The loggers shot the bears and mountain lions for sport. And it was then the Laguna people understood that the land had been taken, because they couldn't stop these white people from coming to destroy the animals and the land [185–86].

Since Tayo has traveled in his quest through other mountains where there has been no sign of the whites, it seems that Betonie must have a purpose for sending Tayo to this particular mountain (Mount Taylor/Tse-pi'na). It is on this mountain that Tayo's own history and loss are simultaneously made apparent through the contrast of the remaining natural features of the mountain with the scars left by the whites.

While searching the mountain for his uncle Josiah's cattle, Tayo finds a high fence of heavy-gauge steel mesh with barbed wire strung across the top and the wire buried into the ground to prevent animals from digging under it. Although the white owner of the land on the other side of the fence claims that it is to keep animals out, "the people knew what the fence was for: a thousand dollars a mile to keep Indians and Mexicans out; a thousand dollars a mile to lock the mountain in steel wire, to make the land his" (188). Tayo's cattle, a particularly tough, hybrid breed from Mexico, are on the other side of the fence; so Tayo, in an effort both practical and symbolic, spends the entire night cutting through the thick wires, leaving a hole twenty feet wide for the cattle to pass through. As Tayo cuts through the fence, he also removes some of the barriers within himself that have prevented him from seeing connections between times and places. The effort to find the cattle and to cut through the fence so intensely occupies Tayo that he ceases to remember and think about the past. He experiences a sense of timelessness on the mountain which he expresses in his thoughts by thinking about the absence of verb tenses in the traditional Laguna language:

> The ride into the mountain had branched into all directions of time. He knew then why the oldtimers could only speak of yesterday and tomorrow in terms of the present moment: the only certainty; and this present sense of being was qualified with bare hints of yesterday or tomorrow, by saying, "I go up to the mountain yesterday or I go up to the mountain tomorrow." The ck'o'yo Kaup'a'ta* somewhere is stacking his gambling sticks and waiting for a visitor; Rocky and I are walking across the ridge in the moonlight; Josiah and Robert are waiting for us. This night is a single night; and there has never been any other [192].

This merging of time, of the mythic with the ordinary, and of people already dead with people still living, all occurring in Tayo's thoughts on a single night on the mountain, leads Tayo to a realization that the past continues to exist within the present, and that the people he has lost, and the lands the Laguna

---

*A gambling spirit who takes advantage of unwary visitors.

people have lost, continue to exist in his thoughts and stories as they were. As long as the memories, the love and the stories still exist, the land and the people continue. In *The Sacred Hoop,* Paula Gunn Allen addresses this notion of the continuous presence of the dead as follows: "Perhaps no one has told him [Tayo] that the departed souls are always within and part of the people on earth, that they are still obligated to those living on earth and come back in the form of rain regularly (when all is well), so that death is a blessing on the people, not their destruction" (124). Complete loss, loss even of memories and stories, is what the destroyers aim to achieve; and it is this sense of complete loss, the forgetting of the continued presence of the dead, that drives people into permanent despair.

Although Tayo is not at the end of his ceremony while on the mountain, his realization that loss is neither final nor complete leads him to overcome his fear of loss and eventually to become well again. The presence of the double history on the mountain, not simply an encounter with nature, prompts Tayo's realization. Near the end of the book, with his healing ceremony almost complete, Tayo again realizes the simultaneity of being:

> He cried the relief he felt at finally seeing the pattern, the way all the stories fit together — the old stories, the war stories, their stories — to become the story that was still being told. He was not crazy; he had never been crazy. He had only seen and heard the world as it always was: no boundaries, only transitions through all distances and time [246].

Tayo's final encounter with a hybrid landscape occurs near the end of the book. Tayo has been living with the mountain spirit woman, Ts'eh, near Pa'to'ch, a sacred mesa to the south of Laguna, when the people of the pueblo become disturbed by Tayo's absence and reportedly odd behavior. His evil rival and a fellow war veteran, Emo, has convinced the people that Tayo is crazy and that he should be captured and taken to an institution. Ts'eh warns Tayo to leave and hide. She also tells him that the conclusion of the ceremony is almost at hand. Tayo leaves, and as he walks along the road, he is picked up by two old friends who, like Tayo and Emo, are also war veterans. Unknown to Tayo, however, the two friends are in on the plot to capture him. Tayo realizes this in time and escapes. He runs to a location where the view is dominated by the Jackpile uranium mine. Here Tayo, while gazing at the mine, contemplates the connection of this sacred area and surrounding locations with the destruction of nuclear weapons:

> Trinity site, where they exploded the first atomic bomb, was only three hundred miles to the southeast, at White Sands. And the top-secret laboratories where the bomb had been created were deep in the Jemez Mountains, on the land the government took from Cochiti Pueblo: Los Alamos, only a hundred miles northeast of him now, still surrounded by high electric fences and the ponderosa pine and tawny

sandrock of the Jemez mountain canyon where the shrine of the twin mountain lions had always been. There was no end to it; it knew no boundaries; and he had arrived at the point of convergence where the fate of all living things, and even the earth, had been laid [246].

As Tayo walks into the mine shaft, he finds yet another sign of hybridity in the rocks of uranium ore that combine the power of destruction and the natural landscape: "The gray stone was streaked with powdery yellow uranium, bright and alive as pollen; veins of sooty black formed lines with the yellow, making mountain ranges and rivers across the stone" (246).

Looking to the sky, Tayo sees again the constellation of stars Betonie had originally told him to find, a constellation that has periodically appeared to Tayo as he has made progress in his quest. This time, however, Tayo notices the constellation forms a map of the places he has visited as part of his ceremony. Land and sky have converged. "For each star there was a night and a place; this was the last night and the last place, when the darkness of night and the light of day were balanced. His protection was there in the sky, in the position of the sun, in the pattern of the stars" (247). This convergence of the earth and the sky at the site of the Jackpile uranium mine place Tayo at the center of the conflict where the life-giving natural forces and the destructive powers of the destroyers meet. As Reyes Garcia notes, "This fused image of earth and sky helps Tayo to feel he is in a place he belongs, at home, part of something larger than himself and which finally encompasses him" (42). If Tayo can survive this last night, the destroyers, temporarily, will be outmaneuvered.

As Tayo hides from his would-be captors, Emo and Leroy, Tayo's former companions, Harley and Pinkie, arrive at the mine. Emo, Leroy and Pinkie gruesomely torture Harley, hoping Tayo will hear his screams and come out to rescue his former friend. Tayo, hiding in the rocks nearby, finds a screwdriver in his pocket and imagines killing Emo, driving the screwdriver into his brain. Tayo, however, ultimately resists the urge to commit violence, thereby thwarting the plan of the destroyers. "He crouched between the boulders and laid his head against the rock to look up at the sky. Big clouds covered the moon, but he could still see the stars. He had arrived at a convergence of patterns; he could see them clearly now. The stars had always been with them, existing beyond memory, and they were all held together there.... The story goes on with these stars" (253–4). Of Tayo's rejection of violence, Cyrus Patell writes in "The Violence of Hybridity in Silko and Alexie," "It is only when he [Tayo] can reject the temptation to kill Emo, can renounce the violence that is Emo's way of life, that Tayo is finally cured. It is, finally, the rejection of violence that proves to be the culmination of Tayo's ceremony" (7). By resisting the urge to commit violence, Tayo has successfully faced and contained the destroyer within himself, symbolized by his white blood. He returns to the Pueblo, now cured, and the elders welcome him into the kiva. And as for the witchery of the destroyers:

> It is dead for now.
> It is dead for now.
> It is dead for now.
> It is dead for now [261].

After completing his ceremony, Tayo has earned the right to pass his story on to the elders. The telling of the story confirms his connection to the land. In an article titled "Writing Nature: Silko and Native Americans as Nature Writers," Lee Scheninger explains the obligation to tell the story: "Language (that unique characteristic that distinguishes humans from other animals) and nature are inextricably connected. The obligation of being human is to see the human connection to nature and to speak it, to tell the earth's story" (52). "The earth, the word, the speaker of the word, and the story are inseparable" (57).

Tayo confronts several instances of hybridity both during the war and during the course of his healing ceremony. During the war, he experiences the convergences of the Japanese soldier and Uncle Josiah and of the Philippines and the Laguna Pueblo. During the ceremony, he finds Josiah's tough, hybrid cattle and a hybrid lover in Ts'eh as spirit and Ts'eh as woman. Most importantly, however, he encounters two hybrid landscapes: Mount Taylor with its conflicting histories, and finally, the Jackpile uranium mine where the ceremony reaches its conclusion, and where Tayo sees the pattern of stars that reflect the sacred places of the land in the constellation of the sky. At each of these convergences Tayo experiences what Homi Bhabha refers to as "the moment of panic which reveals the borderline experience ... [and] resists the binary opposition of racial and cultural groups" (207). As a result of these encounters, Tayo comes to a realization of his own strength and adaptability as a hybrid being, drawing upon his experiences with both cultures. He reconciles the white and the Native American parts of his identity, recognizing within himself the desire to resist destruction, but also, the need to control the powerful urge to destroy.

"Yellow Woman"

Turning to another work by Leslie Marmon Silko, the story "Yellow Woman" is a complex configuration of the environment underscoring the theme of the story as the main character moves through the landscape, passing from her village to the river, to the mountains, and back again. The village represents the ordinary and somewhat monotonous world where the woman, whose name is never given, lives with her mother, grandmother, husband and baby. The woman feels a need for adventure and renewal, a need that first draws her to the river and then leads her straight into the mythical roots of her culture. The river, which runs between the village and the mountains, serves as a place where the woman goes in search of adventure, in particular, a romantic adventure. In "Ritual and Renewal: Keres Traditions in Leslie Silko's 'Yellow Woman,'" A. LaVonne Ruoff writes, "According to Silko, the river in Laguna, where 'Yellow Woman' opens, was always associated with stories as a place to meet boyfriends and lovers" (74). The woman finds a lover, and they head for the mountains. As they travel together through the mountain landscape, the mythic and the ordinary, two seemingly disparate, even incompatible elements, combine and interchange in a perplexing and sometimes disturbing way.

Silko's "Yellow Woman" originates from a long oral tradition of Yellow Woman stories popular among the Keres Indians of the Laguna and Acoma Pueblos in New Mexico. Although the details of the stories differ, the basic plot remains the same. A young woman, alone, encounters a young man and is abducted by him — sometimes with force, but sometimes with her cooperation. The man turns out not to be an ordinary man, but a kachina, a mountain spirit. The two spend time together, have a sexual relationship, and, eventually, Yellow Woman goes home. In some versions she is killed upon her return for her transgressions, but usually, she is welcomed back into her village. The recurring theme of the Yellow Woman stories is renewal. In each telling, the woman gives something new to the pueblo as a result of her excursion into the outside world — new babies, buffalo meat, or in the case of Silko's Yellow Woman story, a new version of the story itself.

In "Earthy Relations, Carnal Knowledge: Southwestern American Indian Women Writers and Landscape," Patricia Clark Smith and Paula Gunn Allen discuss how such mythical interactions of humans and spirits lead to new knowledge that comes to the human through the spirit, but that originates within the land:

> In such comings-together of persons and spirits, the land and the people engage in a ritual dialogue — though it may take the human participant a while to figure that out. The ultimate purpose of such ritual abductions and seductions is to transfer knowledge from the spirit world to the human sphere.... The human protagonists usually engage willingly in literal sexual intercourse with the spirits who simultaneously walk the land and embody it. This act brings the land's power, spirit, and fecundity in touch with their own, and so ultimately yields benefit for their people [178].

Silko's telling of "Yellow Woman" begins with the woman waking up beside the river after a night spent with her lover, whom she met by the river the day before. The woman is keenly aware of the natural environment around her, and the intensity of the colors, textures and feelings indicates she has a heightened awareness of her senses:

> My thigh clung to his with dampness, and I watched the sun rising up through the tamaracks and willows. The small brown water birds came to the river and hopped across the mud, leaving brown scratches in the alkali-white crust. They bathed in the river silently. I could hear the water, almost at our feet where the narrow fast channel bubbled and washed green ragged moss and fern leaves. I looked at him beside me, rolled in the red blanket on the white river sand. I cleaned the sand out of the cracks between my toes, squinting because the sun was above the willow trees. I looked at him for the last time, sleeping on the white river sand [31].

The woman walks along the river, and the feeling that she has entered a magical, mythical place apart from the ordinary world becomes more evident when she looks for, but is unable to see, her village: "I tried to look beyond the pale red mesas to the pueblo. I knew it was there, even if I could not see it, on the sandrock hill above the river" (31).

When the man, Silva (forest in Spanish), awakens, he reminds the woman of the night before and calls her Yellow Woman. When she asks who he is, he replies that she knew who he was the night before and why he had come. She replies, "But I only said that you were him [the kachina spirit] and that I was Yellow Woman — I'm not really her — I have my own name and I come from the pueblo on the other side of the mesa. Your name is Silva and you are a stranger I met by the river yesterday afternoon" (32). She continues to deny that she is living the Yellow Woman story and resists the notion that she and Silva are Yellow Woman and the kachina (or ka'tsina) spirit. "The old stories about the ka'tsina spirit and Yellow Woman can't mean us" (33). As she and Silva head deeper into the mountains, the woman looks for something or someone to reestablish her link with the ordinary world:

> I will see someone, eventually I will see someone, and then I will be certain that he is only a man — some man from nearby — and I will be sure that I am not Yellow Woman. Because she is from out of time past and I live now and I've been to school and there are highways and pickup trucks that Yellow Woman never saw [34].

Continuing within the mythic narrative, the woman and Silva arrive at a hut, and as in the traditional stories, Silva gives the woman a task to do — in this version she fries potatoes. When the woman again denies that she could be part of a Yellow Woman story, Silva confuses her sense of time, stating, "But someday they will talk about us, and they will say, 'Those two lived long ago when things like that happened'" (36). The woman's sense of space also continues to be confused when she tries again to see the pueblo but cannot. Silva persists in identifying himself as the kachina: "I have told you who I am. The Navajo people know me, too" (37). He also confesses to the woman that he is a cattle thief, and when they sleep together that night, the woman feels threatened by Silva, but still feels attracted to him.

By morning, the woman has given herself over to living within the myth. She has the opportunity to escape, but instead she lingers outside the hut: "I found some dried apricots in the cardboard box, and I sat down on a rock at the edge of the plateau rim. There was no wind and the sun warmed me. I was surrounded by silence. I drowsed with apricots in my mouth, and I didn't believe there were highways or railroads or cattle to steal" (38). The woman decides she does not really need to return home — her husband will find someone else and her mother and grandmother will raise the baby. She walks back to the hut, content to stay with Silva, and revels in the beauty of the nature around her. While admiring the scene, however, the edge of Silva's violence intrudes again as she sees the bloody carcass of a slaughtered cow:

> It was noon when I got back. When I saw the stone house I remembered that I had meant to go home. But that didn't seem important any more, maybe because there were little blue flowers growing in the meadow behind the stone house and the gray squirrels were playing in the pines next to the house. The horses were standing in the corral, and there was a beef carcass hanging on the shady side of a big pine in front of the house. Flies buzzed around the clotted blood that hung from the carcass. Silva was washing his hands in a bucket full of ... bloody water with brown-and-white animal hairs floating in it [39].

As they leave to go down the mountain to sell the meat, the woman wonders again if Silva is just a Navajo, pretending to be a kachina. Silva grabs his rifle and they start down the mountain on horseback. Once again the woman looks for some comforting signs of civilization, but when she claims to see the houses of a town, Silva says that she is mistaken, pulling her back into the myth. The landscape continues to be surreally bright and colorful, indicating the "other worldliness" of the mythical mountain environment: "It was hot and the wildflowers were closing up their deep-yellow petals. Only the waxy cactus flowers bloomed in the bright sun, and I saw every color that a cactus blossom can be; the white ones and the red ones were still buds, but the purple and the yellow were blossoms, open full and the most beautiful of all" (40).

Silva and the woman come across a white rancher who accuses Silva of stealing the cow whose meat they carry in gunny sacks. Since it seems violence might break out, Silva tells the woman to go back up the mountain. Not hesitating, she rides back up the path which is so steep she cannot look back. She rides until she comes to a fork in the path, and then she stops to look back. At the fork, she reaches a place of transition. She now cannot see the place from which she has come, where Silva remains with the rancher, and when she looks up, she sees the vapor trails of jets floating in the sky. Next she hears shots. The assumption is that Silva kills the white rancher just as Yellow Woman begins her reentry into the ordinary world. At the sound of the shots, the frightened horse runs away with the woman. They run downhill, toward the river, a direction the woman feels safer going rather than back up the mountain. When they reach the river, the woman gets down from the horse and turns it loose. The woman walks home, first on a dirt wood-hauler's road that soon becomes a paved road as she approaches the village. She walks the last stretch along the river, and as she comes to the place where she first saw Silva, she thinks wistfully of him:

> I came back to the place on the river bank where he had been sitting the first time I saw him. The green willow leaves that he had trimmed from the branch were still lying there, wilted in the sand. I saw the leaves and I wanted to go back to him — to kiss him and to touch him — but the mountains were too far away now. And I told myself, because I believe it, he will come back sometime and be waiting again by the river [43].

The woman heads for home, but she wants to leave open the option for another such adventure in the future, when the monotony of ordinary life again overcomes her. As she reaches the screen door of her house, she hears her husband playing with the baby and her mother telling her grandmother how to make, of all things, Jell-O. As happens in many traditional Yellow Woman tales, the woman decides to tell her family that she was kidnapped by a Navajo. The story ends as the woman wishes her grandfather was still alive, for the Yellow Woman stories were his favorites.

Landscape plays a vital role in Silko's "Yellow Woman." At each stage of the woman's journey into myth and back out again, the landscape gives a visual picture of her subjective state of mind — the brilliant colors, for instance, indicating her heightened senses while living the myth with Silva. The landscape represents her desire for an adventure by the river, her sensual awakening in the mountains, her losing sight of first the ordinary world when she is with Silva, and then the mythical mountain when she is away from him. Finally, the road leads to the mundane ties of the ordinary world that draw her back to her family. The road she walks on becomes more developed, going from dirt to pavement, as she reenters the civilization of her everyday world. Although the woman returns to ordinary life at the end, she has been renewed through her excursion into the mountains by living the story of Yellow Woman, and she returns with a gift — a new Yellow Woman tale to tell.

House Made of Dawn

Related to Silko's use of landscape to portray a character's subjective state of mind is N. Scott Momaday's use of the high desert, the city of Los Angeles, and the beach to symbolically portray the cultural conflict occurring within the character Abel in the Pulitzer Prize–winning *House Made of Dawn*. Abel, like Tayo in *Ceremony*, is a veteran of World War II. When he returns home to the Jemez Pueblo after the war, Abel's memories haunt him, and he is a seriously sick alcoholic. Also like Tayo, who was raised by his Uncle Josiah, Abel has been raised in a traditional way of life by his grandfather, Francisco. But when Abel returns to the reservation after the war, he cannot adjust back to his former way of life.

The book opens with a prologue which first describes the environment Abel was raised in, the high-desert land of Walatowa.

> *Dypaloh.** There was a house made of dawn. It was made of pollen and of rain, and the land was very old and everlasting. There were many colors on the hills, and the plain was bright with different-colored clays and sands. Red and blue and spotted horses grazed in the plain, and there was a dark wilderness on the mountains beyond. The land was still and strong. It was beautiful all around [1].

The description of the land used in this opening immediately ties the scene to Navajo tradition as it is a brief version of a much longer song, a traditional Navajo night chant. "House made of dawn" refers to the earth. Later in the novel, when Abel is living in Los Angeles, more of this healing chant is given when Abel's friend Ben Benally, a Navajo, sings about the land to Abel in order to give him hope and to remind him of his old life. "In *House Made of Dawn*," Susan Scarberry-García claims in *Landmarks of Healing: A Study of House Made of Dawn*, "healing occurs when the characters internalize images of the land by means of the symbolic acts of singing and storytelling" (2). Although Abel is Jemez, not Navajo, there is an indication in the novel that his father may have been Navajo. But even without having a biological connection to Navajo culture, as P. Jane Hafen explains in "Pan-Indianism and Tribal Sovereignties in *House Made of Dawn* and *The Names*," there is a "long history of cooperation among the Pueblo peoples, including the Jemez, and with neighboring tribes. This background helps establish the foundation of Abel's association with Navajo Ben Benally" (11). The chant reminds Abel of the land that holds not only the origins of Navajo culture, but also his own Jemez culture.

Following the opening description of the land, Momaday describes Abel's action within the landscape, again a tie with tradition as Abel, performing a ritual of his tribe, runs in the early dawn:

> Abel was running. He was alone and running, hard at first, heavily, but then easily and well. The road curved out in front of him and rose away in the distance.

---

*Dypaloh is a traditional word in the Jemez language used to indicate the beginning of a story. See Momaday's "Glossary" in *The Names*, pp. 168–69.

He could not see the town. The valley was gray with rain, and snow lay out upon the dunes. It was dawn....

He was naked to the waist, and his arms and shoulders had been marked with burnt wood and ashes. The cold rain slanted down upon him and left his skin mottled and streaked. The road curved out and lay into the bank of rain beyond, and Abel was running. Against the winter sky and the long, light landscape of the valley at dawn, he seemed almost to be standing still, very little and alone [1–2].

Abel performs the ritualistic run in the sacred space of the land, its spiritual nature underscored by his inability to see the town. The race, according to Matthias Schubnell in *N. Scott Momaday: The Cultural and Literary Background*, "is connected with the ceremony of clearing the irrigation ditches in the spring. It is an imitation of water running through the channels, a magic bid for the vital supply of rain, and a ritual act to prevent the harvest from being influenced by evil powers" (132). But there is a feeling of desolation and loneliness to the scene, indicating right from the beginning the struggles that Abel will encounter.

Following the prologue, part one of the novel is entitled "The Longhair." The term "longhair" refers to a Native American who lives by the old traditions. Often the term has a derogatory connotation, and may be used by other Native Americans who are urbanized and who have assimilated into white culture to refer to those whom they see as resistant to change. Francisco is a longhair; he believes in the old traditions and ceremonies. And since Francisco does not have to live outside the Jemez Pueblo, his ways are suited for the environment and the community in which he lives. Francisco is respected for his way of life by the community and is one of the keepers of the traditions. But unlike Francisco, Abel does have to leave the pueblo, and his ties to tradition and his inability to adapt to life outside of it make him a target of ridicule among more urbanized Native Americans. His inability to adapt is viewed as a stubborn resistance to accept change, and while later living in Los Angeles, the term "longhair" is applied to Abel in its derogatory sense.

Abel's road to Los Angeles begins at Jemez. One night while drinking in a bar on the reservation after Abel has returned from the war, he begins a conversation with an albino man. The man had once humiliated Abel by beating him with a rooster because Abel had made a poor showing in a competition; he had beaten Abel until the bird was dead, and bits of its feathers, flesh and entrails covered the ground.*

---

*The competition was a chicken pull. In *The Names* (New York: Harper & Row, 1976), Momaday describes a chicken pull as follows: "Some of the ablest riders of the village participated in this ancient sport, which is decidedly cruel, but also very exciting to see, inasmuch as it requires great skill. The riders convened on their horses at the west end of the plaza. Then someone, an official dressed ceremonially in white pants, a belted tunic, and moccasins, brought a rooster to the center of the plaza and buried it to its neck in sand; the miserable creature made a grotesque

Convinced the albino man is an evil spirit, a witch who can turn himself into a snake, Abel lures the albino outside the bar and murders him in a brutal stabbing. At the trial, a priest speaks in Abel's defense, proposing that Abel's imagination, given his cultural background, could indeed have convinced him that the albino was a witch. Because of the priest's intervention, Abel is given a reduced sentence, and after several years in prison, which he can barely remember, he is released and put into a relocation program that moves him to Los Angeles.

Ben Benally, Abel's Navajo friend in Los Angeles, feels an affinity with Abel through the connection of their similar cultures and their origins within the high desert landscape. Robert Nelson in *Place and Vision* describes their connection through the land: "Ben ... seems to understand, these similarities in culture derive in turn from similarities in the landscapes out of which the cultures emerged" (75). Benally contrasts his homeland with a description of the city environment:

> You have to watch where you're going. There's always a big crowd of people down there, especially after it rains, and a lot of noise. You hear the cars on the wet streets, starting and stopping. You hear a lot of whistles and horns, and there's a lot of loud music all around. Those old men who stand around on the corners and sell papers, they're always yelling at you, but you can't understand them. I can't, anyway [140].

Benally, like Abel, was also raised on a reservation and still has ties with the traditions of his tribe. Benally still sings the chants and likes to pray in a traditional manner, but he does so alone or with Abel, embarrassed to have others see him. Unlike Abel, however, Benally has chosen to adapt to white culture in the city. He holds down a job in a factory and manages to stay clear of trouble. But even though Benally has been able to adapt, he recognizes that Abel cannot. Speaking about Abel, Benally says:

> He was unlucky. You could see that right away. You could see that he wasn't going to get along around here. Milly thought he was going to be all right, I guess,

---

[contininued] sight — the head of a bird, its yellow eyes blinking with fright, its neck craned, its comb flopping this way and that. Then one by one the riders rode running close upon it, each one leaning down to take hold of it and pull it from the ground. Most of the horses were poorly trained to the task, and some of the riders fell in the attempt, to the great delight of lookers-on; but then one of them ... took the rooster up and held it high in the air, its wings beating furiously. He turned then and walked his horse back to the west end, among the other riders, and one of these he began to beat heavily with the rooster about the head and shoulders. The man raised his arms to protect himself, but according to the rules of the game he must stand his ground and try to catch the rooster up in the loop of his reins or under his arm. Inevitably he did so sooner or later, and the game became a tug of war; the adversaries then pulled the rooster apart (I hoped it was dead); its dismembered body was dropped on the ground and left to the dogs; and another poor creature was brought out, and the game was played again, and so on." (144–145)

but she didn't understand how it was with him. He was a longhair, like Tosamah said. You know, you have to change. That's the only way you can live in a place like this. You have to forget about the way it was, how you grew up and all. Sometimes it's hard, but you have to do it. Well, he didn't want to change, I guess, or he didn't know how [148].

Abel's life in Los Angeles nearly kills him. His alcoholism worsens and he loses his job. The more urbanized Native Americans, like Tosamah, ostracize him and break down his spirit. One night he is savagely attacked by a corrupt policeman (a malevolent being reminiscent of the albino/witch) who smashes Abel's hands with a nightstick. Unable to forget the policeman, Abel goes looking for him on another night, bent on revenge. The policeman, however, beats Abel nearly to death, beating his face and body, breaking his nose and the bones in his hands. Gravely wounded and near death, Abel passes out on the beach where he spends three days lapsing in and out of consciousness, remembering the past. A significant portion of the book takes place in Abel's mind as he lies on the beach.

The beach, a hybrid area, exists at the margin of sea and land. It is a borderland in the sense that few animals, and certainly no humans, can adapt perfectly to both land and sea. People need air to breathe as the fish need water, but because of the tides, to stay on the beach in the same spot is to spend at least part of the time outside of one's element, thereby risking death. For Abel, the beach represents the two worlds between which he hangs suspended. It is a place where he must take stock of his environment and decide where he belongs.

While on the beach, Abel comes to terms with his life and relives, through his dreams, the key moments in his past that have formed him. In spite of his pain, Abel comes to realize that he will not make it in Los Angeles, that to stay there will kill him, and that he must return home and try to become well again if he is to survive. As P. Jane Hafen asserts in "Pan-Indianism and Tribal Sovereignties," even though Benally has performed the Navajo night chant for Abel, "the Navajo rite does not and cannot directly heal him; he must return to the Jemez traditions" (13). The beach is an appropriate place for Abel to come to these realizations, because the beach represents a place of dislocation, and if Abel stays there, exposed to the elements, he will die. The danger the beach poses appears in this passage about a particular specie of fish that periodically, crazily, throw themselves up onto dry sand:

> There is a small silver-sided fish that is found along the coast of southern California. In the spring and summer it spawns on the beach during the first three hours after each of the three high tides following the highest tide. These fishes come by the hundreds from the sea. They hurl themselves upon the land and writhe in the light of the moon, the moon, the moon; they writhe in the light of the moon.

> They are among the most helpless creatures on the face of the earth. Fishermen, lovers, passers-by catch them up in their bare hands [89].

As the novel continues to shift between Abel's past memories and his present, he precariously balances between life and death while on the beach; the ocean becomes a void, threatening to pull Abel under:

> Now, here, the world was open at his back. He had lost his place. He had been long ago at the center, had known where he was, had lost his way, had wandered to the edge of the earth, was even now reeling on the edge of the void. The sea reached and leaned, licked after him and withdrew, falling off forever in the abyss. And the fishes... [104].

Wounded and helpless, with his hands smashed into flapping appendages, of no more use than the fins of the fish who writhe in the sand, Abel's dislocation is complete. If he stays on the beach, he will die. Knowing this, Abel gathers his strength and makes it back to his apartment where Benally helps him get to a hospital. In *Place and Vision*, Robert Nelson connects Abel's stay in the hospital with his earlier stay in prison as "institutionalized 'places' through which Abel must pass either to get from Walatowa to Los Angeles or vice-versa" (84). The transitions of prison and hospital, though not described in much detail in the book, serve as portals between Abel's two conflicting landscapes and identities.

Abel decides to leave Los Angeles and to return home, but as he boards the bus, still swollen and disfigured from the beating, with his belongings in a paper bag that tears apart in the rain, it is clear that Abel has a long way to go toward recovery. The difficulties he will face in his journey back to his former life and in relocating himself back on the reservation are reflected in the landscape as he sees it upon his return:

> The river was dark and swift, and there were jagged panes of ice along the banks, encrusted with snow. The valley was gray and cold; the mountains were dark and dim on the sky, and a great, gray motionless cloud of snow and mist lay out in the depth of the canyon. The fields were bare and colorless, and the gray tangle of branches rose up out of the orchards like antlers and bones [193].

Indeed, Abel's return is difficult. His body throbs with pain, he's sick, and he continues to drink until he has no more money. His grandfather Francisco is dying, and Abel cannot understand the words his grandfather says to him. Abel himself can think of nothing to say. He spends six days with his grandfather, losing his sense of time and fading in and out of memories. He wakes up on the seventh morning and his grandfather is dead. Faced with this loss, Abel falls back on tradition, and in the preparation of his grandfather's body, he begins his return to the ways of his culture:

> He drew the old man's head erect and laid water to the hair. He fashioned the long white hair in a queue and wound it with yarn. He dressed the body in bright ceremonial colors: The old man's wine velveteen shirt, white trousers, and low moccasins, soft and white with kaolin. From the rafters he took down the pouches of pollen and of meal, the sacred feathers and the ledger book. These, together with ears of colored corn, he placed at his grandfather's side after he had sprinkled meal in the four directions. He wrapped the body in a blanket [210].

As in Silko's "Yellow Woman," the clarity of Abel's vision in this passage and the emphasis on colors indicate the spirituality of Abel's actions.

After Abel prepares his grandfather's body, finishing shortly before dawn, he notifies the priest and goes out to join the runners in the predawn light. As the sun strikes the horizon, the runners streak away and Abel, still racked with pain, runs on alone. He falls once, but he gets up and runs on. This last scene echoes back and joins with the prologue, thus leading the end of the book back into the beginning and returning Abel to the landscape of his tribal identity. Although it is not clear that Abel will succeed at reintegrating himself back into his traditional culture, it is clear that he has started, and the words of the night chant return to him. Although the chant is Navajo, Abel appropriates it to express the reintegration of his identity with the land of Walatowa. His Jemez identity is also present, however, as the book ends with the word "*Qtsedaba*" (a word used by the Jemez to indicate the end of a story):

> He was alone and running on, and he was past caring about the pain. Pure exhaustion laid hold of his mind, and he could see at last without having to think. He could see the canyons and the mountains and the sky. He could see the rain and the river and the fields beyond. He could see the dark hills at dawn. He was running, and under his breath he began to sing. There was no sound, and he had no voice; he had only the words of a song. And he went running on the rise of the song. *House made of pollen, house made of dawn. Qtsedaba* [212].

In *Place and Vision*, Nelson explains the connection of the land, Abel's running, and the act of healing: "Abel's participation in the dawn race not only confirms the healing power of identity with the land ... but more importantly also grounds the possibility of healing in a specific place, thereby turning the *vision* of healing into an *act* of healing and the idea of regenerative motion into a ceremony of regenerative motion, in this case the running of the Winter Race" (88).

In *House Made of Dawn*, Los Angeles represents Abel's frictional, destructive encounter with white culture and his subsequent resistance to assimilation. Only in a hybrid space, on the beach, can Abel remember his past and begin to reintegrate his identity. As he moves in and out of consciousness on the beach, Abel reaches a crisis that must be resolved if he is to survive. He eventually realizes that if he is going to heal, he must go back home. The desert landscape of Abel's home is so integrated into his identity that it becomes the visible indication of his character and the force that will help Abel to heal the identity split he has suffered.

Bless Me, Ultima

Somewhat the same use of landscape as occurs in *House Made of Dawn*—two contrasting landscapes to represent two conflicting cultures—occurs in Rudolfo Anaya's book, *Bless Me, Ultima*. Chicano author Anaya uses two landscapes to portray the two conflicting cultures that the young protagonist of the book, Antonio Márez, has inherited from his parents. When Antonio learns to integrate the two landscapes, he reconciles the cultural split he has felt since birth. Antonio is only six years old when the book opens, yet he is aware of a split between his mother and his father. The split extends throughout the families on both sides and is tied to a dichotomy between the families' different ways of life as symbolized by the landscapes in which they live — the Lunas, on the mother's side, are a farming family who live in the river valley; the Márezs, the father's family, are vaqueros who herd cattle on the plain (llano). This split in his heritage lives within Antonio, and he has felt torn between his mother and his father all of his young life. In a dream, Antonio learns of the events that surrounded his birth and of the conflict between the two families that has caused the split in his own identity:

> *This one will be a Luna, the old man said, he will be a farmer and keep our customs and traditions. Perhaps God will bless our family and make the baby a priest.*
> *And to show their hope they rubbed the dark earth of the river valley on the baby's forehead, and they surrounded the bed with the fruits of their harvest so the small room smelled of fresh green chile and corn, ripe apples and peaches, pumpkins and green beans.*
> *Then the silence was shattered with the thunder of hoofbeats; vaqueros surrounded the small house with shouts and gunshots, and when they entered the room they were laughing and singing and drinking.*
> *Gabriel, they shouted, you have a fine son! He will make a fine vaquero!*
> *And they smashed the fruits and vegetables that surrounded the bed and replaced them with a saddle, horse blankets, bottles of whiskey, a new rope, bridles, chapas, and an old guitar. And they rubbed the stain of earth from the baby's forehead because man was not to be tied to the earth but free upon it* [5–6].*

Antonio often wonders how two people as opposite as his mother and father could ever have married. Throughout the novel, he struggles with this

---

*The italics used in this and some of the other quotes from *Bless Me, Ultima* indicate passages from Antonio's dreams.

dichotomy that permeates every important aspect of his life, including his beliefs about religion and his notions about what is real. Fortunately, he has the help and guidance of Ultima, an elderly woman who was the midwife at his birth and who comes to live with his family when he is six. Ultima is a *curandera*, a healer who cures with a combination of medicinal herbs and magic. Even as a young child of six, Antonio is aware of her power and senses this awareness through how he views the land on the day Ultima arrives to stay with his family:

> When she came the beauty of the llano unfolded before my eyes, and the gurgling waters of the river sang to the hum of the turning earth. The magical time of childhood stood still, and the pulse of the living earth pressed its mystery into my living blood. She took my hand, and the silent, magic powers she possessed made beauty from the raw, sunbaked llano, the green river valley, and the blue bowl which was the white sun's home [1].

Ultima senses a power within Antonio as well, and she trains him as her apprentice and takes him with her when she goes to heal people or to exorcize evil spirits from their homes. But although Antonio's love for Ultima is strong, he sometimes wonders about the nature of her powers. He wonders if she uses her powers only to do good, or if, as some others believe, she can play the role of the *bruja*, the witch, and use her powers for evil as well.

The nature of both good and evil are just one set of opposites Antonio must deal with. He also struggles with the opposition of orthodox Catholicism, represented by his mother's family, and a pagan religion, based on the legend of a god who turns into a golden carp, represented by his father's family. The legend of the golden carp goes back to a primordial time when a group of people were sent to the valley by their gods. Because they kept their faith in their gods, in spite of years of wandering, the gods rewarded them by bringing them to a land that was fertile and plentiful with game, fresh water and abundant fruits. The only thing that the people were prohibited from taking were the carp fish, as the carp were sacred to the gods. All went well until there was a drought that lasted for forty years, and the people were starving. To save themselves, they caught and ate the carp. The angry gods wanted to kill all of the people, but one kind god intervened on their behalf. The other gods were so touched by his concern for the people that they decreed that the people would live in the river as carp, and changed the people into fish. Worried about the fate of the people, the kind god asked to be turned into a carp as well so he could live among the people and take care of them. His desire was granted, and the gods turned him into a giant, golden carp.

When Antonio hears this story from his friend Samuel, he is disturbed. "It made me shiver, not because it was cold but because the roots of everything I had ever believed in seemed shaken" (81). And when Antonio actually sees the golden carp swim by him in the river, he experiences a feeling of the miraculous, a feeling he has not gotten from orthodox religion. Upon seeing the carp, Antonio exclaims, "This is what I had expected God to do at my first holy communion!" (114). Antonio does not abandon Catholicism, but he is confused by having an alternative choice just as he is confused about what lifestyle to follow, the farming life of the river valley or the herding life of the plains.

The answer as to how to integrate the dichotomies of his life comes to Antonio in a dream, a dream in which Ultima appears and explains to him the relationship of the river to the ocean, and the moon to the sun. The vastness of the ocean and of the plains are frequently linked together within the book:

> *The sweet water of the moon which falls as rain is the same water that gathers into rivers and flows to fill the seas. Without the waters of the moon to replenish the oceans there would be no oceans. And the same salt waters of the oceans are drawn by the sun to the heavens, and in turn become again the waters of the moon. Without the sun there would be no waters formed to slake the dark earth's thirst.*
> *The waters are one, Antonio....*
> *You have been seeing only parts ... and not looking beyond into the great cycle that binds us all* [121].

As a result of this dream, which integrates the river (and the river valley) with the ocean (associated with the plain), Antonio begins to envision a life that is not torn by dichotomy, but that holds the possibility of finding a third alternative that combines both of his heritages. On a drive with his father, Antonio learns that his father is ready to put aside the differences he has had with his wife's family, the Lunas, and he encourages Antonio to find an alternative path:

> "...Perhaps it is time we gave up the old differences —"
> "Then maybe I do not have to be just Márez, or Luna, perhaps I can be both —" I [Antonio] said.
> "Yes," he said, but I knew he was as proud as ever of being Márez.
> "It seems I am so much a part of the past—" I said.
> "Ay, every generation, every man is a part of his past. He cannot escape it, but he may reform the old materials, make something new —"
> "Take the llano and the river valley, the moon and the sea, God and the golden carp — and make something new," I said to myself [247].

As William Clements observes in "The Way to Individuation in Anaya's *Bless Me, Ultima*," "The river ... not only separates, but also provides a linkage between *llano* and village, the two heritages" (135). By seeing the interconnections of the sun and the moon, the river and the ocean, Antonio breaks down the binary oppositions that have characterized his life.

The posing of dichotomous relationships and their eventual resolution is a structure that governs much of Anaya's work. In order for a character to know his or her identity, he or she must struggle with opposing dualities and find either some middle ground, or a third alternative that takes from the two opposing forces and forms something new. In an interview conducted with David Johnson and David Apodaca in 1979, Anaya explains his interest in dichotomies and their resolution as a path towards self-actualization for his characters. Landscape necessarily plays a role in self-actualization, Anaya explains, because people live within an environment and cannot become self-actualized without working out their relationship to that environment in which they live. In a response to a question by Apodaca in which he asks for a clarification of the connection Anaya sees among roots, land and self-actualization, Anaya answers:

> We very often talk in modern terms only of being self-actualized with other people. That is, to be congruent with other people. What I am talking about is that there are many more ways which complete the person. A person to me is the pole of a metaphor. Always searching for the other pole. Usually in tension with it. Male in tension with female. You complete the metaphor by dissolving the tension with the other pole, social or communal, finding some kind of a meeting ground. You also complete that by rediscovering the naturalness of the poles and the metaphor of man in his environment. So that if we have been alienated or disassociated or torn apart from the earth itself, to self-actualize you have to rediscover that [Johnson and Apodaca 34].

According to Manuel Broncano in "Landscapes of the Magical," Ultima "is the link between opposing worlds that seek harmony and quietude, the connection resolving the irreconcilable dichotomies" (128). The two opposing landscapes are what Antonio must resolve within this book, and with the help of the dream sent to him by Ultima, he realizes that he need not make an either/or choice in his life, but can create a hybrid identity.

The Woman Warrior: Memoirs of a Girlhood Among Ghosts

So far, we have talked about natural landscapes as holders of tradition and history, as places of healing, as visible indicators of a character's identity, and as a necessary ingredient in the process of a character's self-actualization. The environment in which such dichotomies and resolutions of dichotomies takes place, however, may not always be a natural setting. Maxine Hong Kingston provides manmade settings — cities and even specific buildings, such as schools and theaters — that play critical roles as the necessary locations in which the characters can work out resolutions to the dichotomies with which they struggle.

In *The Woman Warrior: Memoirs of a Girlhood Among Ghosts*, Kingston uses two schools, one American and one Chinese, to indicate the conflict her semi-autobiographical character, Maxine, experiences within herself as she struggles with growing up as a Chinese American. In the American school only English may be spoken, and Maxine describes her early years in school as characterized by silence: "During the first year I spoke to no one at school, did not ask before going to the lavatory, and flunked kindergarten. My sister also said nothing for three years, silent in the playground and silent at lunch. There were other quiet Chinese girls not of our family, but most of them got over it sooner than we did" (165–66). In the Chinese school, Chinese is spoken and the students perform their tasks as a group. Individual oral readings and participation in discussion are not required. Consequently, the students are more vocal, even boisterous:

> After American school, we picked up our cigar boxes, in which we had arranged books, brushes, and an inkbox neatly, and went to Chinese school, from 5:00 to 7:30 P.M. There we chanted together and not alone with one voice. When we had a memorization test, the teacher let each of us come to his desk and say the lesson to him privately.... Most of the teachers were men. The boys who were so well behaved in the American school played tricks on them and talked back to them. The girls were not mute. They screamed and yelled during recess, when there were no rules; they had fistfights [167].

In "Publish or Perish: Food, Hunger, and Self-Construction in Maxine Hong Kingston's *The Woman Warrior*," Paul Outka aptly describes why Maxine's abilities to speak differ between the two schools:

> Neither Maxine [the protagonist] nor Kingston has trouble speaking Chinese in a Chinese environment. It is speaking English in America that poses such a terrible strain. For a Chinese American to speak in this country is not only to challenge the stereotype of the silent, inscrutable Other, but to link the inner world of the imagination to the outer reality of an often hostile "real" landscape, to bridge the mind and body in a single act, to be linguistically American and racially Chinese at the same time [477].

Since the differences in the schools reflect the larger differences between the two cultures, school becomes the location where Maxine confronts the conflict. There is one Chinese girl, a year older than Maxine, who will not speak at either the American nor the Chinese school. One day Maxine confronts her in the basement of the American school and tries to force her to talk. Desperate in her attempts to make the girl speak, Maxine becomes cruel, pulling the girl's hair and pinching her hard. No matter what Maxine does, however, the quiet girl will not speak, and Maxine herself fears that she too, as a Chinese girl, will be forever without a voice. She sees a mirror image of herself in the other girl, and by abusing the quiet girl, Maxine fights against herself.* Paul Outka and others, including Kingston, have observed that "the girl functions as Maxine's doppelganger, a silent body onto which she projects her worst fears in a furious, violent effort to give birth to her own voice by confronting what keeps her silent" (Outka 478).†

The incident brings about a crisis in Maxine's life, and she suffers a breakdown because of it and stays home in bed, away from school, for eighteen months. When Maxine returns to school, now in junior high, she sees the quiet girl again and comments that she has not changed her appearance since elementary school. Maxine no longer feels threatened by the girl and comes to realize that the quiet girl is a special case — not like her. She also realizes a benefit in being Chinese, as the girl's family takes care of her and protects her:

> I was wrong about nobody taking care of her. Her sister became a clerk-typist and stayed unmarried. They lived with their mother and father. She did not have to leave the house except to go to the movies. She was supported. She was protected by her family, as they would normally have done in China if they could have afforded it, not sent off to school with strangers, ghosts, boys [182].

School continues to be an important location for Maxine, and as she grows, it becomes a source of her sense of self-worth, helping her to define herself as a person of intelligence and also as a writer. Near the end of the book, when Maxine is about to graduate from high school, she suddenly finds the courage to confront her mother based on the confidence she has developed in school:

> One night when the laundry was so busy that the whole family was eating dinner there, crowded around the little round table, my throat burst open.... I'm going away.... I am. Do you hear me? I may be ugly and clumsy, but one thing I'm not, I'm not retarded. There's nothing wrong with my brain. Do you know what the Teacher Ghosts say about me? They tell me I'm smart, and I can win scholarships. I can get into colleges. I've already applied. I'm smart. I can do all kinds of things.... I'm so smart, if they say write ten pages, I can write fifteen.... Things follow in lines at school. They take stories and teach us to turn them into essays.... I'm going to get scholarships, and I'm going away [201].

In spite of finding her voice in speaking to her mother (Brave Orchid), Maxine still has far to go in her task of integrating both the Chinese and the U.S. American parts of her identity. At the time she confronts her mother,

---

*Maxine's encounter with the quiet girl is described in much more detail in chapter five.

†See Arturo Islas' and Marilyn Yalom's interview with Maxine Hong Kingston about the quiet girl in *Conversations with Maxine Hong Kingston* (Jackson: University Press of Mississippi, 1998), 30.

she still does not recognize what her mother has given her in terms of the stories she has told Maxine, stories about women warriors who can accomplish great deeds that are meant to show Maxine, indirectly, what she can accomplish in her own life. In fact, even Maxine's discovery of her abilities in school reflects back to Brave Orchid, who herself, in China, was able to establish her own strong identity in a medical school, where she excelled in her studies and got to "live out the daydream of women — to have a room, even a section of a room, that only gets messed up when she messes it up herself" (*Woman Warrior* 61). Through her school experiences Maxine confronts the conflict of cultures she feels within herself, and it is in school, a location where she both faces challenges and receives affirmation, that she finds the confidence to begin a journey toward establishing her own self-identity as a Chinese American writer.

Tripmaster Monkey: His Fake Book

Most of Maxine Hong Kingston's works take place primarily in northern California (her book *Hawai'i One Summer* being an exception). Kingston grew up in Stockton, California, and since both *The Woman Warrior* and *China Men* are semi-autobiographical, their location in northern California is a given. However, northern California is also the setting for Kingston's first purely fictional novel, *Tripmaster Monkey: His Fake Book*, which takes place in San Francisco. As a city, San Francisco is a manmade place, but its unique blend of disparate elements from Western history and high culture give San Francisco an ambiance unlike that of any other city. In *Landscapes of the New West*, Krista Comer describes San Francisco as follows:

> As the urban seat of the mid–nineteenth-century gold rush, the gateway to the Mother Lode, San Francisco *as a city* overflows with the sense of romance usually reserved for the non-urban frontier West. From the beginning of its economic development and its popular representation in the mid–1800s, San Francisco is characterized as a city in a class of its own, a symbol of beginnings and possibility — above all, like the West itself, of hope [104].*

As a symbol of beginnings, possibility and hope, San Francisco provides the contrasting background for Kingston's *Tripmaster Monkey*. The book opens with the protagonist, a young, Chinese American man by the name of Wittman Ah Sing, walking through Golden Gate Park. The park represents a

---

*Comer points out, however, that this image of the West based on new beginnings, possibilities and hope is often a false image, perpetrated primarily by white males. The West, for example, hardly represents hope for Native Americans or for other minority groups who faced discrimination there.

hybrid landscape, characteristic of the San Francisco Bay Area, combining the natural beauty of the West Coast landscape with the achievements of urban civilization as evidenced by the museums, the aquarium, and the formal gardens that occupy space in the park. The description of the park also gives evidence of San Francisco's more recent history as a center for protest and social reform in the 1960s. But as Wittman walks around the edges of the park, he encounters people who have fallen through the cracks of social reform:

> An old white woman was sitting on a bench selling trivets "@ ½ dollar ea.," which a ducky and a bunny pointed out with gloved fingers. She lifted her head and turned her face toward Wittman's; her hands were working one more trivet out of yarn and bottlecaps.... He looked at her thick feet chapped and dirty in zoris. Their sorry feet is how you can tell crazy people who have no place to go and walk everywhere.
> Wittman turned his head, and there on the ground were a pigeon and a squatting man, both puking....
> Along a side path came another Black man, this one pushing a shopping cart transporting one red apple and a red bull from Tijuana [4, 7].

The cultural progress, as evidenced by the museums and other cultural buildings located in the park, also shows some imperfections:

> He would avoid the Academy of Sciences, especially the North American Hall. Coyotes and bobcats dead behind glass forever....
> Don't go into the Steinhart Aquarium either. Remember *The Lady from Shanghai*? The seasick cameras shoot through and around the fishtanks at Orson Welles and Rita Hayworth saying goodbye....
> No Oriental Tea Garden either. "Oriental." Shit [5].

The multiple histories of the romantic old West, urbanization, social protest, and the poor, simultaneously present in the park, are further overlaid with Wittman Ah Sing's own historical past. While walking through the park, he sees a family of FOBs (a derogatory term for newly arrived Chinese immigrants, meaning fresh off the boat). Despite Wittman's obvious disdain for the immigrant family, the family reflects the history of Asian immigration to California, an important factor in the development of the U.S. American West.

> Immigrants. Fresh Off the Boats out in public. Didn't know how to walk together. Spitting seeds. So uncool. You wouldn't mislike them on sight if their pants weren't so highwater, gym socks white and noticeable. F.O.B. Fashions—highwaters or puddlecuffs. Can't get it right. Uncool. Uncool. The tunnel smelled of mothballs— F. O.B. perfume [5].

In spite of his prejudices against the newly immigrated Chinese, on his walk Wittman recalls aspects of Chinatown, a place where he no longer lives but still has a desire to keep alive in his memory. Chinatowns themselves are places which carry a double history — their inhabitants maintain the traditions and languages of the Chinese homeland, yet Chinatowns played a vital role in the history of the western United States, both as a source of labor for development and in providing a cultural mixing ground for Chinese and U.S. American traditions. Chinatowns exhibit as well the history of racism in the United States as Chinese immigrants congregated together in Chinatowns to form supportive, ethnic communities to protect themselves from the often violent, racist actions of whites.* Wittman reminisces as he walks:

> The last time he had walked along the ocean, he ended up at the zoo. Aquarium and dank zoo on the same day. "Fu-li-sah-kah Soo." He said "Fleishhacker Zoo" to himself in Chinatown language, just to keep a hand in, so to speak, to remember and so to keep awhile longer words spoken by the people of his brief and dying culture [6].

In spite of the fact that Wittman is not a particularly sensitive protagonist (the narrator often chides him for his shortcomings), he does realize that he lacks a community, and as such, feels a sense of loss. He does not really belong in Chinatown anymore, where he is ridiculed for his beatnik appearance, but he does want to maintain a connection with Chinese Americans, and he wants to write a Chinese American work. He puzzles over how to write a novel with Chinese characters, but he decides against a novel because he does not know when or how he would let the reader know that the characters are Chinese or Chinese American. He decides to write a play. "By writing a play, he didn't need descriptions that racinated anybody. The actors will walk out on stage and their looks will be self-evident" (34). And so Wittman begins a play, a play that will "make the world spin in the palm of your hand" (35). As the play eventually comes to fruition, the theater building itself becomes a key site of the novel.

Wittman begins to put together the play, a work that combines and mixes random and seemingly exhaustive bits and pieces from Chinese and U.S. American culture, and the play is performed in a theater over the course of several days. The theater is the structure which allows Wittman to finally create a community. The play contains characters and stories from many traditional Chinese works, such as the heroes of *The Three Kingdoms*, although they appear in and out of stories that may or may not be the ones in which they originally appeared. Wittman eclectically borrows from other U.S. ethnic American traditions as well for the material for the play. The passage below,

---

*See Marlon K. Hom, *Songs of Gold Mountain: Cantonese Rhymes from San Francisco Chinatown* (Berkeley: University of California Press, 1987) for an in-depth discussion of San Francisco's Chinatown, including the reasons why Chinatowns were formed and descriptions of the lives of the Chinese immigrants in the nineteenth century.

for example, includes the Mexican American bandit Joaquín Murrieta and the outlaw gunslinger Three-Finger Jack who appear within a story from the Chinese classic, *The Water Margin*, which also is a tale of bandits. In the story, an innkeeper and his wife are charged with murdering and cooking some of their guests and serving them to other clients. In Wittman's play, the wife, the notorious female bandit the Night Ogress, denies the charges:

> "Oh, no," says she. "What must you be thinking?" She flusters around with the featherduster, just a housewife caught behind on her housekeeping. She picks up a hand. "You're thinking that I — that I — cook and serve and eat —? That this is food? Oh, how could you? Why, you're looking at trophies. These are the pieces of armed and dangerous men with prices on their heads. We don't have room in the house for their whole bodies. I'm not strong enough to bring back their entire remains. I just clip a part for identification — a scalp, a distinctive patch of tattooed or branded skin. This hand is the hand of Three-Finger Jack." Well, there are two fingers missing, all right; the famous trigger finger is still there. "And this head is the head of Joaquín Murrieta" [260].

The play leaps randomly through different texts, time periods and cultures, interweaving the threads of many different histories, opinions, movements and stories until the reader is dizzy with the universality of it all. The play takes days to perform, but at the end of the novel, Wittman has accomplished his goal. The players and the audience have grown in numbers, the audience members have become participants, and the players and the audience have become interchangeable, united into the community that Wittman has been seeking. But, Wittman realizes, maintaining a community takes some effort:

> Wittman was learning that one big bang-up show has to be followed by a second show, a third show, shows until something takes hold. He was defining a community, which will meet every night for a season. Community is not built once-and-for-all; people have to imagine, practice, and re-create it [306].

Within the multiple space of the theater, numerous histories which have formed the U.S. are played out on the stage. The identities of the characters within these histories are performed, and thus become fluid, since within the play blacks can play Chinese, Chinese can play whites, whites can play Mexican Americans, etc., because ethnicity is located in the performance, not in the physical appearances of the actors. The identities of the characters and the histories of these various groups cross over, intermix and borrow from each others' stories to create a composite history that is not rigidly categorized by race, gender or ethnicity. The play becomes a performance of the community that has been the outcome of all of these previous histories, and it resists the long-held tradition of the theater that the "white" view is the norm. Jeanne R. Smith in "Rethinking American Culture: Maxine Hong Kingston's Cross-Cultural *Tripmaster Monkey*," explains Wittman's casting choices: "By insisting on a multiracial cast, Wittman explicitly revises the Eugene O'Neill/ Arthur Miller classic American theatrical tradition with its 'typical' white American family, refusing also to replace it with an all-Chinese American cast" (76).

Through the multiple voices of the theater, and her novel, Kingston portrays the hybridity of the U.S. American community as it can be shown through the arts. In a 1989 interview with Paul Skenazy, Kingston deplores how a multicultural representation of the U.S. is more likely to be portrayed in a beer ad than in the arts, "because we aren't giving it to them in literature or in the movies. Artists aren't doing them" (107). Although multicultural representations in the arts have increased since 1989 (as evidenced by many of the works discussed in this book), portraying the hybridity of the United States, and giving all groups an equal voice, is not an easy task. Lara Narcisi in "Wittman's Transitions: Multivocality and the Play of *Tripmaster Monkey*," compliments the novel in this regard, saying, "It does present the artistic form as a substantive step toward a longer-term solution. The text suggests a utopian dream that the multivocal experience achieved through art might portray and/ or model a potential for a future reality" (106). Maxine Hong Kingston in *Tripmaster Monkey* proves that the arts can create a portrait of a multicultural community, and the theater in *Tripmaster Monkey*, the location where all things can be represented through performance, provides a perfect, multi-layered space for this formation of community to happen.

Conclusion

Whether natural or manmade, spaces may often serve as symbolic holders of various histories and cultural meanings, some of which may be in conflict. By using landscapes and architectural spaces to express the conflicts between different cultures, either through separate sites or through a single site with a double history, authors make concrete the conflicts between cultural groups and also reflect the dichotomies of the self that occur within the complex identities of multicultural characters. But the landscapes and sites discussed above extend beyond symbolic purposes. The simultaneous presence of the conflicting cultures can act as a catalyst to lead a character through a process that *may* result in a reconciliation of the fragmented parts of his or her identity. Through contemplating the culturally hybrid nature of the space (or spaces), the character develops a heightened awareness of the incongruity of the two (or more) cultures. This awareness causes anxiety within the character, who may fear an erasure of his or her cultural norms and beliefs as a result of the conflict. But often, this anxiety forces a character into a reconciliation as he or she creates a new sense of self capable of encompassing both cultures. He or she moves beyond the fear of dichotomy to understanding, and ultimately toward integrating the disparate parts of his or her own identity, forming a hybrid identity. The hybrid identity gives the character the flexibility to understand and adapt to the realities of living as a minority within a dominant culture, yet strengthens the character's ties to his or her own heritage culture. This is not assimilation — when a character adapts fully to the dominant culture at the expense of losing identity with his or her heritage. Instead, as Maxine Hong Kingston states in *The Woman Warrior*, the character learns to make her "mind large, as the universe is large, so that there is room for paradoxes" (29).

I wish to remind the reader that this discussion of forming hybrid identities is meant to understand *fictional* characters as they frequently develop in novels and short stories of ethnic literature. I am not attempting to explain the identities of real people. And even in fiction, characters sometimes do not reconcile living simultaneously within two cultures. Some, like Abel, choose to resist adapting to the dominant culture and find their best option is to return home. On the other hand, some, tragically, stay and end up in a permanent identity crisis, like Moon Orchid in *The Woman Warrior*, who will be discussed in the next chapter.

In chapter three, we will see that in a fashion similar to the way spaces can create hybridity within a multicultural character's identity, so too can figures from myth and legend occupy a component of a character's identity, adding the flexibility of hybridity. The mythical or legendary figure gives the character a resourceful model for coping with the dominant culture while still retaining strong ties with his or her heritage.

Chapter Three

Mythical and Legendary Figures: Forming Fictional Multicultural Identities

What, a reader may ask, is an ancient Aztec goddess doing in a contemporary Chicana work, such as Gloria Anzaldúa's *Borderlands / La Frontera*, which describes the difficulties and intricacies of living along the modern U.S.–Mexican border? Why does a contemporary Chinese American woman like Maxine Hong Kingston write about her girlhood as a legendary, fifth-century woman warrior? Why do some characters in Louise Erdrich's *Tracks* and *Love Medicine* have the same characteristics as a traditional, Native American trickster? Figures from myth and legend make occasional appearances in ethnic U.S. American literature, and other than being ties to the traditional culture, what is their purpose? The answer lies at least partially in how some fictional characters in ethnic U.S. literature base their identity, or a component of their identity, on a traditional mythological or legendary figure. This figure serves as a model for adapting to change and helps the character develop the flexibility to cope with living in a multicultural environment. Tricksters, in particular, through the use of shape changing and a defiant wit, model how characters can resist attempts by the dominant majority to erase their heritage cultures.

The multicultural characters in ethnic U.S. literature have facets to their identity that are formed by more than one cultural background. Just as the chapter on magical realism demonstrated how the magical and the ordinary can occupy the same reality, and the chapter on landscapes and spaces showed how one location can hold a multiplicity of meanings, so also a character's identity can hold a multiplicity of subjectivities. For some characters, as we shall see, mythical and legendary figures can provide the inspiration, or the role modeling, for at least one aspect of their multicultural identities.

Before looking at the development of identities in individual, fictional characters, it is worthwhile to see what role group identification plays in the formation of identity. In a short essay entitled "A Reflection on Marginality," Cho-yun Hsu writes about his experiences as a participant in a conference that looked at the formation of identity for Chinese Americans. Hsu writes: "After two and one-half days of discussion, those who had gathered at the East-West Center to discuss the meaning of being Chinese realized that the only relevant criterion of identity is the self-identity perceived by a person. The bottom line of self-identity is the recognition of one's membership in a collective entity" (240).

Identity in the works of U.S. ethnic writers, as presented through their characters, includes a group identity shared with all of those who claim the same ethnicity, located within an overarching individual identity. While the individual identity contains the group identity, it also has other, multiple aspects to it formed through the specific individual's life experiences. We will begin to look at the formation of ethnic identity by first discussing various characters' responses, based on their group identity, to living in the U.S. Then, we will look at a model for multiple subjectivity that serves as an effective tool for understanding the various subjectivities created by ethnic authors for the fictional characters in their works. Following, in the heart of this chapter, we will discover the roles mythological and legendary figures play in forming this multiple subjectivity in multicultural characters. By allowing figures from myth and legend to enter into the formation of the identities of characters, as a means of preserving traditional culture and of resisting domination, ethnic writers exhibit yet another way in which their writing can contain the hybrid perspectives that characterize much of ethnic writing in the United States.

Group Identity as an Aspect of Individual Identity

From the second half of the nineteenth century until the 1960s, the notion of assimilation dominated the U.S. American view towards minorities living in the United States. Whether the members of a minority group voluntarily immigrated, were originally brought as slaves, or were involuntarily "incorporated" into the U.S., such as the Mexican Americans who became part of the United States as a result of the Treaty of Guadalupe Hidalgo (1848), minorities were expected to assimilate to the dominant cultural norm — then defined as white, Anglo-Saxon, Protestant. Those who seemed unwilling or unable to assimilate were either excluded from immigrating in the first place, as evidenced by exclusionary immigration acts such as the 1882 Chinese Exclusionary Act which banned the entrance of Chinese laborers for a period of ten years, or were expected to leave and go back "home." In 1965, immigration policies became somewhat more tolerant. The Immigration and Nationality Act changed the race-based quota system and redefined national origin to mean one's country of birth as opposed to one's race. Instead of quotas being based on the existing percentage of ethnic populations already residing in the United States, quotas were allocated to individual countries, and set at 20,000 per country.

In a chapter entitled "Roots and Changing Identity" from Tu Wei-ming's edited volume *The Living Tree: The Changing Meaning of Being Chinese Today*, L. Ling-chi Wang, professor of ethnic studies at the University of California at Berkeley, defines five types of identity which he observes among the Chinese who have immigrated to the United States. Although he specifically describes the Chinese, these categories may apply to other immigrant groups as well, including minority groups who originally immigrated involuntarily, such as African Americans, and those who were involuntarily made part of the U.S. without immigrating (Native Americans and some Mexican Americans). The five categories of group identity Wang observes include (1) the sojourner mentality, (2) assimilation, (3) accommodation, (4) ethnic pride, and (5) alienation (188–189). While categorizing actual people into these groupings would be fraught with exceptions and would serve little purpose, these categories are useful as models for understanding a range of positions a minority person might take toward the dominant culture, especially, for our purpose, when looking at fictional characters. Part of a character's group identity stems from how he or she, as a member of a minority group, relates to the majority culture as well as to others of his or her group.

The first of Wang's five types of identity, the sojourner mentality, applies to immigrants who come to the U.S. without the intention of staying. The goal is usually financial gain, and the desire to eventually return home is strengthened if the immigrant faces discrimination. Of the sojourner, Wang writes, "This loyalty to one's home village and pride in one's culture, inculcated from childhood on, is vital to the structuring of one's existence and to the formation of one's identity" (200). The sojourner identity is thus tied to cultural roots in the home country and the home country remains the basis on which the immigrant constructs his or her identity.

Gao Li-wei in Yan Zhen's novel *Bai xue hong chen* (*White Snow, Red Dust: An Episode in the Maple Country*) exemplifies such a character. Gao leaves China and follows his wife to Toronto where she wants to pursue graduate study. With no desire to attend school himself (he was already a professor in China), Gao is left to work at a series of low-paying, menial jobs. He refuses to learn English and becomes obsessed with his goal of earning $50,000. This is the amount he feels will be sufficient to justify his trip to

Canada and will allow him to return home without others laughing at him. Gao exhibits all of the traditional sojourner's attitudes: the desire for financial gain, the firm intention to return home (which is strengthened by the discrimination he faces), and an intense pride in his Chinese culture and language.

The second type of identity, total assimilation, occurs when a minority individual rejects his or her native or heritage culture entirely and tries to thoroughly conform to white, Euro-American, U.S. culture. Wang describes total assimilation as it appears among some Chinese Americans: "It is a mentality that is well captured in the Chinese phrase, *zhancao-chugen*: to eliminate the weeds, one must pull out their roots. In other words, to gain acceptance into white society, Chinese Americans must erase and uproot all traces of their Chinese cultural heritage" (202). Dale, a second-generation Chinese American in David Henry Hwang's play *FOB*, provides an example of a totally assimilated character. The play begins with Dale lecturing at a blackboard on the derogatory characteristics of "fresh-off-the-boat" (FOB) Chinese immigrants. His stereotyping includes such attributions as "clumsy, ugly, greasy FOB. Loud, stupid, four-eyed FOB. Big feet. Horny. Like Lenny in *Of Mice and Men*" (13). Born in the United States, Dale denigrates the newly arrived immigrants and sees no remaining connection between himself and his Chinese heritage.

From the point of view of a Mexican American writer, Ana Castillo's character Fe in *So Far from God* also presents a totally assimilated character. Fe seeks to conform to the white, dominant culture by trying to marry Tom, the manager of a mini-mart filling station. Tom, like Fe, is Mexican American, but he has whole-heartedly adopted the dominant culture's capitalistic point of view. Fe herself, in a desire to accumulate more and more material possessions, volunteers for extra work, performing dangerous tasks at the factory in which she works. Working with increasingly more dangerous chemicals with which she cleans machine parts, Fe's extra volunteer work eventually gives her an incurable cancer that kills her. However, it is only shortly before her death that Fe loses her illusions about the merits of capitalism and realizes that she has been fatally duped by the white managers at the factory.

Accommodation, Wang's third type of identity, in relation to Chinese Americans refers to immigrants who came to the U.S. with the intention of one day returning to the homeland, but because of a change in the political situation in China, as happened during the Communist Revolution in China (1949), they were unable or actually prevented by the U.S. government from leaving the U.S. and returning to China. "Accommodation, in this instance, is a survival strategy in an alien setting one is unable to leave" (Wang 206). Although Wang devised this category in relation to Chinese Americans caught in the U.S. after the Communist Revolution, it can also be extended to other groups who were forced to accommodate to U.S. American society against their wishes: slaves brought unwillingly to the U.S. from Africa, Native Americans resettled from their homelands to reservations, and Mexican Americans who lived in the territories that once belonged to Mexico but suddenly became part of the United States. Some members of these groups acquiesced to the outward lifestyles of the dominant U.S. culture for survival purposes, but often maintained their cultural traditions privately in the home. However, it is easy to see how a prolonged period of accommodation could eventually lead to assimilation. The Native American character Benally, for example, in N. Scott Momaday's *House Made of Dawn*, is relocated from his reservation to Los Angeles. While the main character of the novel, Abel, is also relocated but is unable to accommodate himself to the urban, white culture of Los Angeles, Benally is able to make adjustments in his values and behavior in order to get along in the city. Privately, though, Benally tries to maintain his traditional views and practices, praying in his traditional manner when only he and Abel are present. As time passes, Benally realizes that he is moving further away from his cultural roots, but he sees this loss as necessary for his own survival.

The fourth category of ethnic pride and consciousness, which characterizes many of the ethnic writers discussed in this book, reached prominence during the various ethnic movements of the 1960s. The movements promoted the development of distinct ethnic identities and grew out of the African American Civil Rights and Black Power movements. The purpose of these movements was not only to promote a pride in ethnic identity for the group, but also to demand recognition as a legitimate segment of U.S. American society entitled to all of the rights and privileges that come with living in the United States. Ethnic Studies programs such as African American, Native American, Asian American and Chicano Studies appeared on university campuses, allowing for the study of the past and present histories and cultures of ethnic groups in the U.S. Although these movements recognize and maintain the heritage culture as a source of ethnic tradition and pride, identity based on ethnic pride and consciousness is also firmly rooted in the groups' experiences and histories as part of U.S. history.

The immigrants in the alienation or "uprooted" category, Wang's fifth classification, are similar to those described under accommodation with one significant difference. Those described under accommodation *are not able* to return home, although they want to, whereas those in the uprooted category *choose* not to return home, usually because of the political climate of their home country. This would include, for example, Chinese foreign students studying in the U.S. who chose to stay in the United States after the Tiananmen massacre in 1989. Fearing possible intellectual or political repression if they returned to China, these immigrants chose to uproot and establish a new residence in the U.S., although many still thought of China as "home."

Most of the fictional characters discussed in this book could be identified with the category of ethnic pride and consciousness, because they live as self-identified members of a specific minority ethnic group, maintain ties with their ethnic culture, and yet fully view themselves as U.S. Americans with an integral role in U.S. history and culture. As such, they have chosen to integrate the different cultures that shape their identities rather than to allow one or the other to dominate. Authors writing about characters with this sense of group identity, who also view themselves as both ethnic and U.S. American, produce many of the works discussed here as examples of hybrid perspectives in ethnic U.S. literature. Their characters, however, might also portray any of the positions discussed above in their responses to living as a member of a minority group in the U.S.

Moving on from group identity within minority ethnic groups, we next explore a model for self-identity that contains both group and individual aspects. In keeping with the focus of this book on hybrid perspectives, we will look at a model for self-identity that allows for multiple subjectivities within an individual's overall sense of him or herself.

Multiple Subjectivity

Jane Flax, in her chapter from *Disrupted Subjects* entitled "Multiples: On the Contemporary Politics of Subjectivity," argues that the self is a complex multiplicity, and that to imagine a completely unified subject (or self) is an illusion. (Subject is used here to mean a "self"— one's self or another's — and subjectivity refers to self-identity, but recognizes that one does not have the ability to be entirely objective about defining one's or another's self, and therefore, there is a subjective element in the way one identifies or understands the self.) Flax goes on to explain that not only do we have multiple aspects to our subjectivity, but sometimes the various positions are in conflict with one another, giving evidence of the multiple nature of subjectivity. "It would be more fruitful to treat contradictory elements of subjectivity as evidence for its multiplicity. We will need multiple stories in a variety of styles to appreciate its complexity" (98). But although for Flax the subject cannot attain a perfect unity, and is a multiple subject by its very nature — one brings forward different subject positions that are appropriate for different situations, such as being a sibling, a colleague or a lover — the subject does require a certain coherence among the different positions in order to function. Without the ability to maintain coherence, an awareness of the multiplicity and of the mutual interactions of the different subject positions, "one slides into the endless terror, emptiness, desolate loneliness, and fear of annihilation that pervade borderline subjectivity" (103).

The mental psychoses that may result from a person's inability to create coherence among his or her multiple aspects of subjectivity will not concern us here, although there are many characters in ethnic U.S. literature that exhibit a mental instability as a result of an inability to create new subject positions in order to adapt to extreme, cultural conflicts.* What is applicable to this investigation is the notion that multiple subjects within one person is the normal state of being, and that for the multicultural person (or, as concerns us here, for the fictional, multicultural character) the multiple subjectivity developed by the character will reflect the influences of the cultures involved in the development of that character's sense of self. These different cultural influences, in turn, through the multiple subjectivity that the character develops, will govern the way the character relates to others in his or her social roles as a multicultural individual living in the United States.

In applying the notion of multiple subjectivity to fictional, multicultural characters, we can explore how their life experiences with more than one culture have shaped their identities. A character like Benally in Momaday's *House Made of Dawn*, for example, exhibits multiple subjectivity when he puts aside his traditional views and beliefs while at work or at social gatherings with Native Americans who have fully assimilated to white society, yet practices traditional rituals in private.

Involving the native or heritage culture in the development of a character's subjectivity is thus another way in which ethnic authors in the U.S. add a hybrid perspective to their works. The character embodies the multiple cultural influences within the multiple aspects of his or her subjectivity. Some of these aspects are the result of identification with the character's ethnic group, some are the result of assimilation or accommodation to the dominant group, and some are highly individualistic, formed by the personal experiences and proclivities of the individual.

The Role of Mythological and Legendary Figures in Multiple Subjectivity

A strategy used by some ethnic U.S. authors to integrate the heritage culture into the subjectivities of their characters involves using figures from

---

*Some examples would include Maxine's aunt, Moon Orchid, in *The Woman Warrior* by Maxine Hong Kingston; Abel in N. Scott Momaday's *House Made of Dawn*; Lupito in Rudolfo Anaya's *Bless Me Ultima*; Chang in Sigrid Nunez's *A Feather on the Breath of God*; Sethe in Toni Morrison's *Beloved*; Mulberry/Peach in Nieh Hua-ling's *Sang ching yu tau hong* (*Mulberry and Peach*); and Tien-lei in Yu Li-hua's *You jian zong lu, you jian zong lu* (*Palm Trees Again, Palm Trees Again*).

the traditional myths and legends of the heritage culture. As one aspect of a character's subjectivity, he or she may form an attachment to a particular figure from myth or legend and use that figure as a kind of alter-ego. This phenomenon occurs with such frequency in U.S. ethnic literature that it is worth investigating how authors use these mythical/legendary figures and what they contribute to the formation of the character's identity. It would seem that these figures from the heritage culture provide a model for approaching the adopted culture in a manner that inspires the character to create new subjectivities based on the mythical/legendary figures' flexibility in adapting to change and in reconciling dualities. But because the mythical/legendary figure possesses close ties to the heritage culture, the model also allows the character to adapt while still retaining the cultural values of his or her heritage.

The grandparents of Gloria Anzaldúa, and she and her parents in turn, lost their land and their home country, Mexico, when the United States surrounded them and made them unwilling, de facto immigrants. "*Con el destierro y el exilo fuimos desuñados, destroncados, destripados*— we were jerked out by the roots, truncated, disemboweled, dispossessed, and separated from our identity and our history" (Anzaldúa 7–8). In her book *Borderlands / La Frontera: The New Mestiza*, Gloria Anzaldúa addresses the question of living as a *mestiza*, a person of mixed blood. Mexicans sometimes refer to themselves as *mestizos* (the masculine, plural form of the word) because of the mixed heritage which results from the two populations prominent in Mexican history: Spanish and Indian. Anzaldúa discusses the mixed nature of being Mexican, but she also has a third component to deal with: being Mexican American or *chicana*.

> The *mestizos* who were genetically equipped to survive small pox, measles, and typhus (Old World diseases to which the natives had no immunity), founded a new hybrid race and inherited Central and South America. *En* 1521 *nació una nueva raza, el mestizo, el mexicano* (people of mixed Indian and Spanish blood), a race that had never existed before. Chicanos, Mexican-Americans, are the offspring of those first matings [5].

Although Anzaldúa sees some positive aspects of being *mestizo* and living in the U.S. borderland ("I have the sense that certain 'faculties'— not just in me but in every border resident, colored or noncolored — and dormant areas of consciousness are being activated, awakened...." [Preface]) she nevertheless sees life on the border between two cultures and languages frequently as a negative experience that confuses her sense of self and leaves her shifting back and forth, balancing precariously between the two.

> This is her home
> this thin edge of
> barbwire [13].

In addition to being a mixture of Spanish, Indian, and U.S. American, Anzaldúa is also gay, a fact that causes her to be ostracized from traditional Mexican society. With little help from the cultural groups she lives within, she searches for a place to belong. In her search she seizes upon an event that happened in her childhood and takes it as a sign, signifying where her true identity may lie. The incident happens when she is chopping cotton in the fields with her mother. A snake rattles a warning and bites her leg. Her mother kills the snake with a hoe, and Gloria, crosscutting the fang marks with her knife, sucks out the venom and spits out the blood. She cuts off the snake's rattles and buries them in the cotton field, and that night she dreams: "Rattler fangs filled my mouth, scales covered my body. In the morning I saw through snake eyes, felt snake blood course through my body. The serpent, *mi tono*, my animal counterpart. I was immune to its venom. Forever immune" (26).

From the early experience and identification with the snake comes a mixing of personal experience and myth. Anzaldúa's identity with the snake gains a focus in the myth of the Aztec goddess Coatlicue, the snake goddess of the Earth, birth and death with whom she forms a strong identity.

> *Coatlicue* is one of the powerful images, or "archetypes," that inhabits, or passes through, my psyche. For me, *la Coatlicue* is the consuming internal whirlwind, the symbol of the underground aspects of the psyche. *Coatlicue* is the mountain, the Earth Mother who conceived all celestial beings out of her cavernous womb. Goddess of birth and death, *Coatlicue* gives and takes away life; she is the incarnation of cosmic processes [46].

The goddess becomes the means by which Anzaldúa, reaching back to the Indian narrative of her past, can find a model for integrating the split nature of her own identity. As the goddess of both birth and death, Coatlicue embodies a fusion of opposites and holds the power to reconcile any duality. Her physical appearance is a visual representation of her dual nature and her ability to embody opposites:

> She has no head. In its place two spurts of blood gush up, transfiguring into enormous twin rattlesnakes facing each other, which symbolize the earth-bound character of human life. She has no hands. In their place are two more serpents in the form of eagle-like claws, which are repeated at her feet: claws which symbolize the digging of graves into the earth as well as the sky-bound eagle, the masculine force. Hanging from her neck is a necklace of open hands alternating with human hearts. The hands symbolize the act of giving life; the hearts, the pain of Mother Earth giving birth to all her children, as well as the pain that humans suffer throughout life in their hard struggle for existence [47].

For Anzaldúa, a childhood experience with a snake becomes reinterpreted through a mixture with a myth from her cultural past, the myth of the snake goddess Coatlicue. The identification with the snake becomes the identification with the goddess and an incorporation of the goddess' ability to reconcile duality — a useful skill for one such as Anzaldúa who exists between two different cultures. By following the model of Coatlicue, Anzaldúa develops her mode of coping with a multicultural and multilingual existence. She refers to this mode of living as a "tolerance for ambiguity" (79).

> The new *mestiza* copes by developing a tolerance for contradictions, a tolerance for ambiguity. She learns to be an Indian in Mexican culture, to be Mexican from an Anglo point of view. She learns to juggle cultures. She has a plural personality, she operates in a pluralistic mode — nothing is thrust out, the good the bad and the ugly, nothing rejected, nothing abandoned. Not only does she sustain contradictions, she turns the ambivalence into something else [79].

The "something else" is a new *mestiza* consciousness. It contains pain, Anzaldúa explains, but it is powered by a creative energy that allows a continual flexibility of perception in how she views herself and others so that acceptance of others, understanding, and a reconciling of duality can prevail (80). Through the guiding model of Coatlicue, Anzaldúa creates a multiple subjectivity that provides her with the flexibility she needs to deal with the often conflicting values and viewpoints she faces as a gay woman of mixed race, mixed language and mixed culture.

Richard Rodriguez represents an entirely different case, but one also in which a legendary figure, the Virgin of Guadalupe, plays an important role in leading him back to his cultural roots — roots that he cut off as a young man in order to become fully assimilated into U.S. American culture. In his first book, *Hunger of Memory: The Education of Richard Rodriguez*, he begins with his childhood memories of his family speaking at home in Spanish. Spanish, he realizes early in life, is for close, private moments with the family whereas English is for formal, public moments outside the house.*

As he grows, Richard Rodriguez moves further and further away from Spanish, his connections with Mexican culture, and his family. He is convinced that total assimilation into the white, English-speaking culture is the path to success, no matter what else may have to be sacrificed in the way of cultural heritage or relations with others within his ethnic group. He succeeds in becoming a well-known writer, but at great personal cost.

Fortunately, this is not where we leave Richard Rodriguez, because he writes another book ten years after *Hunger of Memory*. In his second book, *Days of Obligation: An Argument with My Mexican Father*, Rodriguez begins with his current age and writes backwards, ending the book as a child. As the structure of the book indicates, the purpose is to return to his family and his

---

*More on this distinction between public and private language and the roles of English and Spanish in Rodriguez's life occurs in chapter five on multilingualism.

sense of roots — to regain what was lost in his headlong pursuit of assimilation.

Days of Obligation begins with a trip to Mexico to find a village like the one in which his parents grew up. Rodriguez has been given an important assignment by the British Broadcasting Company (BBC) to produce a documentary on the United States and Mexico. The irony of the BBC's choice in making him the presenter of the documentary is not lost on Richard. "A man who spent so many years with his back turned to Mexico. Now I am to introduce Mexico to a European audience" (xvi). When his film crew interrupts a child's funeral taking place in the plaza of a small village, with Bobby Brown blasting from their stereo speakers, Rodriguez realizes how little he knows about Mexico and is sickened by his own ignorance:

> And then I saw the reason for the crowd in the plaza — a tiny coffin was being lifted from the bed of a truck. At the same moment, people at the edge of the crowd turned toward our noisy procession.
> Bobby Brown panted Unh-oh-ahhhhhhhh from our rolled-down windows.
> A village idiot — a cripple — hobbled toward us, his face contorted into what was either a grin or a grimace, his finger pressed against his lips.
> *Silencio. Silencio.*
> "Turn off the music," the producer shouted.
> The production assistant radioed the rest of the convoy: Back up, back up.
> There was no room to turn.
> The van, the two cars shifted in reverse. Then my stomach began to churn [xviii–xix].

Realizing how out of place he is in his parents' homeland, Rodriguez begins a journey to rediscover his Mexican roots. The journey leads backwards not only through past times and places, but through many legends as well. One of these legends in particular, the legend of the Virgin of Guadalupe, helps Rodriguez regain a sense of Mexican identity and lets him create a compatible peace between the Mexican and the U.S. American parts of himself.

As a boy, Richard Rodriguez attended an Irish Catholic school, and Catholicism remains one of the defining features of his identity. It is also a means by which he begins to understand the history of Mexico, not through teachings by nuns or priests, but through the legend of the Virgin of Guadalupe. "The Virgin of Guadalupe symbolizes the entire coherence of Mexico, body and soul. You will not find the story of the Virgin within hidebound secular histories of Mexico ... and the omission renders the history of Mexico incomprehensible" (16).

In the year 1531, the Virgin Mary appeared on a hilltop before an Indian peasant named Juan Diego. At first, Diego saw only a blinding light on the hilltop, but then he heard a woman's voice calling out his name. Even though he covered his eyes with his hands, he could see the image of the Virgin:

> She wore a gown the color of dawn.
> Her hair was braided with ribbons and flowers
> And tiny tinkling silver bells. Her mantle was sheer
> And bright as rain and embroidered with thousands
> of twinkling stars.
> A clap before curtains, like waking from sleep;
> Then a human face,
> A mother's smile;
> Her complexion as red as cinnamon bark;
> Cheeks as brown as pérsimmon.
>
> ...This lady spoke
> In soft Nahuatl, the Aztec tongue
> (As different from Spanish
> as some other season of weather,
> As doves in the boughs of a summer tree
> Are different from crows in a wheeling wind,
> Who scatter destruction and
> Caw caw caw caw)—
> Nahuatl like rain, like water flowing, like drips in a
> cavern,
> Or glistening thaw,
> Like breath through a flute,
> With many stops and plops and sighs...
>   [Rodriguez, *Days of Obligation* 17–18].

The Virgin Mary appears as an Indian and speaks to an Indian in his language, *Nahuatl*. Juan Diego has trouble getting the bishop of Mexico City to recognize the miracle, but when he returns to the bishop a second time with roses from the hillside and the imprint of Mary's face on his cloak, the bishop is convinced. Through the Virgin of Guadalupe, Mexican Catholicism becomes no longer just an imposition by the Spanish, but a uniquely Mexican faith.

The ability to take things Spanish and mix them with Indian sensibilities is the creation of Mexican culture. As Rodriguez understands more of Mexican culture and its ability to reconcile differences and create a new *mestizo* culture, he begins to acknowledge the Mexican part of his heritage and to learn, by example, how to incorporate it into his U.S. American life.

All of the stories that Richard Rodriguez hears on his journey to Mexico contribute to his understanding of the country and its culture. He encounters the places, people and narratives of his parents' homeland and makes them part of his own cultural heritage. The result is that he regains the Mexican part of his multiple subjectivity, and with that, he is able to reconnect with his family.

As in *Hunger of Memory*, Rodriguez ends *Days of Obligation* with a commentary about his Mexican father. The first book ends with a description of his father's growing frailty, his inability to communicate with his father, and his sense of separateness from his parents' lives and culture. The second book, however, ends with a joyful description of his father as a boy in his village in Mexico, a boy who not only communicates well, but is noisy enough to wake up the whole town. The encounters Rodriguez has in Mexico, and the understanding he gains of Mexico as a mixed culture that comes to him through the legend of the Virgin of Guadalupe, give him back his Mexican heritage. He has also regained his father, and because he now understands his father; he hears his voice:

> In Mexico my father had the freedom of the doves. He summoned the dawn. Each morning at five-thirty, my father would climb the forty steps of the church tower to pull the ropes that loosened the tongues of two fat bells. My father was the village orphan and it was his duty and his love and his mischief to wake the village, to watch it stir: the pious old ladies bending toward mass; the young men off to the fields; the eternal sea [230].

These examples from Mexican American literature show how an author can incorporate figures from myth and legend into a character's subjectivity. Turning now to some examples from Chinese American literature, we see similar instances where mythical figures become an active part of a character's subjectivity, guiding his or her interactions with U.S. American culture and society. Maxine Hong Kingston and David Henry Hwang both create such characters. Maxine in *The Woman Warrior* integrates her self-identity so thoroughly with the legendary female warrior Fa Mu Lan, that she speaks of the legend of Fa Mu Lan as part of her own personal history. In the play *F.O.B.* by David Henry Hwang, a newly arrived immigrant, resistant to and disdainful of total assimilation to U.S. American culture as a choice for his own identity, declares that he is the legendary, war-like hero Gwan Gung.

Early in her life, as narrated in her semi-autobiographical book *The Woman Warrior*, Maxine Hong Kingston develops an image of her parents' homeland through comments from her Chinese neighbors and through her mother's talk-stories. However, she receives double messages from these sources about the value of being female—one negative that regards girls as a drain on the family economy, and one positive that tells her about Fa Mu Lan and other courageous swordswomen of Chinese legends.

As a child, Maxine Hong Kingston often heard derisive comments made about girls, attitudes that were directly imported from traditional Chinese society. This negative attitude toward girls had an economic source, particularly in rural areas, which stemmed from traditional marriage customs. When a boy in traditional Chinese society grew up and married, his wife came to live in the home of her in-laws. Not only was she an extra hand to help in the house and fields — usually treated no better than a slave by the mother-in-law — but she often came with a dowry as a payment to her husband's family. To raise a daughter and marry her off was expensive, and so sons became looked upon as economic assets and girls as economic liabilities. Poor families, especially ones that already had some girls, simply could not afford to keep them, and so sometimes they were killed at birth or sold as slaves. Although this treatment of girls has virtually disappeared in modern times, some of the stigma against girls still remains. This is the source behind the negative comments that Maxine remembers hearing as a child.

> When one of my parents or the emigrant villagers said, "Feeding girls is feeding cowbirds," I would thrash on the floor and scream so hard I couldn't talk. I couldn't stop.
> "What's the matter with her?"
> "I don't know. Bad, I guess. You know how girls are. 'There's no profit in raising girls. Better to raise geese than girls.'"
> "I would hit her if she were mine. But then there's no use wasting all that discipline on a girl. 'When you raise girls, you're raising children for strangers'" [46].

This attitude, coupled with another Chinese custom of not directly complimenting one's own children, must have been particularly distressing for a child being raised by Chinese methods within a U.S. American context. If raised in China, Maxine would still have felt the pain of such comments, but she would have been better prepared to pick up on the subtle ways in which her parents showed love for her. To disparage a child in front of friends and neighbors in China, for example, may actually be a sign of affection — the parents show that they have such regard for the child that they must criticize it in order to avoid appearing too proud. From the point of view of tradition, to pay compliments to one's own child would be particularly ill-mannered. But surrounded by stereotypical examples of the way parental love is represented in the U.S., obvious and full of supportive praise for the children, Maxine's parents' way of treating her must have seemed perplexing if not abusive. The subtle, ambiguous signals of love measured against the outward derision must have seemed like little compensation. In addition, there was secrecy surrounding her family's seemingly everyday matters that also confused her. Elaine Kim, in *Asian American Literature: An Introduction to the Writings and Their Social Context*, explains the reasons for the confusion that Maxine experiences in her own family:

> In *The Woman Warrior*, secrecy among the Chinese in America has been made necessary by harsh and racially discriminatory immigration policies. Chinese immigrants changed their names and lied about their ages and ports of entry, sometimes making their lives unintelligible to their American-born children.... In many Asian

immigrant families, culture is lived, not explained. Practices become confusing when customs are observed outside their original context, in a new social environment where they may seem inappropriate [200].

Kingston's mother, however, cares for her daughter deeply, as evidenced by the talk-stories. While the mother outwardly criticizes her daughter, she at other times tells her stories of women with great strength and courage, women who are not slaves to anyone. With the talk-stories, the mother, Brave Orchid, expands Kingston's imagination with the possibilities of what she can become and what she can accomplish. She lets her daughter know, through stories, about the resources and courage she has within her.

The tales of swordswomen are not lost on Kingston, and she develops a strong identity with the woman warrior Fa Mu Lan. She tells Fa Mu Lan's story as if it is her own. Fa Mu Lan becomes lost one day at the age of seven and is taken in by an old man and woman. They train Fa Mu Lan in the ways of Chinese boxing and lead her in the path of a warrior. When Fa Mu Lan returns to her village, her husband and brother are conscripted into the army and taken to war. When it is time for her father to go, Fa Mu Lan decides to take his place. Her parents carve words of revenge on her back, so that even if she is killed, her body can serve as a weapon in the war. She goes to battle and eventually her husband joins her and they lead their army together. Even pregnancy, giving birth, and caring for an infant cannot stop Fa Mu Lan, and she battles on. Eventually, Fa Mu Lan returns home and her final act of courage is to rid her parents' village of an evil baron who has abused the people of the village. Through all of these adventures, Fa Mu Lan remains filial to her parents and faithful to her husband.*

Again, as with Gloria Anzaldúa and Richard Rodriguez, narrative takes a formative role in establishing Kingston's self identity. As an adult, she remembers the story of Fa Mu Lan and acknowledges its place in creating the person she has become:

> After I grew up, I heard the chant of Fa Mu Lan, the girl who took her father's place in battle. Instantly I remembered that as a child I had followed my mother about the house, the two of us singing about how Fa Mu Lan fought gloriously

---

*The story of Fa Mu Lan as it occurs in *The Woman Warrior* is actually a composite of several different legendary characters. In an interview with Kay Bonetti in 1986, for example, Kingston comments on her borrowing from a legend about a male general, Yüeh Fei, for part of her story about Fa Mu Lan: "When the woman warrior has the words carved on her back, that's actually a man's story. It's about a man named Yüeh Fei who had the vow carved on his back by his mother. Now, I took that and gave that to a woman. I gave a man's myth to a woman because it's part of the feminist war that's going on in *The Woman Warrior*, to take the men's stories away from them and give the strength of that story to a woman. I see that as an aggressive storytelling act, and also it's part of my own freedom to play with the myth, and I do feel that the myths have to be changed and played with all the time, or they die" (Bonetti 40).

and returned alive from war to settle in the village. I had forgotten this chant that was once mine, given me by my mother, who may not have known its power to remind. She said I would grow up a wife and a slave, but she taught me the song of the warrior woman, Fa Mu Lan. I would have to grow up a warrior woman [20].

In much the same way that Gloria Anzaldúa learns the "tolerance of ambiguity" from the Aztec snake goddess, Coatlicue, Maxine Hong Kingston learns from Fa Mu Lan a way of reconciling the mixed messages of her youth that she receives while growing up between two very different cultures: U.S. American and Chinese. "I learned to make my mind large, as the universe is large, so that there is room for paradoxes" (29). Elaine Kim, in *Asian American Literature*, addresses the paradoxes faced by Maxine: "*The Woman Warrior* is about women, but it is primarily about the Chinese American's attempt to sort fact from fantasy in order to come to terms with the paradoxes that shape her life as a member of a racial minority group in America" (199). Not all cultural differences need to be resolved, Maxine discovers. Two opposites can exist together as long as one can keep the flexibility and the creativity of a multiple subjectivity to deal with both. For Maxine Hong Kingston, she can be Chinese and U.S. American, and the woman warrior shows her the way through her abilities to transform and to combine opposites such as courage and gentleness, war and peace, male and female, defiance and filial piety. The woman warrior provides an alter-ego for Maxine that allows her to reconcile the dualities she faces in her own life experiences as a Chinese American.

David Hwang's play *F.O.B.* was written and first performed while Hwang was a student at Stanford University. As mentioned earlier in this chapter, the play begins with one of the three characters, Dale, a U.S.–born Chinese American, lecturing at a blackboard on the derogatory characteristics of "fresh-off-the-boat" Chinese immigrants. The play also features two other characters, Grace, Dale's cousin, a first-generation Chinese American who has adapted to U.S. American culture but has not totally rejected her Chinese heritage, and Steve, a newly arrived Chinese immigrant. All three are students. As a second generation Chinese American, Dale has assimilated to the point where he has rejected all aspects of his Chinese heritage. He is rude to Steve and ridicules his Chinese characteristics, as if Dale himself did not share any of Steve's "Chineseness." As Sau-ling Cynthia Wong suggests in *Reading Asian American Literature: From Necessity to Extravagance*, "What Dale refuses to see is the fact that, as a person of Chinese ancestry in race-conscious America, to be 'like anyone else' is an unrealizable dream.... With knowledge of his self-defined deformity [being of Chinese ancestry] repressed, Dale directs all his pent-up spite toward the FOB [Steve]" (107). Steve, in contrast, struggles against assimilation. As a mode of defiance, Steve takes on the identity of the mythical Chinese warrior Gwan Gung, and angrily denounces the unwillingness of U.S. Americans to accept him just as he is.* He introduces himself to Grace as Gwan Gung and assigns to her the identity of Fa Mu Lan. Grace, who has both Chinese and U.S. American subjectivities within her self identity, holds the middle ground and attempts to reconcile her cousin Dale with her new friend Steve. The conflict among the three becomes an analogy for the struggles of all immigrants to gain acceptance, and for the price that is paid by some, in terms of losing one's heritage, in order to gain that acceptance. After the three characters argue the merits of their various positions, Grace opts to go out with Steve, leaving Dale behind. By choosing to go with Steve, Grace symbolically shows her unwillingness to sever all ties with her Chinese heritage and, therefore, rejects Dale's option of total assimilation.

Using a legendary figure to operate as one aspect of a character's subjectivity also appears in Native American literature. As an example, we look again at Leslie Marmon Silko's "Yellow Woman." Earlier in chapter two, we saw how the rich source of traditional Native American myths and legends can provide figures that sometimes become alter egos in forming the subjectivities of Native American characters. The man, Silva, takes on the identity of a kachina spirit and the woman, who remains nameless, slips in and out of an identity as Yellow Woman. She shows her indecision over her own identity when she says to Silva, "But I only said that you were him [the kachina spirit] and that I was Yellow Woman — I'm not really her — I have my own name and I come from the pueblo on the other side of the mesa. Your name is Silva and you are a stranger I met by the river yesterday afternoon" (32).

Eventually, the woman gives herself over to living within the legend and ceases to look for opportunities to escape. She becomes so entranced with her identity as Yellow Woman that she is willing to give up her husband, her baby, and the rest of her family and community. Only when she fears that Silva will kill the white rancher who has caught Silva with stolen meat does the woman decide that life as Yellow Woman may be a little too adventurous. She returns home and reports to her family, in accordance with the traditional Yellow Woman tales, that she was kidnapped by a Navajo. The reader might ask what the woman gained through her experience of living the legend of Yellow Woman, especially since she returns home to the same humdrum life she earlier sought to escape. But although the woman returns, she has been renewed by the adventure and has gained a new appreciation for the comfort and ordinariness of her usual life. She has also brought renewal to her culture in the form of continuing the Yellow Woman tradition by adding a story of her own. As she refreshes the story by adding her new version, we are aware that she too, as Yellow Woman, has been renewed. By adding Yellow Woman to her

---

*Gwan Gung, while a brave and noble warrior, was also noted for his arrogance.

own subjectivity, becoming Yellow Woman temporarily, she has undergone an adventure that has given more depth and meaning to her ordinary life as a wife, a mother, and a daughter, and has left her with hope that the opportunity for a further adventure will come again when she needs it.

Tricksters

A particular type of mythological character bears special mention in this chapter as the quintessential beings for role modeling adaptation to change. These figures are tricksters from traditional myths who possess supernatural powers and who, no matter what cultural tradition they come from, have the ability to transform themselves and events around them. Usually somewhat mischievous, the trickster plays tricks often for his or her own amusement or to undermine authoritative figures and the status quo; but nevertheless, the trickster is tied to his or her culture and people and will use trickery and transformation in times of crisis for the betterment of his or her community. Steven Hawley in "Making Metaphor Happen: Space, Time and Trickster Sign" sums up the trickster's connection with the community: "trickster discourse begins with the premise that in space and time, shit does happen, and that imperfect though they may be, seeing, speaking and knowing in relation to others is still the best way to avoid stepping into the mess" (107). Although the trickster traditions reach back to the indefinite times of oral literature, the tricksters' abilities to adapt and change with the times have made them a natural addition to contemporary ethnic literature in the United States.*

Since tricksters are culturally determined, they should be looked at within the context of the culture from which they come. For those outside of the culture, it may be impossible to ever understand the trickster as those within the culture do. As Franchot Ballinger warns in *Living Sideways: Tricksters in American Indian Oral Traditions*, "We who are acquainted with the stories only in translation must accept that we actually know very little about them, certainly lacking the intimacy that the word *know* suggests. We experience only one of a story's many surfaces and probably little of its depths" (8). In addition, since the traditional trickster tales have their origins in oral literature, and were meant to be heard in the performance of a telling, even more of the story's meaning is lost to cultural outsiders. Ballinger continues, "Even if we had absolutely precise translations that manage to convey all the meanings

---

*Tricksters are tied to the ethnic cultures from which they derive because they originate in the stories from that culture. In this chapter we are concerned with some of the tricksters associated with ethnic minority groups in the U.S., but there are also tricksters associated with Euro–American traditions, such as leprechauns, wizards and fairies, that originated in European folklore.

and nuances of the tale's original language, the text's transformation from orality to print and the absence of both social and performative context would diminish our experience of the story" (9).

However, there are some characteristics that all tricksters, across cultures, seem to share. In "Myth and Symbol" in *The International Encyclopedia of Social Sciences*, Victor Turner discusses the role of myth in general, and of tricksters in particular, during "liminal" periods in the history of an individual, or a culture. "Myths are *liminal* phenomena: They are frequently told at a time or in a site that is 'betwixt and between'" (576). Turner uses the term "liminal" in the sense it was meant by Arnold van Gennep in describing the progression of *rites de passage* in 1909. Van Gennep described a three-step progression of ritual stages in a rite of passage: separation, margin (or limen), and aggregation (Turner 576). Before the margin or liminal stage, the initiates are separated from the rest of the community; after the liminal stage, they rejoin and are reintegrated into the community in their newly achieved status. However, it is the liminal stage in which change takes place. It is the "betwixt and between" part of the ritual when the initiates are between what they were and what they will become. During the liminal stage, the initiates are instructed, often through the telling of myths, and are exposed to the symbolic meanings underpinning their culture. "Liminality," Turner writes, "is pure potency, where anything can happen, where immoderacy is normal, even normative, and where the elements of culture and society are released from their customary configurations and recombine in bizarre and terrifying imagery" (577).

Turner asserts in "Myth and Symbol" that trickster figures are liminal beings, and trickster tales are a particular type of myth that illustrate clearly the aspects of the liminal stage. The trickster reflects the naked, nonlogical initiate during the liminal stage, whose behavior may run the gamut of "destructive, creative, farcical, ironic, energetic, suffering, lecherous, submissive, defiant, but always unpredictable" (Turner 580). Because of their ability to change form, tricksters are androgynous (although they appear more often as male than female) and ambiguous, often taking on forms, such as that of a child, that place them outside of the demands of the social code for proper behavior. "They behave as though there were no social or moral norms to guide them. Self-will, caprice, and lust impel them" (Turner 580). Turner ascribes these other traits as well to tricksters:

> ...combined black and white symbolism, aggression, vindictiveness, vanity, defiance of authority, willfulness, individualism, indeterminacy of stature (sometimes tall, sometimes dwarfish), destructiveness, creativeness (the Winnebago trickster transforms the pieces of his broken phallus into plants and flowers for men — hence he is both single and multiple), and libido without procreative outcome.... Yet wholly

other, they are perfectly familiar to mankind, even jocularly so, for they represent what everyone would secretly like to do [580].

Some of these characteristics we have run across earlier in this chapter. The combination of black and white symbolism, for example, represents the combining of opposites such as the androgynous Coatlique's symbols of birth and death, man and woman, beauty and ugliness. Also the trickster can be both singular and multiple, presenting him- or herself both as one and as many. This combination of multiplicity and unity may serve as a symbol for human subjectivity — multiple subjects within each person's overall subjectivity can be brought into coherence and coordinated to operate within a single individual. We have also seen how other figures, such as the legendary woman warrior Fa Mu Lan, can defy the status quo and train for war. And of course, the liminality of these trickster figures echoes the "betwixt and between" state of the multicultural characters themselves who sometimes exist in a kind of limbo state, belonging neither to one culture nor the other while still being required to participate and function in both. William G. Doty, in a chapter titled "Native American Tricksters: Literary Figuras of Community Transformers," concludes with an affirmation of the trickster's role in preserving cultural norms, even when the trickster is disruptive and the culture is in a state of flux. Tricksters, he writes, "trick hearers and readers into drawing their own morals, even when the stories are lustfully erotic or full of gender ambiguity. By so doing, they affirm ironically the importance of moral standards and set out the task of modeling appropriate change and development as ultimately serious and simultaneously hilarious" (11).

One of these trickster myths, the Chinese story of the Monkey King, has its beginnings in oral literature and then appears in written form in Wu Ch'eng-en's novel *The Journey to the West* (sixteenth century). The story begins like this:

> There was a rock that since the creation of the world had been worked upon by the pure essences of Heaven and the fine savours of Earth, the vigour of sunshine and the grace of moonlight, till at last it became magically pregnant and one day split open, giving birth to a stone egg, about as big as a playing ball. Fructified by the wind it developed into a stone monkey, complete with every organ and limb. At once this monkey learned to climb and run; but its first act was to make a bow towards each of the four quarters. As it did so, a steely light darted from this monkey's eyes and flashed as far as the Palace of the Pole Star [Wu 11].

But Monkey grows to be ambitious, and after studying with a master and learning seventy-two transformations, Monkey feels ready to challenge the throne of the Jade Emperor. He boasts of his skills and his ambitious intentions even to the Buddha of the Western Paradise, who makes Monkey a wager:

> If you are really so clever, jump off the palm of my right hand. If you succeed, I'll tell the Jade Emperor to come and live with me in the Western Paradise, and you shall have his throne without more ado. But if you fail, you shall go back to earth and do penance there for many a kalpa [129,000 years] before you come to me again with your talk [Wu 75].

Monkey, who can jump a hundred and eight thousand leagues in a single jump, looks at the Buddha's hand, barely eight inches across, and thinks he has it made. He jumps as hard as he can. At last Monkey comes to five pink pillars and thinks he has reached the end of the world. Before going back to claim his throne, Monkey decides to leave some kind of record of his presence:

> He plucked a hair and blew on it with magic breath, crying "Change!" It changed at once into a writing brush charged with heavy ink, and at the base of the central pillar he wrote, "The Great Sage Equal to Heaven reached this place." Then to mark his disrespect, he relieved nature at the bottom of the first pillar, and somersaulted back to where he had come from [Wu 75].

Of course when Monkey returns, the Buddha's hand reeks of monkey urine, and poor Monkey is imprisoned inside a mountain as his penance.

After five hundred years, the goddess of mercy, Kuan-yin, releases Monkey to accompany the monk Hsüan-tsang (Tripitaka) on his journey to India to bring back the sacred texts of Buddhism. This part of the story has a basis in history. Hsüan-tsang was an intellectual and devout monk who played a key role in Chinese Buddhism. He traveled abroad in the seventh century for seventeen years (629–45) in order to bring back 657 Buddhist texts from India which he translated (Hsia 117). The monk of the novel, however, is presented as a comic, peevish, bumbling fool, and it is, of course, Monkey who becomes the true hero of the tale. With his trickster abilities to transform, Monkey has the flexibility to tackle every danger and to surmount every obstacle, and he does so in true trickster style, with great humor and audacity.

In *Tripmaster Monkey: His Fake Book*,* Maxine Hong Kingston centralizes the trickster Monkey as a key force in the creation of both group and individual identity within the novel. As the alter ego of the novel's beatnik protagonist, Wittman Ah Sing, Monkey guides Wittman through outrageous antics and creative inspirations, all which eventually lead to the formation of a multicultural community, Wittman's utopian concept of a dream society. Wittman also seeks to integrate the various, multiple subjects of his own iden-

---

*By subtitling this book *His Fake Book*, Kingston pokes fun at those, such as Frank Chin, who have criticized her for manipulating and transforming Chinese traditional tales to further her own contemporary causes. Although the trickster Monkey is meant to be the same as in the traditional novel *Journey to the West*, Kingston realizes she has once again transformed a traditional story and beats her critics to the chase, labeling the text as Monkey's "*Fake Book*" before anyone else can declare her telling of the story to be "fake" (see Smith 67).

tity, and with his seventy-two transformations at hand, Monkey is the perfect master to teach Wittman the art of subjective flexibility.

From the beginnings of the novel, Wittman declares an identification with Monkey that started in his childhood when he sold Doctor Woo's Wishes Come True Medicine while dressed in a monkey suit. He traces his family's U.S. American origins back to his great-great-grandfather, who came to the U.S. with a trunk "big enough to hold all the costumes for the seventy-two transformations of the King of the Monkeys in a long run of *The Journey to the West* in its entirety" (29). Wittman performs Monkey antics in front of his friend, Nanci, and declares: "I am really: the present-day U.S.A. incarnation of the King of the Monkeys" (33). And while exercising his Monkey persona, Wittman loses his job selling toys in a department store by playing a Monkey trick:

> Out of a box, he took an organ-grinder's monkey with cymbals attached to its hands. It had a red fez on its head. He took off its little vest, and inserted batteries in its back. It hopped about, clapping the cymbals and smiling. Its tail stuck out of a hole in its green-and-white-striped pants. "Look here, kiddos," said Wittman, and unboxed a Barbie Bride. He put her on her back with her arms and veil and legs and white dress raised, and the monkey on top of her. Her legs held it hopping in place and clapping her with its cymbals. Her eyes opened and shut as the monkey bumped away at her [65].

To further the identification of Wittman with Monkey, each chapter of Kingston's novel ends with a direct address from the narrator to the reader, just as each chapter in *The Journey to the West* ends with a direct address. The parallel style in chapter endings between the two works strengthens the association between Wittman and Monkey: "Our Wittman is going to work on his play for the rest of the night. If you want to see whether he will get that play up, and how a poor monkey makes a living so he can afford to spend the weekday afternoon drinking coffee and hanging out, go on to the next chapter" (Kingston 35). Compare with the end of chapter six of *The Journey to the West* as translated by Anthony C. Yu, which tells of Monkey's penance spent trapped within the mountain: "We do not know in what month or year hereafter the days of his penance will be fulfilled, and you must listen to the explanation in the next chapter" (Wu 179). Both Kingston's and Wu's novels make use of a traditional narrator who stands outside of the action.* The narrators in both books comment, sometimes sympathetically and sometimes critically, on their monkey protagonists and interfere frequently with the action to address their comments to the reader.

In Kingston's novel, Wittman writes a play based on the Monkey legend,

---

*This type of narrator is a feature in most traditional, classic Chinese novels.

but in trickster fashion, he deviates from the original story and multiplies the viewpoints and voices in the play by adding bits and pieces from other Chinese works, such as *The Water Margin* and *The Three Kingdoms*, and by mixing in random bits of Mexican lore, U.S. American history and pop culture. He draws upon U.S. historical figures, for example, in a scene that explores the complexities of multiple identity. During the play two actors appear in a connecting suit as the Siamese twins Chang and Eng (originally called Siamese because they were born in Thailand [formerly Siam], but the name later came to indicate any conjoined twins). Chang and Eng made their living during the nineteenth century by traveling around the world, appearing as a spectacle. They often would perform tricks such as somersaults and backflips as do the actors in Wittman's play. Taking facts from the real lives of Chang and Eng — their marriages to the Yates sisters, their adoption of the last name Bunker to appear more American, and their ownership of slaves — the twins rename themselves Bones and Jones in Wittman's play and create an identity puzzle that overturns any conventional sense of identity. The twins act out a double identity that is both plural and singular. Another actor enters, also with a complex, double identity, named Miss Narcissus (the translation for the Chinese name of the first Chinese American writer Sui Sin Far — Fah in Kingston's text — who was born to a Chinese mother and British father and named at birth Edith Eaton). Miss Narcissus asks Chang and Eng, "Are you fraternal twins or identical? You certainly do look alike," and Chang answers, conflating the plural and singular identity of the conjoined twins, "I am alike" (291). Miss Watanna (the Japanese name Winnifred Eaton, Sui Sin Far's real-life sister and also a writer, chose to be known as) urges Chang and Eng to adopt a Japanese identity. During the time of the Eaton sisters, Chinese immigrants faced much more discrimination than the Japanese, so Winnifred adopted a Japanese last name. Edith, however, chose to reinforce her Chinese identity by choosing to write under her Chinese name. At the suggestion that Chang and Eng adopt a Japanese identity to make their lives less difficult, "Chang-Eng" reply, "Identity?" and the stage direction indicates, "(He are baffled.)" (292). Chang-Eng indicates the twins' plural identity, and interestingly, is the way Chang and Eng actually signed their letters home to their families when they were on tour. Thus in a short space, several complex and baffling forms of identity are explored, with Chang and Eng being the embodiment of the sense of double identity felt by many minority peoples. As Lara Narcisi comments in "Wittman's Transitions: Multivocality and the Play of *Tripmaster Monkey*," Chang and Eng "suggest an expansive and un-categorizable view of identity" (99).

The twins' double identity is made visible when the audience clamors to see where they are joined, as did audiences who saw the real Chang and Eng. Chang addresses the audience, recognizing their attraction as spectacles.

"We know damned well what you came for to see — the angle we're joined at, how we can have two sisters for wives and twenty-one Chinese-Carolinian children between us.... You want to know if we feel jointly. You want to look at the hyphen. You want to look at it bare" (293). The "hyphen" Chang refers to is the band of flesh, about the width of an arm, that joined the real Chang and Eng at the chest. Audiences used to want to see the band to prove that Chang and Eng were truly conjoined, and not faking their condition. In Wittman's play, the band stands symbolically for the hyphen that connects the two halves of a minority, multicultural identity — Chinese American, for example — that for Wittman indicates a person who is not allowed by white society to be totally American. Jonna Mackin reflects the same view in "Split Infinities: The Comedy of Performative Identity in Maxine Hong Kingston's *Tripmaster Monkey*." She asks key questions about the inequality of race and power in the U.S. that still need answers in the twenty-first century: "This story of Siamese twins embodies the problem of union in a nation of physically and culturally unlike-minded individuals. What *is* the tie that binds? How does each member of the national union achieve power in a system capable of an illogical 'color line'?" (530).

Wittman's goal is to create a play that is all inclusive, a play that leaves no one on the margins. He casts people of different races to play members of the same families, and the actors change characters with the dizzying speed of quick-change artists. The audience grows larger with each night the play continues, and they begin to take part in the performance. The audience begins to come in order to see each other as well as to view the play, and a community is formed. Taking the transformational ability of Monkey as his guide, Wittman creates a play in the trickster spirit, a play that wars against racism and that exists in a liminal time and place. Within the theatre, the audience is not separate from the players and everything that happens is doubled — occurring both as a representation of something that happened in some other time, and as something in itself, happening now. Through the play, Wittman identifies himself and his community, and integrates the two, through a colossal mixing of actions, dialogues and monologues representing the multiple voices and histories of the community.

The relationship of tricksters to the formation of community relates to the trickster's ability to represent the one and the many. In Louise Erdrich's novel *Love Medicine*, the Chippewa trickster Nanabozho lingers in the background of the novel, never centralized like Monkey in Kingston's *Tripmaster Monkey*. No one character in *Love Medicine* is a complete representation of Nanabozho alone. Instead, separate individuals in the community bear characteristics of Nanabozho that when brought together tie them to each other and to their mythical roots.

Like other tricksters, Nanabozho's most important characteristic is his ability to transform. Summing up Nanabozho's characteristics in her chapter "'Stop Making Sense': Trickster Variations in the Fiction of Louise Erdrich," Claudia Gutwirth describes Nanabozho as "an emissary of Kitche Manitou, the Great Spirit. A teacher, helper, and healer, but also a buffoon, Nanabozho possessed the ability to transform himself" (148). His transformational powers demonstrate his ability to transcend the boundaries of his physical being, to go outside and beyond his own body. Jeanne Rosier Smith argues in *Writing Tricksters* that this ability to transcend the physical limits of the individual body is the key to understanding Erdrich's notion of identity — a "transpersonal" identity in which a "strong sense of self must be based not on isolation but on personal connections to community and to myth" (74). In *Love Medicine*, characters demonstrate this ability to transcend beyond their bodies, and it is in these characters, Smith argues, that the identities are the strongest. As an example, Smith shows how Albertine Johnson loses herself in the night sky while lying outside in a field with her cousin Lipsha:

> Northern lights. Something in the cold, wet atmosphere brought them out. I grabbed Lipsha's arm. We floated into the field and sank down, crushing green wheat. We chewed the sweet grass tips and stared up and were lost. Everything seemed to be one piece. The air, our faces, all cool, moist, and dark, and the ghostly sky.... At times the whole sky was ringed in shooting points and puckers of light gathering and falling, pulsing, fading, rhythmical as breathing. All of a piece. As if the sky were a pattern of nerves and our thought and memories traveled across it. As if the sky were one gigantic memory for us all [Erdrich 37].

While looking up at the sky, Albertine thinks of June, Lipsha's mother who has recently passed away. She envisions June in the sky, dancing, and remembers the smell of her perfume, and Albertine transcends, for the moment, the division between life and death. In Chippewa mythology, the Northern lights are created by the dead dancing in the sky (Smith 75).

June herself carries some of the trickster's characteristics in her. Nanabozho is a woodland trickster, and as a young child, June lived with her outcast mother in the woods. When her mother died, the little girl lived on her own, eating pine sap she found in the woods. Marie Kashpaw takes June in to raise her, but June stays connected to the woods, eventually going to live with Marie's brother-in-law, Eli, who also prefers life in the woods. "Sometimes I thought she was more like Eli," Marie muses. "The woods were in June, after all, just like in him, and maybe more. She had sucked on pine sap and grazed grass and nipped buds like a deer" (Erdrich 87). June's son, Lipsha, contains another part of Nanabozho's power — the ability to heal:

> I know the tricks of mind and body inside out without ever having trained for it, because I got the touch. It's a thing you got to be born with. I got secrets in

my hands that nobody ever knew to ask. Take Grandma Kashpaw with her tired veins all knotted up in her legs like clumps of blue snails. I take my fingers and I snap them on the knots. The medicine flows out of me. The touch. I run my fingers up the maps of those rivers of veins or I knock very gentle above their hearts or I make a circling motion on their stomachs, and it helps them. They feel much better. Some women pay me five dollars [Erdrich 231].

Lipsha further shows his connection to Nanabozho as he reenacts part of the Nanbozho myth at the end of the novel when he seeks to find out the identity of his parents. The trickster Nanabozho in the mythological story is told by his grandmother that a powerful wind spirit stole away his mother at his birth, and he goes in search of her, just as Lipsha, after his grandmother tells him that June was his mother, sets off on a journey to discover his father. Nanabozho meets with a gambler, and they gamble over the destiny of Nanabozho's people. Nanabozho defeats the villain, winning the game through trickery. Similarly, Lipsha gets into a card game with his violent half-brother King, also June's son, and wins June's car from King by using marked cards. As the character of his generation who possess the most magic, Lipsha's survival is necessary for the traditional, cultural survival of the community.

Other facets of Nanbozho appear in Lulu Lamartine, Lipsha's grandmother. Her strong sexual appetite bears evidence to the trickster within her, but she also shows the ability to transcend beyond her physical limits. Her sensuality is the key to her transcendent ability:

No one ever understood my wild and secret ways. They used to say Lulu Lamartine was like a cat, loving no one, only purring to get what she wanted. But that's not true. I was in love with the whole world and all that lived in its rainy arms. Sometimes I'd look out on my yard and the green leaves would be glowing.... I'd hear the wind rushing, rolling, like the far-off sound of waterfalls. Then I'd open my mouth wide, my ears wide, my heart, and I'd let everything inside [Erdrich 276].

Lulu also becomes in her later years a keeper of the culture of the tribe. Stressing the importance of not selling land, of preserving the old language, and of maintaining some integrity in the production of native crafts, Lulu becomes a spokesperson for her community.

The most vivid trickster in *Love Medicine*, however, is Lulu's son Gerry Nanapush (Nanapush is an alternate name for Nanabozho), who is also Lipsha's father. Hounded by the law since his youth when he got into a bar fight, Gerry proves himself to be the master escape artist: "Gerry was talented at getting out, that's a fact. He boasted that no steel or concrete shitbarn could hold a Chippewa, and he had eellike properties in spite of his enormous size. Greased with lard once, he squirmed into a six-foot-thick prison wall and vanished" (199–200). Despite being two hundred and fifty pounds and over six feet, Gerry is agile, light, cat-like; whatever prison he is put in, he manages to escape. Albertine comments on Gerry's graceful, almost androgynous movements: "He was bigger than I remembered from the bar.... He was so big that he had to hunker one shoulder beneath the lintel and back his belly in, pushing the doorframe wider with his long, soft hands. It was the hands I watched as Gerry filled the shack. His plump fingers looked so graceful and artistic against his smooth mass. He used them prettily" (205). And again Albertine notices Gerry's agility when he escapes from the police by jumping out of a third-story hospital window: "His body lifted like a hot-air balloon filling suddenly. Behind him there was a wide, tall window. Gerry opened it and sent the screen into thin air with an elegant chorus-girl kick. Then he followed the screen, squeezing himself unbelievably through the frame like a fat rabbit disappearing down a hole" (209).

Gerry's agility, androgyny, disregard for boundaries and defiance of authority make him clearly a trickster figure, a trickster with a political point to make. Racism is what put Gerry in jail to begin with, and his defiance of the law is actually a higher form of justice, flipping the normal assumptions of right and wrong.

After winning June's car away from King, Lipsha drives Gerry to the Canadian border in yet another escape from the police. On this drive, Lipsha realizes that he is Gerry's son. As they say goodbye, Lipsha feels the expansion of himself beyond his physical body: "In that night I felt expansion, as if the world was branching out in shoots and growing faster than the eye could see. I felt smallness, how the earth divided into bits and kept dividing. I felt the stars. I felt them roosting on my shoulders with his hand. The moon came up red and warm" (366).

By placing characteristics of the trickster Nanabozho in various characters within the novel, Erdrich underscores the necessity of community in preserving cultural traditions as a resistance to domination by the white culture. Although they live in the modern world and face discrimination, poverty and other social ills, most of the members of the community in *Love Medicine* carry a piece of tradition within them, and those that do not, such as the violent, wife-beater King, serve as warnings as to what can happen if one completely loses touch with one's tradition. Together, the individuals of the community create a unity brought together by the characteristics of Nanabozho, their symbol for tradition and their resistance to assimilation. The transforming figure of Nanabozho allows for many voices to be heard and many stories to be told.

In a later novel, *The Bingo Palace*, Erdrich further develops Lipsha's trickster connections. Lipsha pleads with a woman who has rejected him, "You've got to listen to me even though I am making no sense. In fact, because I am making no sense, you should listen harder. We'll get to the truth quicker if we don't worry about logic" (111–12). As a trickster, Lipsha knows that language can be reductive, limited to one meaning, and often to one voice. Gutwirth makes this comment on Lipsha's outburst: "As Lipsha suggests, the only remedy is to make ourselves receptive to things that don't make sense: the playful, the multiple, the incoherent. The presence of trickster reminds us to stop making sense, both as a way to avoid the violence that the imposition meaning often entails, and as a means of embracing language's inherent capacity for overdetermination" (161). Like all tricksters, Nanabozho allows multiple perspectives to be displayed, multiple layers of meaning to be revealed, and therefore, represents the diversity and the unity of the community.

In *Tracks*, a novel published after *Love Medicine* but set chronologically in a time period (1912–1924) before *Love Medicine*, Erdrich delineates characters that are even more clearly related to tricksters. Nanapush is an obvious trickster figure. His name, as mentioned above in the discussion of Gerry Nanapush (his future son with Lulu), is an alternate name for Nanabozho. When Lulu is a young woman, Nanapush narrates his portion of *Tracks* to her so that she can know her history and why her mother, Fleur, left the reservation. Explaining to Lulu how he got his name, Nanapush says, "My father said, 'Nanapush. That's what you'll be called. Because it's got to do with trickery and living in the bush. Because it's got to do with something a girl can't resist. The first Nanapush stole fire. You will steal hearts'" (33).

Nanapush portrays the persona of a trickster throughout the novel. More than all of the other characters in the book, except for Fleur, who will be discussed below, Nanapush realizes the value of the land to the community and strives to preserve the land as the essence of what holds the community and its traditions together. He tells Lulu, "I know this. Land is the only thing that lasts life to life" (33). Nanapush also has the power to heal as he shows when he saves Lulu, when she was a young child, from having her frozen feet amputated, and again when he concocts a special stew to try to cure Fleur's spiritual darkness after she is unable to save her second child. When an exhausted and starving Eli, a young man whom Nanapush treats as a son and who acts as a husband to Fleur, goes out to kill a moose in the dead of winter, Nanapush, from far away in his cabin, guides Eli's hunt so that it will be successful. Then, as Eli travels home to bring back the meat, Nanapush beats a drum to guide Eli's footsteps so that he will not hurry too fast, sweat, and possibly die in the extreme cold. Realistically, Eli could not possibly have heard the drum from Nanapush's cabin, but he does hear the beat, and Nanapush saves his life.

Perhaps Nanapush's most trickster-like behavior is his astounding gift for talking. After Nanapush rescues Fleur from her family's cabin, where all but Fleur had died of consumption, Nanapush and Fleur sit for days in a state of near death, too disheartened to eat or care for themselves. Perhaps they would have died, too, except the local priest, Father Damien, comes to visit. Nanapush recounts how talk saved his life:

> My voice rasped at first when I tried to speak, but then, oiled by strong tea, lard and bread, I was off and talking. Even a sledge won't stop me once I start. Father Damien looked astonished, and then wary, as I began to creak and roll. I gathered speed. I talked both languages in streams that ran alongside each other, over every rock, around every obstacle. The sound of my own voice convinced me I was alive [7].

Through talk, Nanapush also saves Margaret, Eli's mother with whom Nanapush lives, from rape. Two young men kidnap them because they resent, among other things, Nanapush and Margaret's attempts to get their neighbors to stop selling off land. Nanapush intimidates the men through talk and teasing, causing them to resort to shaving Margaret's head instead of raping her as a humiliation. Lulu is saved from her extreme frostbite through Nanapush's chanting: "Once I had you I did not dare break the string between us and kept on moving my lips, holding you motionless with talking, just as at this moment" (167).

Like any trickster, Nanapush's talk is often humorous and full of sexual innuendo. He uses humor to cajole or trick his enemies into getting what he wants, and to show endearment for those he cares about. Nanapush's and Margaret's banter, for example, is often suggestive. Once when angry about Nanapush helping her son, Eli, begin a relationship with Fleur, Margaret taunts Nanapush and ridicules his manhood:

> "Old man," she scorned, "two wrinkled berries and a twig."
> "A twig can grow," I [Nanapush] offered.
> "But only in the spring" [48].

Humor pervades Nanapush's life. Even his death, which takes place in Erdrich's later novel, *The Last Report on the Miracles at Little No Horse* (2001), leaves the reader laughing as a moose Nanapush had used to pull his boat to shore (living out a traditional Nanapush story), takes off over land with Nanapush still in the boat (287).

Because of her banter, her sexuality, and her traditional way of living, Lawrence W. Gross suggests in "The Trickster and World Maintenance: An Anishinaabe Reading of Louise Erdrich's *Tracks*" that Margaret is also a trickster figure. While it is true that Margaret can be tricky, she tricks and manipulates others more for her own good than for the good of another or for the community. Her most spectacular "trick" involves finding a way to get control of the money she, Nanapush, Fleur, Lulu and her sons Nector and Eli all earned by stripping and selling bark from cranberry trees throughout an especially arduous winter. The money was to go to pay the tax on Margaret's, Nanapush's and Fleur's land. Because the payment is late, however, the amount owed is more, and Margaret and Nector pay the entire amount of cash to save Margaret's land. Consequently, Nanapush loses his land, but even more distressing, Fleur's land is sold to a lumber company. So Margaret, while often tricky, ultimately betrays those she supposedly loves and tears apart her family and community. Alternatively, Nanapush's tricks are often designed to benefit or guide someone else or to preserve the community — the chief function of a trickster.

Fleur is another strong trickster character in *Tracks*. Pauline, the second narrator of *Tracks*, describes Fleur and other tribe members' fear of her:

> Alone out there, she went haywire, out of control. She messed with evil, laughed at the old women's advice and dressed like a man. She got herself into some half-forgotten medicine, studied ways we shouldn't talk about. Some say she kept the finger of a child in her pocket and a powder of unborn rabbits in a leather thong around her neck. She laid the heart of an owl on her tongue so she could see at night, and went out, hunting, not even in her own body. We knew for sure because the next morning, in the snow or dust, we followed the tracks of her bare feet and saw where they changed, where the claws sprang out, the pad broadened and pressed into the dirt. By night we heard her chuffing cough, the bear cough. By day her silence and the wide grin she threw to bring down our guard made us frightened [12].

Living alone, dressing like a man (androgyny), studying old ways of magic and healing, and shape-shifting into a bear while out hunting solidify Fleur's role as a trickster. In addition to these traits, she also consorts with the lake spirit, Misshepeshu, and crosses the boundary between the living and the dead when she goes to gamble for the life of her second child. Fleur also curses people who have betrayed her, and twice conjures the wind to carry out her revenge. Her last "trick" in the book is to saw the trees around her cabin nearly clear through, and when the lumber men come to drive her off her land, she brings the wind and crashes the trees all around them. Nanapush narrates the scene:

> The wind shrieked and broke, tore into the brush, swept full force upon us.... With one thunderstroke the trees surrounding Fleur's cabin cracked off and fell away from us in a circle, pinning beneath their branches the roaring men, the horses. The limbs snapped steel saws and rammed through wagon boxes. Twigs formed webs of wood, canopies laced over groans and struggles [223].

Clearly Fleur is a powerful old-time trickster, but in the end of *Tracks* she loses everything — Eli, her children, her home, her community, her connection with the lake spirit, her parents' and ancestors' graves, and, worst of all, her land. In spite of the efforts of Nanapush and others to preserve the traditions of the community, change has come, and Fleur lacks Nanapush's ability to shift with the times. She can reap a revenge, but she cannot, or will not, adapt as Nanapush can. Nanapush, surprisingly, even becomes a tribal official at the end of the book, but he makes such an uncharacteristic move so that he can save Lulu and bring her back home from boarding school. Fleur has her power, but not the ability to adjust and change her power in order to deal with the changes society has thrust upon her, and therefore, her power becomes impotent. She leaves while Nanapush stays to continue to resist the disintegration of the tribe.

The second narrator of *Tracks*, Pauline, poses an interesting case. She too, in spite of her bizarre and seemingly psychotic nature, also possesses some trickster characteristics. She develops a morbid attraction for the dead and dying, feeling that at their bedsides she has control over their deaths. When she observes Mary Pepewas' death, she sees herself as cutting the rope that still tethers Mary to life, and after Mary dies, Pauline feels light and free. "A cool blackness lifted me, out of the room and through the door. I leapt, spun, landed along the edge of the clearing.... And that is when, twirling dizzily, my wings raked the air, and I rose in three powerful beats and saw what lay below" (68). The shape shifting into a bird is not just Pauline's unstable imagination, since she is found perched in a tree the next morning.

Pauline has the ability to enter other people's bodies and to manipulate their behavior. She lies in bed at night and practices becoming Sophie, whose young beauty she envies. "I could almost feel what it was like to be inside Sophie's form, not hunched in mine, not blending into the walls, but careless and fledgling, throwing the starved glances of men off like the surface of a pond" (78). When Eli rejects Pauline's awkward advances toward him, she manipulates Sophie and Eli into having sex by seeming to control their bodies. Through her actions, she sets off unintended consequences that further divide the community, including the kidnapping of Nanapush and Margaret mentioned earlier.

Pauline is a plain, skinny young woman who feels herself to be invisible, and particularly unnoticed by men. She is of mixed blood, and longs to be white. "I wanted to be like my mother, who showed her half-white. I wanted to be like my grandfather, pure Canadian" (14). As a person of mixed race, Pauline holds special significance in the novel as both an insider and an outsider. As stated by Lynn Domina in her article "'The Way I Heard It': Autobiography, Tricksters and Leslie Marmon Silko's *Storyteller*," "Since a capacity to shift shapes is among the most prominent and universal characteristics of a trickster, mixed-race identity almost inevitably provides one with a precondition for trickster ability" (46).

Rejecting her own culture and community, Pauline leaves the reservation to go work at the nearby town of Argus, and it is in Argus that she gets to know Fleur. After Fleur wins a pot of money gambling with her male coworkers, a scheme she plotted out for a month or more, the men rape her. Pauline witnesses the rape, yet is too frightened to help Fleur, and she is overcome with guilt. Later, when Fleur conjures a tornado to take revenge on the town of Argus, the men who raped Fleur are trapped in a meat freezer, and all but one die. Pauline may or may not have locked the men in the freezer of her own free will, she may have been controlled by Fleur, but either way she carries the guilt of that murder. She describes the incident with hazy recollection: "Sometimes, thinking back, I see my arms lift, my hands grasp, see myself dropping the beam into the metal grip. At other times, that moment is erased" (27). Whether Pauline actually moved the bar to lock the men in the freezer is ambiguous, but she and Fleur are inextricably linked from then on. Since Fleur shows unusual tolerance for Pauline in later portions of the book, even when Pauline manipulates Eli into having sex with Sophie and Fleur finds out, it would seem that Fleur owes Pauline a debt.

Pauline's rejection of her own culture and racial make-up lead her to live with the nuns, and, significantly, she must deny that she is Indian in order to join the convent. Nanapush tries to save Pauline from abandoning her culture and her people, but she develops a bizarre and demented attachment to her own interpretation of Christianity. She believes Jesus speaks to her: "One night of deepest cold He sat in the moonlight, on the stove, and looked down at me and smiled in the spill of His radiance and explained. He said that I was not whom I had supposed. I was an orphan and my parents had died in grace, and also, despite my deceptive features, I was not one speck of Indian but wholly white" (137).

Pauline performs penances that degrade and, at times, nearly kill her. When Pauline decides that God only wants her to urinate twice a day, for example, Nanapush lures her out of her penance with cups of sweet sassafras tea and a wildly funny story about a young woman swept away by flooding water. By humiliating Pauline into breaking her penance, Nanapush tries to show her the ridiculousness of her extreme behaviors and attempts to bring her back to her tribe. Pauline eventually gives up on God and Jesus, seeing them as too weak to overcome the Chippewa spirits, and she decides she must take Christ's place and eliminate them herself—particularly the lake spirit. "Christ was weak, I saw now, a tame newcomer in this country that has its own devils" (192). She takes Nanapush's leaky boat out into the middle of the lake to do battle with the lake spirit. In great danger from the rough water, Nanapush is the one who paddles out in a canoe and tries to save her. She refuses to be rescued, however, and attempts to overturn Nanapush's canoe, so he has no choice but to leave her to her mission. Eventually the current pushes Pauline's boat to shore, and she does battle with the lake spirit and defeats him. In the morning, Napoleon Morrisey, who had seduced Pauline and was the father of her illegitimate child, instead lies dead on the shore.

Although Pauline has some special abilities and demonstrates some trickster traits, she also seems to contradict some of the basic characteristics of a trickster. She rejects her community, deludes herself into thinking she is white, internalizes white racism against Indians, and she uses her magical abilities largely for self-serving ends. Her magic, though at times it seems real, at other times could also be viewed as just a product of her deteriorating psyche. Though a somewhat pitiable figure, an outcast from a young age, Pauline causes much sadness, death and division within the community. However, unlike Fleur who leaves the reservation, Pauline wipes out her old life by symbolically rolling in dirt and mud on her way back to the convent, becomes a nun with the name Sister Leopolda, and is assigned to become a teacher of Indian children in a Catholic school. She declares, "I have vowed to use my influence to guide them, to purify their minds, to mold them in my own image" (205). While Fleur, unable to adapt to changes in the culture, has to leave; Pauline, frighteningly, stays and perpetuates her self-loathing of her race and culture into the next generation.

Looking at Pauline's character from the trickster point of view does not seem as fruitful analytically as for Nanapush or Fleur. Pauline seems to be more akin to the type of character Sau-ling Cynthia Wong has called the racial shadow. In *Reading Asian American Literature: From Necessity to Extravagance*, Wong devotes a chapter to discussion of the racial shadow. Although she discusses this concept in relation to Asian American literature, the concept can also apply to other literatures of marginalized groups. Wong relates the racial shadow to the psychological process of projection. When a character has internalized (or eaten, to use Wong's terminology) racism against his or her own self and group, projection of those racist thoughts onto another can be a defense. Wong writes:

> Projection, a psychological process that (like bursting and vomiting) reverses the symbolic directionality of eating (introjection), keeps at bay the threatening knowledge of self-hatred. By projecting undesirable "Asianness" outward onto a double—what I term a *racial shadow*—one renders alien what is, in fact, literally inalienable, thereby disowning and distancing it [78].

The double, as Wong explains, thus develops as a defense mechanism caused by repression followed by projection onto another. The character may experience a split or fragmentation of the self, projecting the unfavorable aspects of him or herself onto another version of the self. This alternate self, or double, may be presented as a hallucination or as "a separate, autonomous character in the fictional world" (83). Either way, "the double is symptomatic of a crisis in self-acceptance and self-knowledge: part of the self, denied recognition by the conscious ego, emerges as an external figure" (82).

In the case of Pauline, she exists as a separate, autonomous character, but instead of being one character's alternate self, she seems to provide the function of a defense mechanism for the entire community, other members of which must also feel some sense of racial and cultural inferiority at the incursion of the white culture. Wong briefly mentions Pauline in her book, reinforcing that her "individual psychopathology is shown to be inextricable from — in fact exacerbated and given frighteningly violent shape by — the history of Native American subjugation" (116). Pauline's character is deeply rooted in Chippewa culture, both in terms of her people's subjugation to the white culture, which causes her sense of self-hatred, but also as a trickster. Pauline works on behalf of the community, although indirectly and unwillingly, by absorbing the widespread feelings of cultural inferiority and self-hatred. Her trickster traits are evident as explained above, but when viewed as a trickster that also fills the role of a racial shadow, we understand Pauline's dark character, and also see that Pauline does serve a purpose in her community as the projection of their collective thoughts of self-hatred. Through Pauline, the community can purge these negative feelings, project them on her, and she internalizes them. Thus, in spite of her extreme darkness, Pauline, like all tricksters, ultimately serves a positive role in the preservation of her community's traditions and values despite her negative behavior.

Myth, Legend and Self

It is clear from reading the authors whose works occur in this chapter that narrative can be a powerful tool in creating one's sense of oneself. Mythical and legendary figures can provide models and offer solutions that can be adopted as a means by which to approach life. Their liminality, their flexibility, and their abilities to avoid being trapped all make these figures from myth and legend desirable role models, especially when one lives a life that tends to be characterized by seemingly irreconcilable dualities that must be negotiated. Stories from the past heritage can provide a connection between one culture and another by offering alternate subjectivities that become part of the character's self and group identity. Each of the authors mentioned above takes a figure from a narrative and reinterprets it in a way that suits the present circumstances of the character. From these mythological and legendary figures, the characters gain a hybrid perspective, additional insight, into how to deal with conflict and into how to reconcile a double heritage without losing a part of oneself.

Chapter Four

Comedy and Tragedy: The Ironic Double Spaces of Ethnic Humor

Humor sometimes depends upon the ironic intermingling of two meanings, occurring simultaneously, to make us laugh. To understand only the literal, surface meanings of the words of a joke, for example, is to miss the joke. Much humor depends on underlying connotations and double entendres, and it is this doubling of meaning, especially when the meanings create an incongruity, that makes humorous discourse funny. Doubling also gives humor its great flexibility, making it suitable for undermining the status quo while at the same time appearing to maintain it. Just as we have seen in previous chapters with magical realism, landscapes and multiple subjectivity, the doubling of meanings within the common space of one humorous discourse creates a hybrid perspective. In the case of ethnic humor, hybrid perspectives within humorous discourse can be used as instruments of subtle subversion against an oppressor, or can mitigate a tragedy, combining the tragic with the comic. In these capacities of mitigating and subverting, humor gives an outlet for reacting against discrimination and for battling the frustrations of living within two cultures.

Humor as a Means to Overturn the Status Quo

As Nancy Walker wrote in *A Very Serious Thing: Women's Humor and American Culture*, "An essential purpose of humor is to call the norm into question" (71). Humor told by ethnic authors and comediennes that focuses on racial or ethnic hierarchies attempts to overturn the status quo, put the underdog on top, and allow those who are normally silenced to take control. The reversal may only be temporary, lasting only the time it takes to tell and enjoy a joke, or it may only occur amongst a small group of people, perhaps only the joke teller and one listener, but the power of humor can also be far reaching and can bring about lasting changes in how people view each other and their society.

Joanne R. Gilbert, both a scholar of humor and a former stand-up comedian, emphasizes humor's power to invert and critique the status quo in her book *Performing Marginality*: "Within the topsy-turvy world of stand-up comic performance, hierarchies are inverted, power relations are subverted.... Because it can avoid inflaming audiences by framing incisive — even incendiary — sociocultural critique as 'mere entertainment,' comedy is undeniably a unique and powerful form of communication" (xii). In Gilbert's view, social critique that also can make people laugh has the power to break down barriers and influence social change. Jennifer Andrews in "In the Belly of a Laughing God: Reading Humor and Irony in the Poetry of Joy Harjo" also notes humor's power to transform human hierarchies in Native American texts, especially if the humor contains irony, an essential tool for humorous social critique: "Humor can channel anger, celebrate survival, and even unite Native and non–Native readers by allowing otherwise disparate groups of people to laugh together. Irony, in turn, often tempers the playful elements of humor by reminding readers of the legacy of oppression that has shaped the lives of Native North Americans for centuries" (200). As humor told by ethnic writers and comediennes expands beyond the simple joke told by one person to another, and reaches ever larger audiences through television, films, literature, and other media, humor's ability to change attitudes, alleviate frustrations, and reverse the status quo also gains in power.

Looking at an example of Native American humor that contains a dose of irony, the following passage from Sherman Alexie's *The Lone Ranger and Tonto Fistfight in Heaven* clearly illustrates how humor can invert and subvert social, hierarchal categories. In this passage, Victor, a Coeur d'Alene Indian, while taking some powerful drugs with his friends, has a vision in which he sees his friend Junior on stage singing and playing the guitar. In Victor's vision, Junior says:

> *Indians make the best cowboys.* I can tell you that. I've been singing at the plantation since I was ten years old and have always drawn big crowds. All the white folks come to hear my songs, my little pieces of Indian wisdom, although they have to sit in the back of the theater because all the Indians get the best tickets for my shows. It's not racism. The Indians just camp out all night to buy tickets. Even the president of the United States, Mr. Edgar Crazy Horse himself, came to hear me once [18].

This passage strikes the reader as humorous because of the irony. The discriminatory practice of seating people according to race, with the lower status group in the back, this time falls upon whites instead of Native Americans. Also, the assumption that the president of the United States is a Native American named Edgar Crazy Horse overturns (as Barack Obama actually did in 2008) the biased notion that only a white man can be president.

The use of humor as a subversive form of criticism, to invert the social hierarchy and put the underdog on top, is not unique to minority groups in the contemporary United States; humor has served such a purpose throughout the ages. In *The Dialogic Imagination*, Mikhail Bakhtin discusses the unique liberties granted to humorous discourse in the Middle Ages, which ridiculed the ruling classes, as long as it stayed within boundaries. "The Middle Ages, with varying degrees of qualification, respected the freedom of the fool's cap and allotted a rather broad license to laughter and the laughing word" (72). But in the United States, subversive humor by ethnic groups has expanded beyond boundaries and has, like the ethnic literature that has been discussed thus far, become a part of mainstream humor. In a chapter entitled "Outsiders/Insiders," in *Rebellious Laughter*, Joseph Boskin discusses the rise of ethnic humor among U.S. minority groups and the transformation ethnic humor has produced in the national humor of the United States.

> Struggling on the knife edge of urban environments, their jokes and routines offering an ongoing summons, minorities have recast the language, character and tempo of national humor. Nineteenth-century Irish immigrants, later joined by incoming Jews, migrant African-Americans, and women and other groups after the 1950s forged a style and practice of comedy that was subversively wicked and sly, prodding and absurdist, indirect and undercutting. A mélange of masks — the trickster, the con man, the affable rogue, the role-reversing jokester — emerged as minorities coped with the discriminatory practices and stereotypes, turning negative features into virtues [38–9].

The irony within ethnic humor, like humor in general, juxtaposes incongruous elements sharing the same space, and points out contradictions. What distinguishes much ethnic humor from non-ethnic humor, which may also rely on incongruity as a means to provoke laughter, is that the incongruities in ethnic humor often result from clashes between different cultures, such as misunderstandings or discrimination between different races or ethnicities, and the incongruous elements create a humorous juxtaposition out of what in other circumstances might only be a bitter, or even tragic, situation.

When put into a context that contains cultural incongruities, humor deals with the clashes between cultures by finding the comic element. The following joke about a WASP (white, Anglo-Saxon Protestant) illustrates how a serious cultural clash can become a source for humor:

What do you get when you cross a WASP with an orangutan?
I don't know, but it won't let "you" into its cage [Boskin 147].*

The joke ridicules the stereotypical image of the WASPs as wanting to keep minorities out of their neighborhoods, but also, more subtly, implies that such tendencies are less than human (more like an orangutan), suggesting that those being kept out are actually more civilized than those being let in. Of course, the joke could not exist if there was not some truth to the stereotype of the exclusive WASP, and so humor criticizes the majority group, emphasizing a point of conflict, but also at the same time mitigates the conflict, providing a release from the tension that arises from being a victim of an injustice. As Gilbert states, "Clearly, marginal humor is an aggressive response to domination. Although it is not always overt, the aggression in marginal humor may be discerned as cultural critique" (158). The aggression in the above joke, therefore, serves a positive, active role both as a release of tension and as a social critique.

Because of the "*you*" in the joke cited above, and because of its critique of WASP exclusiveness, this joke provides a good example of the complicated relationship of joke teller to joke listener in ethnic humor discussed by Lois Leveen in her article, "Only When I Laugh: Textual Dynamics of Ethnic Humor." Leveen delineates four basic combinations of joke relationships that exist in the telling of ethnic jokes: "1) a group member telling a joke to another member; 2) a member telling a joke to a non-member; 3) a non-member telling a joke to a member; and 4) a non-member telling a joke to a non-member" (33). "A joke text," Leveen writes, "may have a different meaning when told in each of the four basic joke act situations" (33). Considering the orangutan joke above, we can see that only under the first possibility, a group member telling a joke to another member, and, in this case, both being members of a minority group, does the joke have a humorous effect. If both the teller and the listener were members of the white, majority group, the joke would not make sense—neither would try to exclude the other on the basis of race. If the teller were a member of a minority group and the listener was a member of the majority group, the joke also would not make sense, since the punch line is about the exclusive tendencies of the majority. If the teller were white and the listener a member of a minority group, the joke would take on a racist meaning and become offensive, as the white teller would seem to be supporting the exclusionary practices of WASPs and ridiculing the minority person. The only combination that supports the humorous intention

---

*This is just one example of the genre of WASP jokes. For more examples see Joseph Boskin, *Rebellious Laughter: People's Humor in American Culture* (Syracuse: Syracuse University Press, 1997), 147–50.

of the joke, therefore, is if both teller and listener are members of a minority, marginalized group (though they would not necessarily have to be members of the same minority group). Only in this last circumstance does the joke serve its intended function as a critique of the white majority that helps to temporarily lighten minority frustrations over discrimination.

Even when minority humor is self-denigrating, it still can place the member of the minority ethnic group on top through a subtle criticism of the majority group. For example:

"Tell me, Lord, how come I'm so black?"
"YOU'RE BLACK SO YOU COULD WITHSTAND THE HOT RAYS OF THE SUN IN AFRICA."
"Tell me, Lord, how come my hair is so nappy?"
"YOUR HAIR IS NAPPY SO THAT YOU WOULD NOT SWEAT UNDER THE HOT RAYS OF THE SUN IN AFRICA."
"Tell me, Lord, how come my legs are so long?"
"YOUR LEGS ARE LONG SO THAT YOU COULD ESCAPE FROM THE WILD BEASTS IN AFRICA."
"Then tell me, Lord, what the hell am I doing in Chicago?" [Boskin 44–45].

The African American in the joke feels the separation between himself and members of the white majority group. He demands an explanation for his otherness, a difference that he locates within his physical features. The fact that he is physically so well adapted for life in Africa (according to the joke) creates the humor, as he lives in Chicago — an incongruity. Yet when he asks what he is doing in Chicago, the answer is evident — African Americans (for the most part) are victims of a historic forced displacement, of past slavery. Again, an incongruity resulting from a past tragic event creates humor and points obliquely at the tragedy. With subtlety, the joke criticizes the majority group that continues to inflict discrimination on the minority group, and secedes the moral high ground to African Americans.

When a joke teller who is a member of a minority group tells a self-deprecating joke about his or her own group, there is some risk that the stereotype will be taken seriously, even by the teller him- or herself. As Leon Rappoport warns in *Punchlines: The Case for Racial, Ethnic and Gender Humor*, "A more serious side of self-critical humor can be seen occasionally when it crosses the border into self-hatred" (36). Generally, however, self-deprecating humor exaggerates stereotypes, and through ironic humor, a stereotype is held up to ridicule for listeners (or readers) to see the absurdity in such thinking. Jennifer Andrews stresses this point, stating that "irony [coupled with humor] may remind readers of the ridiculousness of a situation or stereotype that might otherwise be entirely devoid of humor" (202). The joke teller, therefore, presents the stereotype, but simultaneously disproves it, thereby attaining a position superior to those who would believe such a stereotype. Such jokes,

Rappoport writes, indicate that "members of ethnic groups are in effect proclaiming a form of ethnic pride" (37). As an example of such self-deprecating humor, Lois Leveen provides a joke told by the Chinese-American comedian Phil Nee: "It's not always fun being Chinese. My girlfriend left me last week, for a guy who looks exactly like me" (43). Nee holds up the stereotype that "all Chinese people look alike" for ridicule, but instead of reinforcing the stereotype, as the surface meaning of the joke might indicate, the stereotype strikes the listener as absurd (and funny) because of the obvious improbability of the assertion that Chinese people cannot tell each other apart.

As we have seen with Native American and Chinese American humor, Chicano and Chicana writers share instances of humor based on language and cultural juxtapositions of clashing elements, usually between the Chicano and Anglo* ethnic groups. As with other ethnic groups, humor gives a means to highlight and to work through the dualities of the two cultural systems in a manner that downplays the potential seriousness of the situation.

Building a career on the phenomenon of cultural incongruities between Mexican American and Anglo ethnic groups, José Antonio Burciaga founded a comedy group known as Culture Clash. He also has written books of collected comic sketches that poke fun at Mexican American and Anglo customs, and particularly at the disjunctures that occur when the two cultures collide. In *Spilling the Beans*, he writes: "Putting incongruous things together, things that don't necessarily go together can be funny. Mexican culture and Anglo-American culture have as many incongruities between them as commonalities" (176). The following passage occurs in the selection "Ramblings on NAFTA" from *Spilling the Beans* (NAFTA stands for the North American Free Trade Agreement negotiated between Canada, Mexico and the United States and put into effect January 1994). The inversion of social hierarchy evident in this joke and the subtle criticism of the dominant U.S. group are by now to us familiar functions of ethnic humor:

> During the early part of the Civil War President Abraham Lincoln called General Mariano Guadalupe Vallejo to Washington on business. During their conversations, General Vallejo suggested to President Lincoln that the United States build a railroad into Mexico, believing as he said, "it would be a benefit to both nations."
> A smiling President Lincoln asked, "What good would it do for our people to go down to Mexico even if the railroad were built? They would all die of fever and according to your belief, go down yonder," with a motion of his hand towards the supposed location of the infernal fires.
> "I wouldn't be very sorry about that," General Vallejo answered coolly.
> "How so?" President Lincoln asked, "I thought you liked the Yankees."
> "So I do," was the answer. "The Yankees are a wonderful people! Wonderful!

---

*I use the term Anglo here, because it is the term most commonly used by Chicanos to refer to members of the white majority group.

Wherever they go they make improvements. If they were to emigrate in large number to hell itself, they would somehow manage to change the climate" [32–33].

In this joke, "General Vallejo" ridicules the Anglos' inflated assessment of their own abilities through an exaggeration — suggesting they could even improve upon hell if they went there. Paired with this critique, however, is a defense of the Mexican people, humiliated by "Lincoln's" comment that the U.S. has nothing to gain from working with Mexico, a common sentiment expressed during the negotiation of NAFTA. Although the joke is fictional, and set in a distant time so as not to be too offensive, the exchange nevertheless sharply resists the U.S. notion of Anglo superiority that persists in the present time. The joke, then, not only critiques Anglos' prejudices, but also enhances group solidarity for Mexican and Mexican American people who have shared in bearing the brunt of Anglo "superiority."

Humor as a Means to Enhance Group Solidarity — Coyote Stories Old and New

Although it is true that contemporary times and conditions have seen an explosion of ethnic humor, humor has long been used in what is now the United States to enhance group solidarity and to criticize members of other groups. The first inhabitants of North America used stories, including humorous ones, within their separate tribes to identify themselves as a group and to distinguish themselves from other tribes. Traditional Coyote stories, for example, give evidence that ethnic concerns and beliefs in the otherness of neighboring tribes were prevalent in North America, even before its colonization by Europeans. These Coyote stories are found throughout North America and are not limited to particular tribes or geographical areas. The time of their origin cannot be fixed, but they are known to have their beginnings in pre–Columbian oral literature.

Regardless of the variations in the stories that occur among different tribes, Coyote is a recognizable character with distinguishing characteristics. Since his shape may transform, it is not his body type as a coyote that identifies him, but rather his trickster characteristics. In *Giving Birth to Thunder, Sleeping with his Daughter: Coyote Builds North America*, Barry Lopez writes:

> Those who are familiar with the mythology and folklore of the American Indian know already, perhaps that Coyote was not necessarily a coyote, nor even a creature of strict physical dimensions. He was known as the Great Hare among many eastern tribes and as Raven in the Pacific Northwest.... He was Trickster, Imitator, First Born, Old Man, First Creator, Transformer, and Changing Person ... all names derived from his powers, his habits and his acts [xv].

Coyote stories originally served to reinforce tribal identities and to demonstrate proper behavior (although Coyote was usually an example of how *not* to behave). Coyote's antics not only entertained, but provided a comic relief for frustrations and the releasing of social tensions in much the same way that clowns functioned, according to Lopez, in Native American religious ceremonies, serving to reinforce, through contrast, the moral structure of the tribe (xvii).

Coyote stories are seasonal, meant to be told at evening during the winter months. In the foreword to Lopez's book, Barre Toelken specifies that Navajo Coyote stories, for example, were to be told only after the first killing frost and before the first thunderstorm, the telling at other times being taboo. Restrictions as to who could tell the stories were also probably in place at one time, but many of the restrictions have since been lost. The stories could be short or long, or a series of interconnected stories that might be told over longer periods of time, such as a month. They were never meant to be written down but to be a living, transforming oral tradition. To retell a coyote tale is a risky business, as they are believed to hold a power that is not to be released by just anyone. But to possess the power, the tale must be told in the correct manner, at the correct time, and by the right person. Telling the tale in writing instead of orally, for instance, robs the story of its magic right at the start. Therefore, the Coyote stories I am about to retell are only vague shadows of the real thing. Retelling a Coyote story that one has read in a published book reveals no secrets and, I hope, causes no offense.

Coyote stories, both traditional and modernized, provide a rich resource of Native American humor and, particularly for our purposes, humor that sometimes deals with ethnic difference. A Nez Perce story included in Barry Lopez's collection relates how Coyote created human beings belonging to different tribes. The humor in this story derives from Coyote's ability to trick his foe, using only his wits to outsmart the monster. By "pulling one over" on the monster, Coyote gains the upper hand and is able to change the destructive behavior of the monster into a beneficial act of creation. The story begins as follows: Before the creation of human beings, a huge monster with a voracious appetite was loose on the earth and was eating everything in sight. Soon all of Coyote's friends were gone, devoured by the monster, and Coyote determined the eating had to come to a stop. Coyote tied himself to the top of a tall mountain and dared the monster to eat him. The monster could not because Coyote was tied too tightly to the mountaintop, and the monster could not pull him off. The monster decided to make friends with Coyote, and one day Coyote asked to see the animals in the monster's belly. The monster agreed to this request, and Coyote entered his stomach and saw all of his friends, still alive and well. Coyote built a fire and cut down the monster's heart, killing the monster and allowing all of the animals to escape. In honor of the event, Coyote decided to create a new type of animal — human beings. To do so, Coyote cut the monster up and threw the pieces in all directions, and when the pieces landed, they became the different tribes of human beings. When finished, Coyote's friend Fox said that no one had been created to live in the spot where they were then standing, and so Coyote washed the monster's blood from his hands, mixed it with water, and sprinkled the mixture to create the Nez Perce: "'Here on this ground I make the Nez Perce. They will be few in number, but they will be strong and pure.' And this is how the human beings came to be" (Lopez 8).

Putting oneself or one's tribe in a superior position over another (at the other's expense, of course) is a common occurrence in Native American humor. To come out on top through trickery is considered funny. The adversary is never completely defeated, however, because there is always the chance that the underdog will come up with a better story that will put him or her on top again. The following Coyote story told by the Shoshone explains the ethnic differences between tribes in terms of physical beauty. As one would expect, the Shoshone are presented as one of the more beautiful tribes.

One day Coyote sees a tall, beautiful woman and follows her to her home. Ocean Old Woman is her mother and Coyote teaches both women how to copulate. Both give birth to many small children, all at once, and they put the children in a water jug. When Coyote returns from hunting, they tell him it is time for him to go. They put the water jug on his back, telling him to open the stopper at certain points along the way on his trip back home.

> At Saline Valley he opened the stopper a little way. Tall dark people, very good looking got out and ran away. They were the best looking people in the jug.... In Death Valley he opened it again. More good-looking people came out and ran away. The women all had long, dark hair, very beautiful. When he came to Ash Meadows, where we are, he opened it up again and the Shoshone people and the Paiute came out. These people were very good-looking too. At Tin Mountain Coyote let some others out but they were not too good-looking. Then at Moapa he opened the jug up all the way and short ugly people came out, very poor. The girls had short hair and lice. They all had sore eyes. The people over there are still like that today [Lopez 10].

In true trickster fashion, Coyote is not limited to time or place, and modernized Coyote tales are common in contemporary times. The subject matter and Coyote's attitudes have been updated, but a similarity exists between the traditional tales and the modernized versions, and Coyote's humor and mischief remain the same. This contemporary Coyote tale, told by a storytelling character named Samuel, can be found in Sherman Alexie's book *The Lone Ranger and Tonto Fistfight in Heaven*. Note the similarities with the tales already mentioned above that explain ethnic differences, but in this case, the differences explained are those between Native Americans and whites:

> "Listen," Samuel said. "Coyote, who is the creator of all of us, was sitting on his cloud the day after he created the Indians. Now, he liked the Indians, liked what they were doing. *This is good*, he kept saying to himself. But he was bored. He thought and thought about what he should make next in the world. But he couldn't think of anything so he decided to clip his toenails. He clipped his right toenails and held the clippings in his right hand. Then he clipped his left toenails and added those clippings to the ones already in his right hand. He looked around and around his cloud for somewhere to throw away his clippings. But he couldn't find anywhere and he got mad. He started jumping up and down because he was so mad. Then he accidentally dropped his toenail clippings over the side of the cloud and they fell to earth. The clippings burrowed into the ground like seeds and grew up to be the white man. Coyote, he looked down at his newest creation and said, *Oh, shit*" [Alexie 134–35].

As well as inverting the racist hierarchy of white over Indian, the story also serves another role of humor mentioned above, that of mitigating sadness. Before Samuel tells the story to a group of children, he worries that his stories have become corrupted and useless due to his own failings, and therefore, he, as a storyteller, may have lost his purpose in life. Samuel sees the value of his stories in their power to teach, to show how life ought to be lived. And, "at the very least, he could tell funny stories that would make each day less painful" (Alexie 134).

Modernized Coyote stories that point out differences between whites and Native Americans can become very specific in their criticisms, precisely pinpointing just who and what are the sources of irritation as they fight the battle of cultural clash. Anthropologists, an especially targeted group in Native American humor, are the butt of the following Coyote story heard on the Warm Springs Indian Reservation in Oregon and retold by Barre Toelken in the foreword to *Giving Birth to Thunder, Sleeping with his Daughter*. The story begins when an anthropologist comes across a coyote caught in a trap:

> "Please let me out of this trap; if you do, I'll give you lots of money," the coyote said.
> "Well, I'm not sure. Will you tell me a story, too?" asked the professor.
> "Sure I will; I'll tell you a real, true story, a real long one for your books."
> So the anthropologist sprung the trap, collected a big handful of bills from the coyote, and then set up his tape machine. The coyote sat, rubbing his sore legs, and told a long story that lasted until the tape ran out. Then he ran off.
> The anthropologist went home and told his wife about what happened, but she wouldn't believe him. When he reached in his pocket to show her the money, all he came out with was a handful of fur and dirt.
> And when he went to play his tape for the other professors, all that was in the machine was a pile of coyote droppings [xii].

Although updated, contemporary Coyote stories share more commonalities with the traditional stories than they do differences. According to Leslie Marmon Silko, the same can be said in reference to other types of Native American stories and their traditional antecedents. When Silko was asked by an interviewer, Laura Coltelli, in 1985, if there is a difference between the use of humor in traditional stories as compared to contemporary ones, Silko responded by stressing the similarities:

> You know I haven't really thought about whether there's a difference. I'm so attuned to seeing the many similarities. Same thing, referring to the same incident, especially areas in justice, loss of land, discrimination, racism, and so on, that there's a way of saying it so people can kind of laugh or smile. I mean, I'm really aware of ways of saying things so you don't offend somebody, so you can keep their interest, so you can keep talking to them [Coltelli 62].

In this comment, Silko clearly connects stories, old and new, to the cultural and historical bonds that tie people together into a community. She also mentions humor's ability to cross cultural lines and to get people of different backgrounds and experiences to talk with each other without taking offense. And, with a segue into the next section of this chapter, she refers to the ability of humor to alleviate pain and sadness, "so people can kind of laugh or smile" about situations and conditions which, at base, are not so funny.

Humor as a Means of Mitigating Tragedy

As can be seen from the above examples, the abilities of humor to subvert, criticize, and to invert stereotypes combine with its abilities to create group solidarity and to mitigate tragedy. In *The Dialogic Imagination*, Bakhtin comments on this close association between humor and tragedy. Comedy, Bakhtin explains, contains an underlying tragic element because it developed from cultic rituals often surrounding death. This comic/tragic duality is evident in the plays of Aristophanes, who uses the "ritual of food, drink, ritual (cultic) indecency, ritual parody and laughter as an approach to death and new life" (218–19). Then, using Elizabethan drama as a later example, Bakhtin writes: "The comic and clownish scenes in Elizabethan tragedy reveal a profound kinship [with the tragic] ... and this is especially true in Shakespeare (the nature of laughter, its association with death and with a tragic atmosphere)" (219–20). Humor thus lends its double space to events with both tragic and humorous aspects. Tey Diana Rebolledo in her chapter, "Walking the Thin Line: Humor in Chicana Literature" (in *Beyond Stereotypes: The Critical Analysis of Chicana Literature*), writes that Chicana literature treads the fine line between laughing and crying; laughter lightens the oppression of day-to-day struggles and disappointments and allows people to see new, creative possibilities in situations that could otherwise only be considered tragic. Ana Castillo, in an interview conducted by Elsa Saeta in MELUS, expresses a similar idea when she explains that celebration and joy are a means of softening tragedy and thus are a key to survival in the Chicano community. And in regard to Native American humor, Leslie Marmon Silko, when asked how humor fits into her writing in a 1977 interview conducted by Dexter Fisher, had this answer:

> It's generally double-edged. It seems with humor, there's always something beyond just the laughing — that when you're laughing, you have to think beyond to greater considerations.... Generally while you're laughing, you have an awareness of something great. You get a sense of history insofar as you remember all the other stories like that. Sometimes they were funnier, and sometimes they weren't so funny at all.... Whatever just happened, it would be related to other things that had happened, and finally the function of the stories would be to keep you from feeling that God had just dropped a rock on your head alone or that you had been singled out in some way ... because the stories remind you that this isn't the first time.... So pretty soon, after the whole thing is over with, things are back in perspective [Fisher 27–28].

The connection between comedy and tragedy frequently occurs in the ethnic literature that will be discussed in the remainder of this chapter. At times the humor can become dark, and what appears to be humorous at the first encounter, when repeated and intensified, may become quite tragic. Such is the case in Gerald Vizenor's novel *Griever*, which gives a bleak critique of Chinese society through the eyes of a Native American teacher who considers himself to be a reincarnation of the Chinese trickster, the Monkey King. John Lowe points out about *Griever* that "beneath the comedy ... lies death and tragedy; Griever's affair with a Party leader's daughter results in pregnancy and ends in the woman's murder" (109). Just as likely, however, in ethnic literature a tragic event may be dissipated by humor, and an individual who has become isolated from the community because of a tragedy may be brought back into society through humor. At times humor serves only as a coping mechanism, mitigating sadness, but more often it works as a slow and steady force for social change by opening the possibility for creative solutions to difficult problems. It also works to change opinions, expose stereotypes, and strengthen the cohesion of a community.

Sherman Alexie's short story, "The Approximate Size of My Favorite Tumor," in the collection *The Lone Ranger and Tonto Fistfight in Heaven*, plays on the power of humor to mitigate a tragedy and to reintegrate an individual who has suffered a tragedy back into the community. The narrator of the story, Jimmy, suffers from a fatal cancer. Jimmy uses humor to alleviate the pain and the fear he feels, making light of his disease by comparing one of his tumors to a baseball and imaginatively transforming himself into a baseball star: "I told her [his wife, Norma] to call me Babe Ruth. Or Roger Maris. Maybe even Hank Aaron" (157). Jimmy goes on to imagine himself in the Baseball Hall of Fame on display with his x-rays pinned to his chest. While presented humorously, the equation of Jimmy's cancer to baseball is not arbitrary. Joseph L. Coulombe, in "The Approximate Size of His Favorite Humor: Sherman Alexie's Comic Connections and Disconnections in *The Lone Ranger and Tonto Fistfight in Heaven*," argues that Alexie uses Jimmy's cancer as a symbol for the great harm the U.S. has done to Indian people, and connects Jimmy's cancer with baseball to underscore the insult that Indians still endure because of the present-day use of Indian mascots in sports: "The connection to the national pastime renders Alexie's provocative humor all the more poignant, as images of Indians have long been used — from the Boston 'tea party' to the Atlanta Braves — by white America to symbolize what is quintessentially American" (100). Ironically, Indians are held up as a symbol of what is unique, strong and admirable about America, yet at the same time they are parodied by mascot figures that make them appear ridiculous. This ridicule through mascots is, of course, symbolic of the far greater irony that whites spent hundreds of years trying to eradicate Indians from the U.S., yet simultaneously viewed them as an essential ingredient in the American national character (see Philip Deloria's *Playing Indian*).

Eventually Jimmy jokes so much about his cancer that Norma threatens to leave him if he makes even one more joke. Extending his humor beyond the appropriate level, Jimmy is unable to stop even though his joking causes his wife pain. Norma does indeed leave him, as Jimmy's incessant joking cuts off all possible serious communication between them. Jimmy's joking also alienates him from his friends, which would seem to go against the notion that humor reintegrates a person who has suffered a tragedy back into the community. However, Norma eventually returns to Jimmy *because* of his humorous spirit. She misses his humor, which is similar to her own temperament, so she returns to be with him and to help him die. The community comes to understand that Jimmy is not in denial about the seriousness of his disease, but that humor has the power to alleviate some of the pain and sadness.

The role of humor in mitigating sadness occurs in the ethnic literature of all of the groups discussed so far. In the next section, we will look closely at several examples from Chicano/a literature that clearly indicate a close intertwining of the spiritual, the tragic and the comic.

Humor, Religion and Mitigating Sadness in Chicano/a Literature

Moving beyond ethnic stereotyping and inverting social hierarchies, a type of humor that has made an appearance in recent Chicano writing is popular, religious humor based on the saints and other religious figures, including the Virgin of Guadalupe, who have made a place for themselves in Chicano pop culture. Although these figures retain their religious significance, once outside the church walls and on the streets as part of everyday life, they develop human-like characteristics in the minds of their followers that lead to humorous situations. The humor has religious connections, but these connections of humor to faith are important not only as religious expressions as such, they are also a means of pointing out the incongruities that usually exist between the ideal, spiritual world and the ordinary world. The combination of humor and faith serves as a popular expression of religion and appeals to people who find religion in everyday matters and in their ties to the community.

Jose Antonio Burciaga confirms the role of saints and other religious figures in the creation of unity within a community when he writes about the Virgin of Guadalupe in *Spilling the Beans*. Although the Virgin of Guadalupe was an important religious symbol in Mexico for centuries, Burciaga claims that it was in the 1960s during the United Farm Worker movement started by Cesar Chavez that the Virgin of Guadalupe took on a special role as a symbol of Chicano identity, power and unity in the United States. Her image became popularized, and she appears today on everything from murals, to votive candles, to T-shirts, to tattoos on bare skin. She, along with the enormous pantheon of popular saints, has an importance that extends well beyond the church and into the lives, rituals and celebrations of the community. The saints are part of what holds Chicano communities together (see Burciaga 102–23). In the true comic tradition, humor involving the use of saints seeks to create communities and to promote well-being. This is not to say that there is no sadness behind the humor, there often is a sad origin, but the humor itself becomes a means of healing the sadness, as we have already seen, and of bringing about happiness through the reintegration of the individual into the community.

"Little Miracles, Kept Promises" appears in Sandra Cisneros' short-story collection entitled *Woman Hollering Creek and Other Stories*. It is a story made up entirely of ex-votos (written prayers attached to the walls or statues of a church that either petition or give thanks to a particular saint). Mary Pat Brady in her article "The Contrapuntal Geographies of *Woman Hollering Creek and Other Stories*" explains ex-votos, their purposes and their connections with the community: "Ex-votos traditionally commemorate a miracle or blessing received, or record a promise should a petition be answered. More importantly, they are public expressions that form an archive of a community's needs and concerns" (132–133). Although many of the ex-votos in Cisneros' story are not funny, but actually tragic, some that could potentially be tragic are mitigated by the humorous manner in which they are written. For example, in an ex-voto written by a man who has been cheated out of money owed to him by his employer, although the situation itself is not funny, humor is created by the detailed and familiar manner in which the man addresses the Virgin of Guadalupe:

> Virgencita de Guadalupe,
> I promise to walk to your shrine on my knees the very first day I get back, I swear, if you will only get the Tortillería la Casa de la Masa to pay me the $253.72 they owe me for two weeks' work. I put in 67.2 hours that first week and 79 hours the second, and I don't have anything to show for it yet. I calculated with the taxes deducted, I have $253.72 coming to me. That's all I'm asking for. The $253.72 I have coming to me.
> Arnulfo Contreras [120].

This familiar form of address to a saint creates an incongruity that has a humorous effect on the reader. The reader may sympathize with the petitioner's plight, but the tone prevents the ex-voto from being taken too seriously. Sometimes the petitioner addresses the saint in so familiar a manner that the petitioner feels comfortable enough to threaten the saint, to comic effect, as in the following ex-voto:

> Dear San Antonio de Padua,
> Can you please help me find a man who isn't a pain in the nalgas. There aren't any in Texas, I swear. Especially not in San Antonio....
> I'll turn your statue upside down until you send him to me. I've put up with too much too long, and now I'm just too intelligent, too powerful, too beautiful, too sure of who I am finally to deserve anything less.
> Ms. Barbara Ybañez [117–18].

Other forms of address not usually considered suitable for addressing a saint appear in other ex-votos from the story. Even one offering thanks for an answered prayer contains the incongruous tone of a business deal:

> Saint Sebastian who was persecuted with arrows and then survived, thank you for answering my prayers! All them arrows that had persecuted me — my brother-in-law Ernie and my sister Alba and their kids — el Junior, la Gloria and el Skyler — all gone. And now my home sweet home is mine again, and my Dianita bien lovey-dovey, and my kids got something to say to me besides who hit who.
> Here is the gold milagrito I promised you, a little house, see? And it ain't that cheap gold-plate shit either. So now that I paid you back, we're even, right? 'Cause I don't like for no one to say Victor Lozano don't pay his debts. I pays cash on the line, bro. And Victor Lozano's word like his deeds is solid gold.
> Victor A. Lozano [120–21].

The humor in the ex-voto above results not only from the wheeler-dealer manner of address used by Victor, but also from the fact that what he prayed for was for his in-laws to move out of the house — not exactly a selfless desire. Another incongruity in this ex-voto, Spanish language articles used with the kids' English names, results in combinations like "el Junior" that also add to the humor.

Other ex-votos derive their humor from the nature of the request in the petition. In the cases below, the everyday character of the requests contrasts humorously with the otherworldly esteem in which one normally regards a saint.

> Dear San Lázaro,
> My mother's comadre Demetria said if I prayed to you that like maybe you could help me because you were raised from the dead and did a lot of miracles and maybe if I lit a candle every night for seven days and prayed, you maybe could help me with my face breaking out with so many pimples. Thank you.
> Rubén Ledesma [121].

> Saint Jude, patron saint of lost causes,
> Help me pass my English 320, British Restoration Literature class and everything to turn out ok.
> Eliberto González [124].

These ex-votos with their seemingly trivial requests are humorous, but avoid becoming merely ridiculous, because the reader can visualize the petitioner behind the ex-voto. And while the request may seem funny to the reader, the sense that, nevertheless, the request is important to the petitioner is never lost.

Altogether, the ex-votos in "Little Miracles, Kept Promises" give the reader a glimpse into the community and the concerns of its members. Here, in keeping with the topic of this chapter, only humorous ex-votos are discussed. But even in the cases of tragic ones (such as a short one that reads, "Teach me to love my husband again. Forgive me" [119]), the tragedy is softened by two factors: the knowledge that the petitioner believes in the intercession of the saint and therefore has the hope that the situation will improve; and the petitioner has a public forum in which to express his or her desire, grief, hope or fear. The comic ex-votos mix with the tragic ones to give an overall depiction of the community, and the community, in turn, provides the sense of belonging and support that the petitioners seek.

So Far from God by Ana Castillo also begins in tragedy and ends in the formation of a community. In the middle, spiritual quests, faith healing and political activism all interact with comic and tragic events to lead the novel to a hopeful end. The story revolves around Sofi, a woman deserted by her husband, and her four daughters, three of whom carry the names of the three virtues: Esperanza (Hope), Caridad (Charity), and Fe (Faith). The fourth and youngest daughter acquires the name La Loca Santa (the crazy saint), because of her miraculous death and resurrection at the age of three. Not exactly a model saint, however, "Santa" is soon dropped from her name when the neighbors discover that she does not intend to perform the usual saintly duties, such as giving blessings and performing miracles. Although La Loca is the only "official" saint in the family, Caridad also has her spiritual pursuits. After she is attacked, brutally beaten and left for dead, Caridad has a miraculous recovery, brought about through the prayers of La Loca, and spends a year living in a cave as a recluse. Sofi's other two daughters, Esperanza and Fe, are more politically inclined and become involved in their own causes — Esperanza in the Gulf War, and Fe in protesting environmental hazards.

The sainthood of La Loca (the reader never learns her original name) begins when she is three years old. The little girl suffers an epileptic attack and is pronounced dead at the hospital. Days later, at her funeral, she suddenly revives and sits up in her coffin:

> The lid had pushed all the way open and the little girl inside sat up, just as sweetly as if she had woken from a nap, rubbing her eyes and yawning. "¿Mami?" she called, looking around and squinting her eyes against the harsh light.... Then, as if all this was not amazing enough, as Father Jerome moved toward the child she lifted herself up into the air and landed on the church roof. "Don't touch me, don't touch me!" she warned [22–23].

And so begins the odd sainthood of La Loca Santa. From that time on, humans repulse her because of their smell. She claims that they all carry the stink of the places she had passed through while dead. She refuses to allow people to see her, and she spends her life in the seclusion of her home, only allowing her mother and occasionally her sisters to be near her. Her one saintly task is to pray for others, and on the occasions that she performs this task, she has some amazing results.

All four of Sofi's unusual daughters come to tragic ends. Esperanza, the newscaster and political activist, is captured and then killed while reporting on the Gulf War. Fe dies of cancer after she goes to work in a weapons factory and is given toxic chemicals to work with in order to clean weapon parts. Caridad falls in love with an Indian woman from Acoma, and while visiting her mesa home, the two jump off the mesa in response to a call from a spirit. And La Loca, the recluse, somehow inexplicably dies from AIDS. Influenced by her four daughters' beliefs in social causes and out of the grief she feels after their deaths, Sofi decides that things in her town of Tome must change for the better. To instigate change, Sofi decides to run for mayor of Tome, even though Tome, as yet, has never had a mayor.

As the result of Sofi's efforts, the neighbors pull together and start a cooperative business that benefits them all. Sofi herself donates her meat market to the cause, and gains the respect of the townspeople as the originator of their improved lives. Thus Sofi, who lived much of her life separate from the people of Tome because of La Loca's oddities, the problems with her other daughters, and the shame she felt over having been deserted by her husband, finds herself reintegrated into the community with a new identity as La Mayor. The tragedy of her daughters' deaths, although laced throughout the novel with comic episodes, leads Sofi to consider the social responsibilities one has towards one's community, and then leads her to activate a plan to improve the community. Out of appreciation, the community gives Sofi new respect and reintegrates her into the communal life. The work with the community, in turn, mitigates Sofi's tragic losses and helps her to recover.

Comedy mitigates the tragedy of another child's death in María Amparo Escandón's *Esperanza's Box of Saints*, a novel previously discussed in connection with magical realism. The story begins with a tragedy, the death of Esperanza's twelve-year-old daughter Blanca. While in the hospital for a routine tonsillectomy, Blanca contracts a deadly, highly contagious disease that the doctor cannot name. Adding to the mystery surrounding the death, Blanca's body is so contagious that no one is allowed to see it, including her mother. Never seeing the body, Esperanza is not convinced that her daughter is truly dead and turns to a saint, San Judas Tadeo, for assistance. She relates her attachment to this particular saint in a confession to her parish priest:

> The night of the funeral I prayed to San Judas Tadeo, our saint for desperate cases. You know how miraculous he is. Why is he so good to me? I guess that's why he's a saint and I'm not. It takes a good-hearted kind of person to become a saint. He's been among my favorite ones ever since I was a little girl [14].

And then when she prays to the saint while in her kitchen:

> And then, what happens to me, of all people? A week ago his image appeared before me, on my oven window. I was baking pollo al chipotle for the funeral guests. I can never get that sauce right [14].

Esperanza's negligence in cleaning the oven has had a divine purpose, for without the grime on her greasy oven window, San Judas Tadeo would not have been able to appear to her. She describes his appearance to the priest along with the saint's mysterious message:

> I looked real hard at the oven window, and there he was. He wasn't flat like a painting. He had depth. Weight. He floated toward me, like a piñata dangling from a rope. The grease dripping shone like amber. He looked directly into my eyes. He was so beautiful. His hair was blond and a little curly. He had a beard, just like Jesus Christ. He said, "Your daughter is not dead" [16].

The appearance of the saint lets the reader know early in the novel Esperanza's character. She is a domestic woman with a fervent belief in the saints and faith in their abilities to assist people. She finds her faith in the articles of her everyday life, seeing the spiritual within the ordinary. She believes the saints are approachable, that one can speak openly to them, and at times, they will take the initiative and appear with important messages. Although Esperanza talks frequently to her priest in confession, she never feels she needs an official from the church to act as an intermediary between her and the saints; she deals with them directly in her own kitchen. She describes to her priest the saint's second appearance as follows:

> This time I was making stuffed chicken breasts. I closed the oven door, and right away I checked the window. I moved my head this way and that to get a better look at the grease drippings, until, suddenly, there he was, talking to me, calling me by name. He said, "Esperanza, you must find your daughter. Find her. No matter what you have to do. She is not dead, she is...." I tried touching the image and whispered, "Where?" but he disappeared without giving me more specific instructions [38].

Esperanza lives alone with her comadre, Soledad. Both Soledad and Esperanza lost their husbands in the same bus accident years before when Blanca was just a baby. From that time, Soledad and Esperanza have lived isolated lives, concentrating their efforts on jointly raising Blanca, and not looking for any relationships beyond their friendship. Although Esperanza and Soledad are very different from each other and sometimes do not get along, Esperanza says to her priest about her friend:

> But whether I like it or not, I don't see myself living without Soledad. We're meant to share the rest of our lives with each other. When both our husbands hurled down the Cumbres de Acultzingo ravine in that bus twelve years ago, may they rest in peace, God decided that Soledad and I should raise my daughter Blanca together [20].

Although the friendship between the two women has served them well in the loneliness they have shared since the death of their two husbands, neither has had the opportunity to move on with her life and relieve her isolation. Neither has sought another husband nor has had a purpose to her life beyond doing what was needed to raise Blanca. With Blanca no longer there, they begin to realize how isolated they have been. They have their first serious divergence of opinion over Blanca's death. Esperanza clings to the notion that Blanca is still alive, while Soledad tries unsuccessfully to get Esperanza to accept Blanca's death.

Esperanza adored her daughter, lived for her daughter, and is not willing to let her go. She is so convinced that Blanca is not dead that she goes to the cemetery and digs up her grave. She is unable to get the lid off of the casket, but she thumps the top and decides that the sound is hollow and, therefore, the casket must be empty. As a result of this and other desperate acts, the people in her town begin to think Esperanza has gone crazy. Even Soledad does not believe her when she describes Saint Judas Tadeo's appearance in the oven window. So, Esperanza acts alone as she searches for Blanca.

When Esperanza learns that the doctor who treated Blanca has also disappeared, her thoughts connect into a series of assumptions that lead her to think that the doctor perhaps kidnapped Blanca and sold her into slavery as a prostitute. Esperanza becomes so convinced that this is what happened that she begins to believe that Saint Judas Tadeo was the one who told her this piece of information. Esperanza frequently uses the saints as a means of discovering her own inner convictions and strengths, but in this case she confuses her own thoughts with what she thinks came from the saint. As a result of the belief that Blanca has been kidnapped, Esperanza first decides the best way to find Blanca is to work in a brothel as a maid, then later, she decides to become an actual prostitute:

> Esperanza wondered if passing as a prostitute would be a better way to know where Blanca might be. Men tell their secrets to prostitutes. Perhaps she could be one for a while. She could blend in. She could go from brothel to brothel and from oven to oven. It could be an option [82].

Certainly a novel about the death of a child and her mother's desperate search for her from brothel to brothel, believing that her daughter is still alive, could be a very depressing story, but this is not the case. Esperanza's buoyant faith in her saints not only keeps her from harm (and from actually having to have sex with her clients in her newfound profession), but also creates friends and helpers out of such unlikely characters as pimps, prostitutes, transvestites and Johns. Esperanza's faith gives her the resources to draw upon her own ingenuity, and situations that would normally be quite tragic are ironically flipped into hilarious misadventures through which Esperanza passes unscathed.*

One day after returning to Mexico, Esperanza decides to take a bath. While relaxing in the tub, she suddenly detects the scent of mangoes, a smell she associates with the scent of Blanca's skin. She describes what happens next to her priest:

> Then I looked toward the wall, by the sink. There is a great rust stain from a leaky pipe dripping down next to the medicine cabinet and all the way to the tile. In

---

*The novel, *Esperanza's Box of Saints*, seems to adapt the narrative genre of the *picaresque*, which features a "fool" who travels through contemporary society, observing and commenting on what he or she encounters. Although the fool has misadventures and often misunderstands what is seen, he or she manages to travel through the world unscathed. One major difference, however, is that Esperanza, while very naive and innocent, is never portrayed as merely foolish. In fact, her insight into people and events is often what saves her. In the end, she proves to have a knowledge of both life and religion that are envied by those who once doubted her sanity.

that stain, I saw Blanca's face. She was wearing a beautiful Jarocha costume. She said, "Mommy, you and me, we'll always be together." Oh, Father Salvador, I'm so grateful to God I never got around to calling the plumber. She said, "I'll always be here for you, Mommy" [244].

Esperanza realizes that her message from Saint Judas Tadeo was incomplete. "If only I had let my saint finish his sentence, after 'Blanca is not dead...,' I would have heard, 'Blanca is not alive.' Now I know where she is" (245). Blanca's appearance in a mundane rust stain adds to the humor, and the joy, of Esperanza's discovery. Esperanza believes that Blanca is in between life and death — in the world of the saints. Although it is not like having her alive, Blanca will also never be gone. Esperanza now accepts Blanca's death and is able to decorate her tomb, painting it a bright color of pink.

With Blanca's whereabouts decided, Esperanza can marry Angel, the man she loves, and can continue with her life. Angel wants to marry Esperanza and start a family with her in Los Angeles. With Soledad also getting married, there is nothing left to keep Esperanza in her town — nothing that is, except the rust stain on the bathroom wall. Still, Esperanza's faith, Angel's love, and a happy, comic ending prevail:

> They passed a sign that read: UNITED STATES BORDER 200 KILOMETERS. Esperanza's box of saints was in the back of the truck along with a couple of suitcases. Next to them, tightly fastened with ropes, was an entire wall from Esperanza's bathroom, complete with tile, sink, medicine cabinet, light fixture, toilet, pipes, and the rust stain [253].

Through Esperanza's humorous escapades, during which she mixes deep despair, challenges to her faith, and whimsical observations on the people and situations she encounters, both she and Soledad are set free. Having once lived in isolation, both women at the end of the novel have become reintegrated into life. Although their reintegration into community is through the standard comic convention of marriage, their marriages are not simply a rehanding of their lives over to husbands, but unions chosen by women who have come to know and to rely upon themselves. Esperanza searched for her daughter, but as in any quest, what she discovered is herself.

Certainly the tragedy and irony behind the humor is apparent in all three of the Chicana works discussed above — the problems of the petitioners in "Little Miracles, Kept Promises"; the disease, pollution, violence and war that take Sofi's four girls in *So Far from God*; and the mysterious disease that kills Esperanza's young daughter in *Esperanza's Box of Saints*. But these are stories in which the humor outshines the tragedy. The humor lessens the sadness and also points the way toward a creative solution that eventually reintegrates the character, happily, back into the community.

Humor, Cultural Displacement and Community in Maxine Hong Kingston's Works

The perspective stated previously that humor can be a means of advocating for social change describes Maxine Hong Kingston's humor in *Tripmaster Monkey*. The traditional Chinese trickster, Monkey, like the Native American Coyote, shows himself to be adaptable to the change in times. Monkey adroitly makes the transition from criticizing the elaborate Chinese bureaucracy and religious structures of traditional China to lampooning aspects of contemporary U.S. cultural conditions and social hierarchies that affect contemporary Chinese Americans. As discussed in the previous chapter, the Chinese American protagonist of *Tripmaster Monkey*, Wittman Ah Sing, takes his place as a contemporary Monkey King and uses his trickster antics to criticize both Chinese American and white racist stereotypes. When a girlfriend, also Chinese American, comments that a poem Wittman wrote seems conservative to her, he responds in a manner that ridicules whites and Chinese alike:

> "Conservative like F.O.B.? Like Fresh Off the Boat?" He insulted her with translation; she was so banana,* she needed a translation. "Conservative like engineering major from Fresno with a slide rule on his belt? Like dental student from Stockton? Like pre-optometry majors from Gilroy and Vallejo and Lodi?" But I'm an artist, an artist of all the Far Out West. "Fee-see-no. Soo-dock-dun," he said, like an old Chinese guy bopping out a list poem [19].

Later, when Wittman first meets Taña, a white woman with whom he will start a relationship and eventually marry, he is both attracted and put off by her dabblings in Chinese culture. Again he plays with white stereotypes of Chinese Americans. When he tells Taña his name, she wants to know his other, Chinese name. Wittman makes up one:

> "My other name is Joang Fu...."
>
> "Joang Fu is a secret name, isn't it? Have you given me your secret name and power over you, Joang Fu?"
>
> "No, that's a white-man superstition. Do you throw the Ching?† My name is number sixty-one, which they translate Inner Truth. You can look it up." I am

---

*Banana refers to a person who is yellow on the outside, white on the inside. In other words, a Chinese American who has assimilated to white culture to the point where he or she is only Chinese on the surface. Other foods are used with the same meaning for other ethnic groups: apple for a Native American, coconut for a Mexican American, and Oreo for an African American. Although derogatory in meaning, these terms are sometimes used by members of a minority ethnic group to criticize other members of the same group.

†Reference is to the *I Ching*, the *Book of Changes*, an oracle book dating back to ancient China that became a popular means of fortune telling in the 1960s. The book is consulted by tossing coins or sticks, which leads to a configuration of six lines, or two trigrams. Each set of six lines has a number assigned to it, which in turn leads to a particular text within the book— Wittman refers to text sixty-one. The text gives the reader a current view of the state of change

True Center. Core Truth. Truth is a bird carrying a boy in her talons. She can look it up for herself. He hoped nobody Chinese was eavesdropping. Can't stand hippy dippies who trade on orientalia [128].

Maxine Hong Kingston uses her character Wittman Ah Sing to rail against stereotypes and to speak out against discriminatory practices. He is an example of what Kingston refers to as writing "against the stereotype" (Fishkin 164).

As an energetic, humorous, iconoclastic figure, Wittman at least partially succeeds in creating a multicultural community through a surrealistic drama. Within his theatrical extravaganza, as we saw in the previous chapter, he uses humor to overthrow the norms of ethnic hierarchies in numerous ways. Wittman, as John Lowe describes him in "Monkey Kings and Mojo: Postmodern Ethnic Humor in Kingston, Reed and Vizenor," learns to direct humor in a positive direction by "developing his already innate joking relationship with the world and turning it from a negative, sarcastic stance to a loving, mischievous, creative one" (122).

Part of Wittman's extravagant play addresses ethnic jokes specifically. He complains, "All my life, I've heard jokes — maybe the same joke in fragments — that they quit telling when I walk in" (316). Together Wittman and the audience members fill in the unheard parts of a joke, fully sharing in its racist, sexist and homophobic language. By constructing the joke together as a group, the audience and the actors take away the secrecy, hang the joke out for all to hear, and, thereby, somewhat ameliorate the bigotry and hatred that goes into such a joke. Lara Narcisi, in "Wittman's Transitions: Multivocality and the Play of *Tripmaster Monkey*," describes how this neutralizing of a racist ethnic joke can occur: "This scene suggests that the more potent evil lies not in speaking such a joke aloud, but in whispering it in undertones as a means of conscious exclusion. By collectively reconstructing such jokes, the audience shouts out what has previously been silenced, using a linguistic tool of separatism [the racist, sexist joke] as a mechanism, instead, for unification" (104). The joke remains racist and sexist, but brought out into the open before a diverse group of people, the joke itself becomes the object of ridicule.

If subversion of the norm is the task in *Tripmaster Monkey*, Kingston's first book, *The Woman Warrior*, succeeds in combining the tragic with the comic within the same literary space. She takes the serious consequences of cultural dislocation and puts them into a humorous context so that the reader, while laughing, still feels the sad twinge of the character's discomfort. In an interview Kingston did with Arturo Islas and Marilyn Yalom in 1980, Yalom

[continued] as it exists in the world at the time the coins or sticks are tossed, and what changes are likely to follow. Given this information, the one who consults the text can plan his or her actions in accordance with the present state of affairs and in anticipation of the changes to come.

comments on the simultaneity of tragic and comic elements surrounding the character Moon Orchid, Maxine's aunt who comes from China to reclaim her husband and, through her inability to make a cultural adjustment to the U.S., goes mad. Yalom states, "There is the character of the aunt, Moon Orchid, who comes from Mainland China. There it's explicit — she goes mad in America. You were speaking earlier about humor, and she is so funny! We can't help but laugh, but it is also tragic" (Islas and Yalom 29). As insensitive as Yalom's comments may seem, since she speaks about a character that not only goes mad, but who eventually dies from her condition, nevertheless, Moon Orchid is a humorous character.

Moon Orchid is a timid woman with a kind nature who comes to the United States at the urging of her sister, Brave Orchid, in order to find her husband. Her husband had emigrated from China to the United States thirty years before, and although Moon Orchid received money from him in China, he has never sent for her to join him. Moon Orchid stays with her sister's family, but she is never able to fit in, finding the speech, mannerisms and customs of her sister's children, especially, to be beyond her comprehension. In an attempt to understand their actions, she stands over the children and humorously describes them aloud as she watches:

> She followed her nieces and nephews about. She bent over them. "Now she is taking a machine off the shelf. She attaches two metal spiders to it. She plugs in the cord. She cracks an egg against the rim and pours the yolk and white out of the shell into the bowl. She presses a button, and the spiders spin the eggs. What are you making?"
> "Aunt, please take your finger out of the batter."
> "She says, 'Aunt, please take your finger out of the batter,'" Moon Orchid repeated as she turned to follow another niece walking through the kitchen [140].

Moon Orchid proves hopelessly inept at life in the United States. In the family laundry, the only job she successfully performs is folding towels. She is terrified of the confrontation that Brave Orchid plans for her and her estranged husband, and when she finally comes face to face with him, she can only whimper as her husband rejects her. Unlike Moon Orchid, her husband has had thirty years to acculturate, and he evidently has done a thorough job of it. He chastises Moon Orchid for coming to the U.S. to find him:

> "You weren't supposed to come here," he said, the front seat a barrier against the two women over whom a spell of old age had been cast. "It's a mistake for you to be here. You can't belong. You don't have the hardness for this country. I have a new life."
> "What about me?" whispered Moon Orchid....
> "I have a new wife," said the man.... "You go live with your daughter. I'll mail you the money I've always sent you. I could get arrested if the Americans knew

about you. I'm living like an American." He talked like a child born here [152–53].

In spite of his cruelty and the thirty years that have passed, Moon Orchid's husband knows her well. She is not a strong person and lacks the ability to adapt to the new culture. Moon Orchid takes her husband's advice and goes to live with her daughter in Los Angeles, but before long the shock of being rejected by her husband, coupled with living in a country that she cannot understand, drives Moon Orchid into paranoia:

> That week a letter came from the niece saying that Moon Orchid had become afraid. Moon Orchid said that she had overheard Mexican ghosts plotting on her life. She had been creeping along the baseboards and peeping out windows. Then she had asked her daughter to help her find an apartment at the other end of Los Angeles, where she was now hiding. Her daughter visited her every day, but Moon Orchid kept telling her, "Don't come see me because the Mexican ghosts will follow you to my new hiding place. They're watching your house" [155].

Brave Orchid takes Moon Orchid back to live with her, but none of the remedies Brave Orchid tries can restore Moon Orchid to health. As Sau-ling Cynthia Wong states in *Reading Asian American Literature: From Necessity to Extravagance*, "Moon Orchid's ineptness at work, her lack of serious purpose, her aesthetic bent, her air of distracted innocence, all put her in the rank of the doomed" (197). Even Moon Orchid's name indicates her weakness, composed of two passive *yin* characters: Moon and Orchid.

Moon Orchid's inability to communicate or to understand even the simplest, everyday actions in her new environment at first seem humorous, yet eventually she becomes profoundly isolated, lonely and terrified. As a result of her inability to adapt to the cultural differences she encounters in the United States, particularly the language, Moon Orchid first succumbs to mental illness, then is hospitalized, and finally she dies from her disorder.

Terror, mistreatment and dislocation combine with comedy in Kingston's second book, *China Men*, as well. *China Men* relates the partially historical and partially fictional accounts of Maxine Hong Kingston's male ancestors and their various immigrations to the United States. One of her grandfathers, Ah Goong, already a little crazy from having been bayoneted in the head by a Japanese soldier during Japan's invasion of China, comes to the United States to make his fortune working on the railroad. Ah Goong, like many of the Chinese workers, receives the most dangerous job assignments. Because of his slight build, Ah Goong becomes a basketman and is lowered over the sides of high cliffs in a light wicker basket to plant gunpowder charges into the sides of cliffs. Sometimes the basketmen are blown up and sometimes they simply fall out due to strong winds or a weak basket. But even living under the stress of such terrifying work, with no women in the camp for companionship, Ah Goong manages to find the comic element in his life while hanging precariously, thousands of feet above the ground:

> One beautiful day, dangling in the sun above a new valley, not the desire to urinate but sexual desire clutched him so hard he bent over in the basket. He curled up, overcome by beauty and fear, which shot to his penis. He tried to rub himself calm. Suddenly he stood up tall and squirted out into space. "I am fucking the world," he said. The world's vagina was big, big as the sky, big as a valley. He grew a habit: whenever he was lowered in the basket, his blood rushed to his penis, and he fucked the world [133].

The double meaning of "fucked the world" is clear. On the one hand, Ah Goong physically experiences an orgasm while looking, sensuously, at the scenery spread out before him; but, he also resists domination by insulting the world/society that puts him in such a dangerous position in the first place. He realizes that because he is Chinese, his bosses consider his life to be expendable, and therefore, he and his fellow Chinese are given the most dangerous jobs. While he makes love to the beauty of the scenery, he simultaneously tells the racist society to "fuck off."

These three works by Maxine Hong Kingston all examine dislocation, culture clash and the need for community experienced not only by first-, but also by second- and later-generation immigrants who belong to a marginalized, minority group. Although it would be naive to think that humor can solve every problem — humor doesn't do much to solve Moon Orchid's problems, for instance, especially since she is the object of the humor and not, herself, in on the joke — but humor can often, as we have seen, overturn hierarchies and lessen the severity of a difficult situation. At times, in the hands of a gifted writer or a comedienne, humor can go even further and actually become a tool for change, bringing new perspectives to old ways of thinking and drawing people together into a more tolerant community. But does even a more tolerant community give a member of a minority group the possibility of fully participating in U.S. society? Next, we look at three different perspectives from Chinese American literature on the meaning, achieving, and withholding of the American Dream.

Humor and the American Dream in Chinese American Literature

One of the most humorous contemporary Chinese American authors is Gish Jen. In her novel *Typical American*, Jen not only mitigates the anguish of cultural displacement with humor, but also manages to combine humor with violence in a manner that first amuses and then horrifies the reader. The main character, Yifeng Chang (Ralph), comes to the United States before the Communist Revolution to study engineering, but although he has his goals clearly in mind, and written down on paper, his plans start to unravel as soon as he arrives in the United States. He is arbitrarily given the name Ralph by a young, female secretary in the Foreign Student Affairs Office, an indication that his sense of self is already slipping away. His schoolwork does not go well, his visa expires, and he begins to have trouble with the Department of Immigration. All of this occurs while the revolution in China takes place, and Ralph loses his connections with his family back in China as well as his chance to return home. Hopelessly lost in the United States, Ralph moves from one slum apartment to another, trying to avoid being caught by immigration officials. When his last hope, an advisor named Pinkus, turns on him, Ralph contemplates suicide, moves again and escapes into a deep sleep.

> Once moved, he slept and slept, his days and nights marbled together as though so much vanilla batter, so much chocolate, cut into each other with a knife. He had stopped going to work; as much as he had hoped anything, he hoped Little Lou would come and find him. But Little Lou didn't come, didn't come, didn't come; and then Ralph didn't care anymore if he came or not. He lay waiting to see what happened. Anything could happen, this was America. He gave himself up to the country, and dreamt [41–42].

In this passage, Jen critiques the concept of the American Dream — the promise that material gain, social mobility and happiness await those who immigrate into the United States. Ralph believes in that dream so much that he thinks his luck will change and that good things will come to him, even if all he does is sleep. Although we laugh at Ralph's misconception of the dream, we also realize that many of the misfortunes he has encountered thus far are because of his race and nationality. Contrary to the American Dream, which promises that each can be the master of his or her own fate, Ralph's fate seems arbitrary and out of his control.

Ralph may have stayed in bed forever if the couple living above him had not made love so energetically that the ceiling came down on him. Covered with plaster dust, Ralph goes out for a walk. He sits on a park bench and when it seems as though things cannot get worse, a miracle happens. Ralph looks up from his seat on the park bench and standing before him is his sister, Theresa, newly arrived from China.

With his sister's help and a series of happy coincidences, Ralph receives amnesty for his visa violation, gets back into school, graduates with his Ph.D., gets a teaching job at the university and even receives tenure — all through chance happenings rather than through any major effort of his own. The American Dream seems to fall on Ralph in abundance, but since he does not really do much to deserve his good fortune, he feels insecure and out of control. Ralph, his wife Helen, and Theresa live together, and together they learn how to get by in the United States. However, while the two women actively engage their lives in their new home, doing what they can to survive and make their lives better, Ralph continues to rely solely on the advice and help of others. He is not so much an active participant in his own life as he is one who is affected by the actions of others. He feels insecure and indecisive in the United States, and frequently takes his frustrations out on his wife. Ralph begins to knock on Helen's head to get her attention and to make fun of her light, barely perceptible breathing. At first, his actions are amusing and even Helen does not feel threatened. However, Ralph's knocking becomes more violent each time it is repeated:

> Ralph knocked at Helen's skull. *"Nothing to say? Anybody there? Come on, open up."* Knocking made Ralph feel fierce, but it made Helen go blank — which made him knock more, and command her to breathe, and accuse her of holding her breath on purpose (which she wasn't, really, she wasn't, she wasn't) until she ran away into another room. Sometimes she would blockade the door; he would bang and bang, unable to stop himself* [73–74].

As Ralph's sense of failure and lack of confidence in his own decisions increases, so does his violence against Helen:

> Ralph's thumbs hooked themselves around her windpipe. His face looked strangely melancholy and sallow; his hands might have been candles, he might have been about to bless her like a priest on Ash Wednesday. When she should have stood up from the altar rail, though, he squeezed, almost courteously, as if he only meant to be holding her breath for her, and just for a moment. Still the room spun before he came to his senses and shoved her back away from himself, out of his murderous hands. He shouted then, like a parent, *"Xiao Xin!"*— Be careful! But it was too late. Glass tinkled; she felt the impact afterward, the firm, cool glass, breaking through [263].

Helen survives her two-story plunge through the bedroom window, and for a time, Ralph is sorry. But when he sees Grover, a supposed friend of his who hints at having had an affair with Helen, Ralph's violence surfaces again. He forces Helen to go for a ride in the car with him, and driving recklessly, he nearly crashes them into a tree. Arriving back home, still angry, Ralph pulls too quickly into the driveway and strikes down his sister, Theresa.

Later, while waiting in the snow for a taxi to take him to the hospital to see Theresa, Ralph has become nearly paralyzed with indecision:

> His coat stiffened around him, a prison.
> What escape was possible? It seemed to him at that moment, as he stood waiting and waiting, trapped in his coat, that a man was as doomed here as he was in

---

*In the novel, Gish Jen uses italics to indicate speech that the characters are meant to be speaking in Chinese.

China. *Kan bu jian. Ting bu jian.* He could not always see, could not always hear. He was not what he made up his mind to be. A man was the sum of his limits; freedom only made him see how much so. America was no America [295–96].

Shirley Geok-Lin Lim describes Ralph's "bleak understanding" in her chapter "Immigration and Diaspora" in *An Interethnic Companion to Asian American Literature* as his realization of the contradictory nature "of American culture, which has composed a fiction of seamless yet contradictory values: progressive social mobility and community cohesiveness, increasing wealth and intensifying consumer patterns, hyperindividualism and strong family bonds," which make fully participating in U.S. society difficult for anyone, but particularly those with a marginalized status (301). It seems as though Ralph will never stop a taxi, will never learn how to cope with life in the United States, will never know what to say to Theresa, and will be permanently immobilized by indecision. But suddenly, Ralph recalls a scene from the previous summer. He remembers his sister and his friend, Old Chao, floating on rafts in a swimming pool. Thinking about them floating in the pool, sipping their lemonade, Ralph is suddenly heartened. The thought of friends and family — and the odds they have overcome — gives him the courage to continue trying to hail a cab, even though he has some uncomfortable moments ahead when he has to face Theresa. The book ends with Ralph still standing on the curb, but the reader feels that if he persists, he will survive. He will get a cab, make it to the hospital, and will somehow restore his relationship with his sister and with his wife. His decision to persist in spite of difficulty is the clue that Ralph has turned a corner, and has decided to act. Although he had hit bottom only moments before, when Ralph determines to get to the hospital, and acts on his decision, he begins anew to build a life with his family. Perhaps he will never fully prosper materially or completely adjust to life in the United States, but with his final impression of friends and family, he realizes what is important to him — and perhaps that is Ralph's dream. The reader is left with the feeling that Ralph will succeed because he finally takes control of his life and makes his own decision, instead of relying on the material promise of an ultimately unattainable dream.

Ralph's lack of agency in governing his own life at first leads to many humorous happenings in the novel, but as the story progresses, Ralph's inability to act and to make decisions on his own become frightening. He becomes someone completely subject to the whims of others and loses his sense of himself. As a result of his dislocation in the United States, he becomes frustrated over his lack of control and turns to violence. It is only when he begins to recover his ability to act that it seems his life will get better.

While humor mitigates sadness and violence in *Typical American*, the humor of Gish Jen also illustrates her method of inverting stereotypes. In

Jen's novels and short stories, she juxtaposes one minority group against another, having her characters sometimes choose to adopt the characteristics of another minority group in the United States as opposed to having them choose to follow the customs of the white majority. Mona, a Chinese American teenager in *Mona in the Promised Land*, for example, chooses, much to her mother's dismay, to become Jewish. Although Mona's mother, Helen, wants Mona to become Americanized, she is not sure that becoming Jewish is becoming more U.S. American. Mona argues with her mother:

> "You are the one who brought us up to speak English. You said you would bend like bamboo instead of acting like you were planted by Bell Telephone. You said we weren't pure Chinese anymore, the parents had to accept we would be something else."
>
> "American, not Jewish." Helen assigns Mona a piece of pork to slice while she herself cleans the fish, and it calms them both down to see what a nice job Mona can still do — thin and across the grain. (Lucky for them, Mona is the reformed kind of Jew that does not observe the many rules regarding fins and hoofs, mollusks and ruminants.)
>
> "Jewish is American," Mona says. "American means being whatever you want, and I happen to pick being Jewish" [49].

Having Mona decide to follow the religion of another minority group rather than that of the majority overturns the reader's stereotyped preconceptions of what a member of an ethnic minority group should want. Even Mona's rabbi recognizes that Mona's parents just "want to be Wasps" (53). The reader, no matter what his or her ethnicity may be, assumes that members of ethnic minorities want to be more like the majority, not more like another minority — especially one that has suffered persecution and discrimination. It takes some uncomfortable analysis to realize exactly why Mona choosing to become Jewish is funny, and the answer is that we are locked into believing in social hierarchies that put the white majority group into the higher and thus, we think, more desirable position. When someone chooses to move across the social stratification from one ethnic minority group to another, instead of moving closer to the majority group, there is an incongruity, and we laugh.*
But for Mona, the freedom to choose to become Jewish is part of her vision of America, a place where she can choose to be whatever she wants.

In her article "Delivering the Punch Line: Racial Combat as Comedy in Gus Lee's *China Boy*," Christine So notes a similar instance of a minority child, in this case a Chinese American boy, of wanting to be like another minority as opposed to the majority. The underlying message in Gus Lee's *China Boy*, however, according to So, conveys that because of Kai Ting's Chi-

---

*A Jewish friend of mine also pointed out that Mona *choosing* to be Jewish is also a humorous incongruity since Jews are the *chosen* people (not the ones doing the choosing).

nese ethnicity, he is as unlikely to fully realize his American identity as he is unlikely to become a member of another non–Chinese minority. She writes:

> The comedy is especially heightened when Kai attempts to adapt not into mainstream America but into an African American community.... Lee's narrative uses the uneasiness that the mixing of races and ethnicities produces and transforms that tension into humor. In so doing, he rewrites the traditional story of an American underdog's triumph from a Chinese-American perspective, even as jokes about his character's alien identity and its incompatibility with other minority cultures ensure that Kai Ting's American identity will never be fully realized [143].

So's view that *China Boy* demonstrates the inability of minorities to "triumph," by gaining full acceptance into mainstream U.S. society, reflects a complicated, dark side of Lee's and Jen's comedy. Still, as with most comedy, there seems to be hope held out — Kai Ting eventually wins his fight against a bully who has tormented him and stands up to his racist stepmother, and Mona, as discussed above, exercises her right of choice, as an American, to become Jewish.

In the case of Kai Ting, his only relationship with a white character is the one he has with his abusive stepmother. As Cheryl Alexander Malcolm suggests in "Going for the Knockout: Confronting Whiteness in Gus Lee's *China Boy*," perhaps Kai Ting has no desire to integrate into white society. As Kai Ting finally stands up to his stepmother, Edna, at the end of the book, "his boxer stance, raised finger 'like a small flag,' and black English combine to suggest that Kai Ting contests not only his stepmother's authority in the home but also the notion of America being defined by whiteness, Edna's whiteness" (421). As Malcolm points out, Lee's portrait of black America in *China Boy* contains diverse characters, including both street bullies and close friends. Kai Ting also has a Jewish friend and a Latino boxing coach. The only white character is Edna — a mentally and physically abusive woman (421–22). Thus it seems that Mona and Kai Ting, two Chinese Americans, have different motives for wanting to become part of another minority group over trying to join the majority. In both cases, the two might not be fully accepted by the majority group, as So suggests, because of their race, but Mona chooses to become Jewish because, in her mind, part of being American is to have the freedom to choose one's religions and associations. Mona's choice, therefore, brings her closer to the mainstream's stated values. Kai Ting, however, questions the merit of belonging to the white society, even if he were accepted. Since his white stepmother will not even allow him in his own house during the day, white society, as he knows it, does not seem very inviting. Instead, Kai Ting prefers a multiracial society, apart from white society, and finds his place within the marginalized groups. The humor in *China Boy* thus resists the notion that all members of minority, marginalized groups would prefer, if they could, to be part of the dominant group.

These three novels deconstruct the notion of the American Dream. In all three cases the main characters' dreams turn out not to be a shared national notion of material well being and social mobility, but an individual assessing of what is important in one's life and what is achievable given one's circumstances. The ways in which these characters' dreams deviate from the norm provides the humor for these texts — a man who literally thinks he can "dream" his way to a fulfilling life, a teenage Chinese girl who chooses to be Jewish, and a young Chinese boy who chooses not to integrate into the white society. As comic novels, however, all of them end on a note of hope. Each character determines what is important to him- or herself, and each ultimately acts according to his or her own desires; all reject the notion that their dreams can be imposed upon them from the outside by a dominant society.

Humor as a Hybrid Perspective

The capacity for humor to contain a double space qualifies it as a technique by which ethnic writers can create hybrid perspectives within their works. The use of double meanings of words and the interweavings of contradictory elements such as tragedy and comedy or violence and humor, allow for two different, simultaneous viewpoints of the same situation, reflecting the duality of ethnic identity. As Lois Leveen describes humor in relation to ethnic identity, "In terms of ethnicity, the dualism becomes even more complicated. Distinctions arise between the individual self and the collective (i.e., ethnic) identity; between the assimilated self and the ethnic self; and between the self as object and the self as subject — a situation that arises whenever an ethnic speaking subject tells a joke of which, in terms of ethnicity, s/he is also an object" (41). Through the creative use of the humorous double space, ethnic writers are able to subvert the status quo while appearing to uphold it, to invert stereotypes and social hierarchies based on ethnicity so that the group normally relegated to the lower position can, at least momentarily, gain the upper hand. The double space of humor also allows for the coexistence of opposite emotions, allowing the reader/listener to experience the multiple facets of a given situation, the comic as well as the tragic elements. This intermixing of emotions and doubling of meanings draws ethnic humor and the literature that contains it closer to the way that we perceive actual life. Life never seems all comic or all tragic, but is a constant shift and flux between one and the other. Surface meanings, we find in our daily experiences, are rarely the whole story. Because of its ability to mirror the complexities of life, ethnic humor possesses an appeal that reaches beyond the members of the author's own ethnic group and thereby plays a role in bringing ethnic literature away from the margins of society and into the center.

Chapter Five

Multilingual Expression: Hybrid Perspectives Through Language

The first characteristic of a minor literature as defined by Gilles Deleuze and Félix Guattari in their examination of Franz Kafka's work in *Kafka: Toward a Minor Literature* concerns "that [literature] which a minority constructs within a major language ... that in it language is affected with a high coefficient of deterritorialization" (16). The example used by Deleuze and Guattari is the German Jewish literature of Warsaw and Prague. Jewish writers in these cities found themselves in the difficult position of not having a viable language in which to write. In Prague, the Jews spoke Prague German, a minority language separate from their Czech territoriality. Unable to write in Czech without increasing their sense of dislocation, writing in German also proved difficult. Although the Jews were part of the German-speaking minority in Czechoslovakia, they were oppressed by the non–Jewish Germans within that minority, and consequently, their writings did not find acceptance among the German-speaking nor the Czech-speaking audience. Nevertheless, the Prague Jews also faced what Deleuze and Guattari describe as "the impossibility of not writing because national consciousness, uncertain or oppressed, necessarily exists by means of literature" (16). So although the Prague Jews felt compelled to write, the language they had at their disposal and the topics they needed to write about were only appropriate for a minority literature, destined only to reach a limited and marginal audience. "In short," write Deleuze and Guattari, "Prague German is a deterritorialized language, appropriate for strange and minor uses" (17). Recognizing that the deterritorialization of language is not limited to this one example, they also add parenthetically, "This can be compared in another context to what Blacks in America today are able to do with the English language" (17).

If we view the deterritorialization of language as the inability of an ethnic writer to use his or her native language, or heritage language in the case of minority writers for whom English is a first language, to write for an audience within the adopted country, then much of the ethnic literature written in heritage languages within the United States, up until recently, has been minority literature. However, a growing trend in ethnic U.S. literature incorporates the native or heritage language into the work, forcing English to share the page with other languages. This practice incorporates a hybrid perspective within the works by means of multiple languages. By including the ethnic language in the U.S. American context, writers claim their literature through the use of their languages and propose that their languages can stand side by side with English in the creation of U.S. American works. This practice centralizes the ethnic language along with English, and thereby resists a hierarchal, binary relationship between the dominant and the subdominant language.

In his essay "Discourse in the Novel" in *The Dialogic Imagination*, Mikhail Bakhtin points out that all literature contains a variety of forms and registers within its national language, a characteristic he refers to as heteroglossia. Heteroglossia, however, may also include the use of different languages as well as a multiplicity of varieties within one language, and the interactions of these languages and their varieties are essential to the genre of the novel.

> The novel can be defined as a diversity of social speech types (sometimes even diversity of languages) and a diversity of individual voices, artistically organized. The internal stratification of any single national language into social dialects, characteristic group behavior, professional jargons, generic languages, languages of generations and age groups ... languages that serve the specific sociopolitical purposes of the day ... this internal stratification present in every language at any given moment of its historical existence is the indispensable prerequisite for the novel as a genre.... Each of them permits a multiplicity of social voices and a wide variety of their links and interrelationships.... These distinctive links and interrelationships between utterances and languages, this movement of the theme through different languages and speech types, its dispersion into ... social heteroglossia, its dialogization — this is the basic distinguishing feature of the stylistics of the novel [Bakhtin 262–263].

In light of Bakhtin's theory of heteroglossia, the inclusion of languages other than English in U.S. American literature is a natural development for the U.S. novel. Ethnic minorities and their languages are part of the social stratification of the United States, and therefore, a mixture of languages within a novel, and varieties within those languages, are a reflection of the dialogue that occurs regularly within the United States.

Expressing this necessary condition of heteroglossia within Mexican American works, while also emphatically centralizing the languages of the borderlands, Gloria Anzaldúa explains the use of multiple languages in *Borderlands / La Frontera: The New Mestiza*:

> The switching of "codes" in this book from English to Castillian Spanish to the North Mexican dialect to Tex-Mex to a sprinkling of Nahuatl to a mixture of all of these, reflects my language, a new language — the language of the Borderlands. There, at the juncture of cultures, languages cross-pollinate and are revitalized; they die and are born. Presently this infant language, this bastard language, Chicano Spanish, is not approved by any society. But we Chicanos no longer feel that we need to beg entrance, that we need always to make the first overture — to translate to Anglos, Mexicans and Latinos, apology blurting out of our mouths with every step. Today we ask to be met halfway [Preface].

Contemporary ethnic U.S. American literature abounds with examples of multilingual uses of language. The range varies from texts that are written almost entirely in a language other than English, to those that are nearly equal mixtures of two or more languages, to those that may contain only a few significant words or phrases in the non–English language.* Others may use English words but with radically different meanings, such as the practice of "Signifyin'" found in some African American works. There are also instances of metalanguage, where narrators or characters express their attitudes and feelings about language and discuss the different characteristics of their native or heritage language versus those of English. And finally, there are silences, instances in the text where the narrator or a character is unable to express him- or herself because of an inability or an unwillingness to use language. All of these aspects are instances of an author's use of languages to convey a hybrid perspective, and all occur within the pages of contemporary ethnic U.S. literature.

U.S. Works Written Primarily in Languages Other Than English

The reasons why ethnic American authors choose to write in their heritage languages vary, of course, depending on the author, but some generalities may be discerned. An obvious reason to write in a native language is that some immigrant writers, especially those who have recently immigrated, simply feel more comfortable writing in their native language than writing in

---

*Some linguists would argue that insertions of single non-English words in an otherwise English-language literary piece does not constitute code-switching. However, since this chapter is focused on the artistic affect of switching between languages, the extensive discussion of code-switching versus borrowing is beyond the scope of this book. For a discussion of the differences between borrowing and code-switching, see Carol Myers-Scotton, *Duelling Languages: Grammatical Structure in Codeswitching* (Oxford: Clarendon, 1993), 163–207.

English, but this is not the case for many immigrant authors who easily express themselves in either language. Some ethnic American authors feel that if they write for an English-language audience about being ethnic American, they will have to cater to the tastes of mainstream Americans and restrict their writing to suit mainstream expectations. Xiao-huang Yin in *Chinese American Literature Since the 1850s*, elaborates on this problem of expectations in relation to Chinese American authors writing in Chinese:

> Chinese American authors who write in English, especially immigrant writers, sometimes (and understandably) are silent on problems in American society and tend to present an image that fits the public's imagination. By contrast, because Chinese-language writers seek affirmation and recognition only from their own community, they do not worry about responses from outsiders. Hence they are more outspoken about problems, both in the Chinese community and society at large. They have consciously created a unique perspective from which to explore the Chinese American experience [165].

Still other ethnic American authors may feel that writing in their native (or heritage) language reaffirms their connection with their heritage culture. Some may even see the use of English in their writing, even though they reside in the United States, as a betrayal of their heritage country, people, and language. When the author Ha Jin decided to become a permanent resident (and later citizen) of the United States, he felt a sense of betraying his homeland, China, when he used English to write. In his collection of non-fiction essays titled *The Writer as Migrant*, Ha Jin expresses this feeling in his essay "The Language of Betrayal":

> The antonym of "betrayal" is "loyalty" or "allegiance." Uneasy about those words, the migrant writer feels guilty because of his physical absence from his native country, which is conventionally viewed by some of his countrymen as "desertion." Yet the ultimate betrayal is to choose to write in another language. No matter how the writer attempts to rationalize and justify adopting a foreign language, it is an act of betrayal that alienates him from his mother tongue and directs his creative energy to another language. This linguistic betrayal is the ultimate step the migrant writer dares to take; after this, any other act of estrangement amounts to a trifle [31].

Explaining his own use of English in writing his creative works, Ha Jin comments that when asked why he writes in English, he often replies, "For survival" (32).

When an ethnic American author writes an entire work in a language other than English, but uses this language to express uniquely U.S. American ideas and experiences, a multiplicity of concepts occurs, brought about by associations with the language used juxtaposed with the U.S. cultural concepts portrayed. Such instances of hybrid perception occur in the works written in Chinese by Chinese American author Nieh Hua-ling. The novel *Sang ching* *yu tau hong* (*Mulberry and Peach*)* is written in Chinese and follows a young Chinese woman's journey to the United States, giving her perceptions of U.S. American culture. Although the stresses of her life and immigration cause the woman to develop schizophrenia and to split into two personalities, Mulberry and Peach, her observations on U.S. and on Chinese culture nevertheless illustrate the clash between cultures experienced by many immigrants. The tensions created between the situations the woman describes and their expression in the Chinese language aptly portray the "betweenness" experienced by the woman, creating an irony for the reader who understands both the Chinese and the U.S. American interpretations of a given situation. The primary audience for such a book would be Chinese Americans with a knowledge of both languages and cultures, therefore the ironies would not be lost on the book's readers. A secondary audience would be Chinese living in China, but with a particular interest and knowledge of U.S. culture — such as former Chinese overseas students who have returned to China — and therefore, they too would notice the tension between the Chinese and the U.S. American interpretations of a given situation.†

While in the U.S., the woman protagonist of *Sang ching yu tau hong* applies a Chinese concept of eating people (a symbolic depiction used in China to portray the inhumaneness with which people treated each other under the traditional Confucian government) to the eating of people at Donner Lake (a grisly legend of pioneer wilderness survival). The use of cannibalism as a means of demonstrating ways in which people are inhumane to each other echoes back to Lu Hsun, the well-known Chinese writer of the 1920s and '30s, whose literary works criticized traditional rituals and customs in China, such as filial piety, and the Confucian system of government. His story "A Madman's Diary" consists of the fictional diary entries of a young man thought to be insane. But although the young man's family and neighbors

---

*The quotations I will be using from the novel are from the translated version: Hualing Nieh, *Mulberry and Peach: Two Women of China*, trans. Jane Parish Yang with Linda Lappin (Boston: Beacon Press, 1981).

†Te-hsing Shan in a chapter titled "Redefining Chinese American Literature from a LOWINUS Perspective: Two Recent Examples," in *Multilingual America: Transnationalism, Ethnicity, and the Languages of American Literature*, ed. Werner Sollors (New York: New York University Press, 1998), distinguishes three main groups of Chinese American writers: 1) those who write and publish in Chinese, were educated in China (or Taiwan), and who have established reputations in Chinese literature; 2) those who write about China and "things Chinese" in English; and 3) those who were born in the U.S. and who write in English about "things (Chinese) American" (117). LOWINUS in the title of Shan's chapter stands for Languages of What is Now the United States. This is a Chinese and Asian American literature project of the Longfellow Institute that seeks to explore "the possibility of multilingual American literature, putting the concept of multi-ethnicity and especially multilingualism into practice, and unearthing [U.S. American] literatures not in English that have long existed yet been unduly neglected" (Shan 118).

consider him crazy, in his madness, the man sees what he perceives to be the true and cruel nature of people under the influence of the Confucian bureaucracy, and he comes to see the long history of China as a string of incidences of people eating (taking unfair advantage of) other people.

The notion of eating human flesh for medicinal purposes and for increasing one's courage is another practice that Lu Hsun references in "A Madman's Diary" to criticize outmoded, traditional Chinese culture. "A few days ago a tenant of ours from Wolf Cub Village came to report the failure of the crops, and told my elder brother that a notorious character in their village had been beaten to death; then some people had taken out his heart and liver, fried them in oil and eaten them, as a means of increasing their courage" (Lu 9).

The young protagonist in "A Madman's Diary," appalled by the eating, comes to realize that he, too, could be eaten. In his madness, he sees signs of cannibalism throughout Chinese society and culture.

> In ancient times, as I recollect, people often ate human beings, but I am rather hazy about it. I tried to look this up, but my history has no chronology, and scrawled all over each page are the words: "Virtue and Morality." Since I could not sleep anyway, I read intently half the night, until I began to see words between the lines, the whole book being filled with two words—"Eat people" [Lu 10].

Nieh Hua-ling continues the theme of cannibalism in *Sang ching yu tau hong*, although in a different manner from Lu Hsun. Nieh Hua-ling uses cannibalism as a means of portraying the inhuman treatment of people in general towards others, whereas Lu Hsun specifically uses it to portray injustices done by those in China who cling to Confucian traditions and refuse to progress. As mentioned above, the young woman protagonist of *Sang ching yu tau hong* suffers from a split personality; she calls one personality Mulberry, the name she is known by in China, and the other personality Peach, which she develops as a reaction to her traumatic shock of leaving China and coming to the U.S. The split in her personality, however, begins earlier in Taiwan where she and her husband and daughter live in hiding in a small attic for eight years. They live in hiding because her husband has embezzled money from the government treasury. The attic is small: "The attic is the size of four *tatami* mats. The ceiling slants low over our heads. We can't stand up straight; we have to crawl on all fours on the *tatami* mats. Eight-year-old Sang-wa can stand up. But she doesn't want to. She wants to imitate the grown-ups crawling on the floor" (Nieh 118).

Living in fear for so long in this confined space, Mulberry begins to lose her sanity and to develop signs of schizophrenia. Listening to the rats gnawing in the attic, Mulberry begins to imagine the rats eating her brain. Both she and her daughter, Sang-wa, fantasize stories about ghouls that eat people and

Sang-wa envisions the world outside the attic as one where people eat other people in grotesque and bizarre ways.

Once in the United States, Mulberry (now having taken on the identity of Peach) hears about the story of cannibalism at Donner Lake and resolves to visit the place. Although the story of the Donner Party is told to her by a U.S. American as one of unavoidable disaster and as a story of the willingness on the part of people to do anything to survive, including eating the dead, Peach is already familiar with the trope of cannibalism from her own culture as a sign of human cruelty. In the U.S., Peach develops a fascination with cruelty and sees U.S. Americans as violent and inhumane people. She interprets the story of the Donner Party through her conception of eating people as a symbol of mankind's inherent inhumanity. The story of starving people eating the dead intrigues her and draws her to the lake.

Originally, I read this novel as it was first written, in Chinese, but it also has been translated into English. I have read the translated version as well. It is interesting to note that the ironies of Chinese versus American views of the cannibalism at Donner Lake discussed here do not seem as prominent when reading the book in English translation. In the English version, Peach's thoughts of cannibalism seem more to be the product of her deranged state of mind than due to a tension between the Chinese and the U.S. American perspectives. The Chinese version, simply by being in Chinese, calls up for the reader the connections of cannibalism with Chinese history and literary tradition. The Chinese version thus more sharply contrasts Peach's interpretation of the situation at Donner Lake as an example of inhumanity, with how the same situation is explained to Peach by a U.S. citizen, as a gruesome but necessary act for survival.

Ironies arising from descriptions written in Chinese of American cultural phenomena also occur in the novel *White Snow, Red Dust: An Episode in the Maple Country*.* This novel, written in Chinese by Yan Zhen, exemplifies works written by overseas Chinese students who are studying in the United States or, in this case, Canada. Although the author was himself an overseas student in Canada, the main character in his novel, Gao, is fictionalized. Gao Liwei is a university professor in China who follows his wife, Lin Siwen, to Toronto where she is a graduate student.

Gao frequently misinterprets ordinary situations in Canada and sees them as discrimination against him for being Chinese. Once when he sees a crossing

---

*To my knowledge, there is no translated version of this book, but although the book is written in Chinese, oddly, the title is given in both Chinese and in English — perhaps simply to express the multilingual experience of a Chinese overseas student. *White Snow, Red Dust: An Episode in the Maple Country* is the English title; the Chinese title, however, translates only as *White Snow, Red Dust*.

guard in front of an elementary school helping a child cross the street, Gao calls for the boy to come over and see him. Quickly the crossing guard warns the boy not to go, and the boy hurries away. Not understanding that Canadian children (like U.S. American children) are warned not to talk to strangers of any type as a safety precaution, Gao assumes the child is afraid and the crossing guard is suspicious merely because he is Chinese. A similar incident occurs when he tries to talk to a black child in a park, and he comes to the same conclusion: Canadians are discriminatory toward Chinese people. Although in some instances Gao experiences true discrimination, he often misinterprets the actions of the Canadians. The reader, conscious of the cultural conditions that cause the Canadians to act in the way that they do, is forced to re-see the situation through Gao's eyes — someone not familiar with the customs. In this manner, the author defamiliarizes an accepted situation and causes the reader to critically reevaluate a particular cultural attitude and to wonder why attitudes are as they are. Why, for example, are children taught to be afraid of strangers in the U.S. and in Canada? The answer, of course, reminds the reader that we live in a violent society. By these means, the author is able to criticize North American culture in an indirect and subtle manner by causing the reader to recognize the sometimes unpleasant reasons behind the actions that North Americans consider to be normal, everyday behavior.

Works written in the United States that are entirely, or almost entirely, written in a language other than English tend to be highly critical of U.S. American culture. This is not surprising since the language in which one chooses to communicate strongly indicates one's ethnic self-identity. Ethnic writers who write solely in their native or heritage language are not interested in attracting readers from the mainstream U.S. society. It is of little importance to them that most U.S. Americans cannot read their work. Still, these works cannot be considered marginal if one takes the concept of marginal to mean that they are overshadowed by a dominant culture. These works represent striations of U.S. society that center themselves on their own ethnic languages and cultural groups. By centering their own language in their literature, these writers create their own satellite centers, independent from the mainstream of U.S. American culture. Unlike Kafka's Jews in Prague that felt no identification nor ethnic pride in the Prague German they spoke, ethnic writers in the United States who write in their native languages are expressing a strong identity with their languages and their ethnic groups, and from their established centers, feel secure enough to even criticize the dominant, English-speaking culture. Since the 1950s and 1960s, increased immigration, progress in civil rights for minorities and the growth of ethnic pride among minority groups in the United States have helped to bring about this greater sense of freedom and security. Consequently, literature in languages other than English has found audiences and an atmosphere in which to develop.

Code-switching

A common bilingual use of language found in ethnic U.S. American literature involves code-switching, actually writing the work in two languages, switching between the two to create a desired aesthetic affect. Code-switching occurs commonly in areas where bilingualism exists on an extensive scale, such as in the southwestern region of the United States. Code-switching, as the name suggests, is a form of communication in which the speaker or writer has knowledge of the vocabulary and grammar of two different language systems and mixes the two languages in speaking or writing. In the Southwest, code-switching has become a common form of communication among bilingual Chicanos who use both English and Spanish, with varying degrees of proficiency, particularly in informal interactions with other bilingual Chicanos. Although code-switching may appear to be the arbitrary use of one language or the other, close analysis reveals that there are linguistic and social factors that combine to determine the appropriate uses of code-switching. Because of the complicated nature of code-switching, an in-depth discussion of how Spanish and English code-switching occurs in Chicano speech follows below. Although writing is often more formal in style than speaking, most of the rules of code-switching for speech apply to writing as well.

As a variety of Chicano speech, code-switching is sometimes viewed by non–Chicanos, including Anglos, Mexicans and other Latin Americans, to be a low-prestige mode of communication. Fernando Peñalosa in *Chicano Sociolinguistics* refers to the derogatory term *pocho* as it is used by Mexicans to refer to Chicano code-switching:

> The mixed code could be considered a language variety which in certain loci or for certain purposes may be the predominant one. This variety has no widely recognized name but is often called *pocho* or *pochismos*.
> The term *pocho* originally meant "discolored, faded" or referred to a horse whose mane and tail had been clipped. But it was used by Mexicans to refer to their Americanized compatriots in the United States, particularly with reference to their habit of substituting English words in their Spanish speech [Peñalosa 73].

In spite of the negative attitudes that some hold regarding code-switching, linguists who have studied Chicano speech tend to have a positive reaction to the increased linguistic options code-switching provides. Not only does the speaker or writer have the resources of both languages available, but can add further meaning by choosing when and in what situations to change languages. Alvino E. Fantini, in a chapter entitled "Social Cues and Language Choice: Case Study of a Bilingual Child," expresses the versatility a bilingual speaker possesses as follows:

> Not only does he command several "styles" of speech like everyone else, but he also has another option — that of switching from one entire language system to another. He can change from code to code in addition to modifying his speech style within the same code. It is now well documented that such changes in language are not arbitrary nor erratic behavior, but rather are related to identifiable social factors [Fantini 89].

To be able to switch codes, in addition to having knowledge of two different language systems, the speaker must also have an awareness of what social conditions make the use of one code or the other more appropriate. Often the situation determines which code will be used by speakers. The formality or informality of the conversation can determine the code, but there are other considerations that pertain to the situation. For example, some Chicanos have a higher proficiency in English than in Spanish in technical vocabulary; therefore, a discussion of a technical topic, even in an informal situation, may prompt a switch from Spanish to English. Also, some Chicanos will switch to English when conversing with speakers of standard Spanish out of a fear of being criticized for their non-standard word usage or grammatical structures.

Another situation that may precipitate the use of code-switching occurs when the speaker feels a need to establish his or her ethnic identity, even though the proficiency in English may be greater than in Spanish. In such cases, the speaker feels pressured by peers to demonstrate some proficiency in Spanish and may choose to code-switch over speaking in Spanish or English. As the example below demonstrates, such a speaker would be likely to interject Spanish connecting words and adverbials into his or her predominantly English discourse: "I've been interested in this as a sociologist pero también as a person who has lived in an area of dynamic transition en los últimos años y I explain it this way. This is discounting that there is a lot of negative feeling por los gringos toward things that are traditional" (Sanchez 151).

Two additional significant factors in determining whether or not code-switching will occur in a conversation are the age of the speakers and the language of the addressee. The older generations are more likely to speak in Spanish with each other, particularly if they are first-generation immigrants, while the younger generations, often born in the United States, are more likely to use English or code-switching. However, an older person might use English when addressing a young person, and a young person is quite likely to use Spanish when speaking to an elder, particularly if the elder is not proficient in English. But when parents address their own children in Spanish, and the parents are proficient in English, the children are likely to respond in English or in code-switching. Thus, the two factors of age and the language of the addressee work together to determine which code is selected for communication.

Although aspects of the situation, the age, and the language of the addressee all function to determine the selection of code, the reason for a code-switch often lies in the effect the speaker (or writer) wishes to produce and in the purpose underlying the speech. Consider the following conversation in which Jaime and the son of the family he is visiting are both of the younger generation, approximately the same age:

> FATHER: Le sale una plaga al trigo, que se como el granito ... Y otro día iban a fumigar porque hay un avión que fumiga y ... los trigos....
> JAIME: ¿Esto lo hace el gobierno o...?
> MOTHER AND SON: — No, él, él.
> JAIME: ¿Es de ellos el aeroplano?
> FATHER: No, no, ellos rentan. Sí.
> JAIME: You gotta have those. In Mexico they do that...
> MOTHER: Y luego tienen una cosa pa hacer agujeros....
> SON: About a half a million dollars, Jaime, American money, worth of farming equipment from the United States [Sanchez 142–143].

In the preceding conversation, the son is the speaker who uses code-switching according to what we would expect in terms of his age and to whom he is speaking. When he addresses Jaime, his peer, he uses English. However, he occasionally begins to use Spanish with Jaime, but then switches to English. When the son addresses his parents, he uses Spanish. More interesting, however, he switches to English when he wants to boast about the extent of his uncle's land holdings and wealth. This switch is more a matter of style than consideration for the addressee. Rosaura Sanchez, author of *Chicano Discourse*, has found that when young Chicanos make evaluative statements, they tend to switch to English. Sanchez speculates that perhaps this is because in the use of Spanish and English among bilingual Chicanos, English is often considered the language with more prestige and power. Therefore, in making a boast, a speaker might choose English, thinking to add validity to his or her statement.

Sanchez presents another example that indicates a particular purpose of code-switching. In the following, the shift from Spanish to English softens a comment, making it a teasing statement instead of a harsher complaint:

> 1. ¿Qué *peace and quiet* sin la televisión!
> 2. ¿Qué *paz y tranquilidad* sin la televisión! [Sanchez 162].

Because the phrase "peace and quiet" is a common saying in English, it does not carry the more serious connotation, a strong dislike of T.V. noise that the complaint has when spoken in Spanish. Thus code-switching may also occur when the speaker wishes to mitigate or soften a statement.

Often the choice of English over Spanish conveys a different connotation even though the words in Spanish seem like an almost direct translation of the English. In many cases, the connotation of a statement will vary according to whether the speaker chooses English or Spanish, even when saying what would appear to be the same message in either language. For another example, consider the following conversation in which an adult asks a child at school what work her father does:

¿Dónde trabaja tu papá?
En el Hilton.
¿Qué hace ahi?
Es un manager y un bartender [Sanchez 163].

About this exchange, Sanchez explains that the word *cantinero* has no prestige in the community. It would connote that her father worked at a local bar. The word "bartender," on the other hand, carries more prestige, particularly when the name of the Hilton is also used. Thus code-switching is much more than a shifting from one language to another, it can also change the level of meaning of what is said. The shifting goes beyond mere translation, as connotations can change significantly depending on which language is used.

Linguists who study the phenomenon of code-switching have discovered that code-switching can operate on a metalinguistic level as well. Switches may be used to begin or to end a discourse, or as a transition to continue the flow of narration. Switches between a statement made in one language and an expansion of that statement made in the other language are also common. Or, points may be repeated for emphasis, stated first in one language and then again in the other.

Rhetorical shifts are also common in code-switching in literature as well as in everyday conversations. These shifts may restrict or increase the levels of meaning an expression carries by changing the form of the expression (from Spanish to English or vice versa) and thereby changing the connotation of the expression. These switches may be metonymic (expressing semantic connections), metaphoric (expressing shared or identical markers), or synecdochic (expressing genus-species relations) (Sanchez 171). The shifts convey a relationship between the expressions, although they may be in different languages, because of the underlying features they have in common. Of course, for the rhetorical expression to have its full meaning, both the speaker and the addressee must have knowledge of both languages and of whatever cultural assumptions are necessary for interpreting the connection.

Understanding the rules and conditions for code-switching is not only necessary for understanding Chicano speech, but for comprehending Chicano literature as well. In recent years, Chicana and Chicano writers have gained prominence in literature, and particularly since the 1970s, almost all use code-switching to some extent in the literature they write. In his book *Chicano Poetics*, Alfred Arteaga explains how the heterotext (a mixture of Spanish and English) reflects the hybrid nature of the mestizos (the Mexican race created from the mixture of Spanish and Indian blood). He writes in particular about Chicano authors who must span the differences not only between their Spanish and Indian ancestry, but also between the Mexican and Anglo races and cultures. Their use of the heterotext expresses the split they struggle with in their identity as Chicanos and as U.S. Americans (Arteaga 24–43).

The work of the Chicana author Gloria Anzaldúa offers a clear example of Arteaga's notion of the heterotext. As was shown in the beginning of this chapter, in the preface to her book *Borderlands/La Frontera: The New Mestiza*, Anzaldúa explains her use of code-switching in her writing. Languages she uses include English, Castilian Spanish, a North Mexican dialect of Spanish, Tex-Mex, and even some of the Aztec language, Nahuatl. These languages together create the language of the borderlands.

Gloria Anzaldúa, however, does more than explain her use of codes in *Borderlands* as a reflection of her mixed heritage; she makes an impassioned plea for the acceptance of her language. She recognizes the low prestige accorded to Chicano speech by Anglos and by speakers of more standard forms of Spanish, and she angrily refuses to apologize for it any longer. Indeed, in *Borderlands/La Frontera: The New Mestiza*, she demonstrates the versatility and artistic potential of code-switching in the hands of a gifted writer.

As one reads Anzaldúa's book, it is possible to see many of the rhetorical, situational and functional uses of code-switching that have been discussed in this chapter. In a metaphorical code-switch, for example, she vividly describes the border as an open wound: "The U.S.–Mexican border *es una herida abierta* where the Third World grates against the first and bleeds" (Anzaldúa 3). By using Spanish to express the open wound, "*es una herida abierta*," Anzaldúa accentuates who it is that bleeds and which culture it is that suffers. The English words surround the Spanish, and with their harsher sounds (such as the "x" in Mexican, and the long "a" in grate and the "ee" in bleeds), the English words violently clash against the softer tones of Spanish, aurally emphasizing the meaning of her words.

Anzaldúa uses language to emphasize, illustrate and bring alive the splits she sees in herself and in her borderlands culture. The splits and multiple facets of her heritage both frighten and fascinate Anzaldúa as shown in her description of herself gazing at her reflection in a mirror. Switching in the last line to Spanish, she emphasizes the multiplicity of her character, as it manifests itself in her appearance, through the multiplicity of language:

> During the dark side of the moon something in the mirror catches my gaze, I seem all eyes and nose. Inside my skull something shifts. I "see" my face. Gloria, the everyday face; Prieta and Prietita, my childhood faces; Gaudi, the face my mother and sister and brothers know. And there in the black, obsidian mirror of the Nahuas is yet another face, a stranger's face. *Simultáneamente me miraba la cara desde distintos ángulos. Y mi cara, como la realidad, tenía un caracter multiplice* [Anzaldúa 44].

(The Spanish sentence translates as "Simultaneously, I saw my face from various angles. And my face, like the reality, had a multiple character.") The switch from English to Spanish in Anzaldúa's description of her face does not jar the flow of her writing. As an artist of both languages, Anzaldúa shows how code-switching is not so much a change from one language to the other as it is a continuous discourse, drawing upon the resources of both languages to express coherent thoughts and images. The flow from one language to the other, in this case without the "grating" of the previous example, emphasizes Anzaldúa's own efforts to integrate the different aspects of her multiple character.

In a stanza from the poem "*El otro México*," Anzaldúa uses repetition in both English and Spanish to describe and emphasize the split she feels not only physically, but culturally, as one who lives along the border:

> 1,950 mile-long open wound
>   dividing a *pueblo*, a culture,
>   running down the length of my body,
>   staking fence rods in my flesh,
>   splits me   splits me
>   *me raja   me raja* [Anzaldúa 2].

Anzaldúa uses Spanish twice in this passage, first to refer to the Mexican people, *a pueblo*. The use of Spanish in this instance underscores her identification with her people, a common use for code-switching. She then translates "split me" into Spanish, "*me raja*." In each language she repeats the words, emphasizing the emotional intensity of feeling culturally, linguistically, and even physically torn apart. Here Anzaldúa's poetry works with the contrasting sounds of both languages and with the visual surface of the page to show aurally and visually the split that so characterizes her life.

The mixture of cultures and languages along the Mexican/U.S. border can have a synergistic effect, creating a third mode of expression that leads to a more multidimensional understanding of human life in general. In *Chicano Poetry: A Response to Chaos*, Juan Bruce-Novoa writes about how expression in two intermixing languages transcends what cannot be expressed by either language alone: "The mixing of two languages I call interlingualism, because the two languages are put into a state of tension which produces a third, an 'inter' possibility of language. 'Bilingualism' implies moving from one language code to another; 'interlingualism' implies the constant tension of the two at once" (226n).

Interlingualism proves particularly effective for expressing the intermixing of cultures in the borderlands. Cultural figures such as the Virgin of Guadalupe encompass more than one culture, and in her case, she represents tolerance and acceptance as opposed to division and ostracism. As the legend goes, the Virgin of Guadalupe appeared to Juan Diego in 1531 with dark features: dark hair, skin and eyes. She spoke to Juan Diego in Nahuatl, the language of the Aztecs. She combined the Spanish culture of Catholicism with the language, appearance and culture of the Indians, thereby symbolizing a melding of the different cultures. To this day, the Virgin of Guadalupe has tremendous appeal to Mexicans, Mexican Americans and others who live along the border. She serves as a mediator between cultures, and in Catholic belief, as a mediator between God and humans; she defends the oppressed of all groups. Discussing the mediating qualities of the Virgin of Guadalupe, Anzaldúa, fittingly, uses both English and Spanish, but she goes beyond the literal meanings of what is said in both languages. She achieves the third possibility of interlingualism:

> During the Mexican Revolution, Emiliano Zapata and Miguel Hidalgo used [the Virgin of Guadalupe's] image to move *el pueblo mexicano* toward freedom. During the 1965 grape strike in Delano, California and in subsequent Chicano farmworkers' marches in Texas and other parts of the Southwest, her image on banners heralded and united the farmworkers. *Pachucos* (zoot suiters) tattoo her image on their bodies.... In Texas, she is considered the patron Saint of Chicanos. *Cuando Carito, mi hermanito*, was missing in action and, later, wounded in Viet Nam, *mi mamá* got on her knees *y le prometió a Ella que si su hijito volvía vivo* she would crawl on her knees and light novenas in her honor [29–30].

This passage illustrates Anzaldúa's use of Spanish within an English narrative to accomplish several different purposes. She refers to the Mexican people in *el pueblo mexicano*, and as would be expected, she states the phrase in Spanish to show her identification with her people. The Spanish slang term *Pachucos* appears in Spanish to refer to a particular group of young Mexican American men that have been born in the United States, have taken on U.S. ways, yet dress in a manner that expresses their rebellion against mainstream U.S. culture and speak in a distinctive Spanish/English slang (the word *Pachuco* is an example of this particular slang). When speaking of her little brother, Carlito, and of her mother (both references to family), Anzaldúa's language is Spanish, the language of the home. Finally, the most intensely felt line, *y le prometió a Ella que si su hijito volvía vivo* (and she promised her that if her son returned alive), is expressed in Spanish, the language used within the family, to foreground the emotion of the mother's promise and her intense concern for her son's life. Furthermore, Anzadúa's switch to Spanish when speaking about her younger brother reveals the irony of a young Spanish-speaking Chicano caught up in a war perpetrated by a dominant, white culture that does not fully accept him or his language. Working together, all of these switches between Spanish and English underscore not only the bicultural identity of the Virgin of Guadalupe, but also portray the bicultural tensions within the author herself.

Lorna Dee Cervantes, also a Chicana poet, uses the two languages in a manner similar to Anzaldúa to create a linguistic split that portrays the cultural inbetweenness expressed by the narrator in her poem "Refugee Ship." Although the last line merely repeats in Spanish the meaning of the previous line in English, it is a repetition with a difference. The use of the two languages in the repetition deepens the meaning of the lines and reveals to the reader how adrift the narrator feels between the two languages and the two cultures. The repetition also gives a sense of finality; the ship will never dock, and the narrator, in this instance, will never find a home port. The last two lines, in the two different languages, intensify the feeling of dislocation much more so than when the same poem is written entirely in Spanish (see Cervantes 40).

These brief examples show how code-switching can intensify as well as visually and aurally convey the meaning of an author's words. So too in everyday speech, code-switching adds extra layers of meaning, defines situations, and expresses ethnic identity simply through the chosen language. As has been shown, code-switching is not the arbitrary use of one language or another, nor the interference of words from one language in another, nor an indication that the speaker lacks the ability to communicate completely in either language. It is a structured system that allows the speaker to make shifts according to the situation and according to the effect he or she hopes to produce in a reader. As one becomes familiar with the rules and social determinants of code-switching from Spanish to English, one can gain a deeper understanding of Chicano speech and of the aesthetic accomplishments of Chicano literature.

While some bilingual authors, like Anzaldúa, boldly write with code-switching, often incorporating long passages in Spanish without translation, others code-switch more sparingly. These authors may be concerned that they will lose their monolingual English-speaking audiences if they code-switch too frequently, and therefore, may only code-switch from English to Spanish with single words or short phrases. In *Movements in Chicano Poetry*, Rafael Pérez-Torres comments on this concern:

One practical problem in teaching Chicano poetry — or writing about it — has to do ... with the audience's proficiency in languages. At the very least, one would hope that an aversion to Spanish would not preclude communication. Although for many people responding to a "foreign" language on the printed page is disorienting, to find this "foreign" tongue *interalia* imprinted within native speech approaches a violation [212].

Authors concerned about losing their monolingual English audience, however, have employed numerous techniques to avoid alienating these readers. For instance, an author might work an English translation into the flow of the text or might use a form of code-switching, such as the synecdochic (expressing genus-species relations) discussed above, to make the Spanish intelligible to a reader who may not know any or only very little of the language. Both translation and synecdochic code-switching appear in Pat Mora's novel, *House of Houses*. First some examples of translation:

> He sits with us at the blue kitchen table, and in his rough, teasing mode asks his sister who sees only shadows, our oldest living relative, "*Y tú cómo estás? No me digas que estás enferma otra vez*," entreating her not to say she's sick again [Mora 1].
>
> ****
>
> "*Planta flores con nombres religiosos como Varitas de San José*," says Mamá Cleta, my great-great grandmother exhorting me to plant flowers with religious names.... I make a note to look for *Manto de la Virgen*, Virgin's Bower, *Flor de San Juan*, Evening Primrose in English, and *Flor de Santa Rita*, Indian Paintbrush [Mora 9].

Often Mora will incorporate Spanish into dialogue, allowing her to translate the Spanish into English by replacing a simple "he said" or "she said" with a phrase such as "entreating her not to" or "exhorting me to" that allows her to provide an explanation in English of what has been said in Spanish. In this way the reader has the cultural flavor of hearing/reading Spanish, yet feels as though he or she understands the language. Mora rarely allows the non–Spanish-speaking reader to be left behind. When she does use Spanish without translation, the phrases are short, simple, and are either understandable from context or are phrases which most U.S. readers would be familiar with even if they have never studied Spanish, such as "*¿Cómo estás?*"

Synecdochic code-switching also includes the reader who does not understand Spanish by making it possible for the author to state the subject of discussion in English first, and then to provide the details in Spanish. Even if the reader misses the details, he or she will not lose the meaning of the passage overall. This works especially well when the details are either discernible by context or are words that even a non–Spanish-speaking reader might know. Mora makes use of this type of code-switch in *House of Houses* as seen in the following examples:

> December 31, 1899, the end of a century. Mamá Nina looks around her living room at her entire family, formally dressed, sleepy after the soup-to-dessert dinner, *sopa*

de verduras, pollo, arroz, camote, natillas y galletitas con café, poised to welcome the new year [Mora 49].

****

In Spanish, Señora de la Torre's daughters teach my mother and her brothers their catechism and to beware of *los Protestantes*. "Never walk in front of a Protestant church. Cross the street." The Delgado children learn their prayers,

> *Santo ángel de mi guardia,*
> *Mi dulce compañía*
> *No me desampares*
> *Ni de noche, ni de día* [Mora 58].

Although the reader may not understand every Spanish word, he or she is not left behind because the context for the Spanish is clearly given in English. In the first example, the Spanish words are obviously foods. In the second example, what follows the English is clearly a prayer. Through the use of Spanish, made understandable to the English-speaking reader, the author allows the reader to enter into the culture of the novel by means of language and to share in the intimacy of the family.

In their article "Marked and Unmarked Choices of Code Switching in Bilingual Poetry," Eva Mendieta-Lombardo and Zaida A. Cintron look at the nature of code-switching in terms of marked (unexpected) and unmarked (expected) choices made by a poet regarding when to code-switch. First they divide bilingual poems into two groups, one that does not require a bilingual readership and one that does. The first group is characterized by code-switching that "consists mainly of culturally loaded Spanish words and phrases, items intimately connected to ethnic identity, yet familiar to those outside the bilingual community" (567). Although for a general audience this type of code-switching would still be considered marked, if only to a slight degree, for a bilingual audience, the switch would seem expected and, therefore, unmarked. The second category of bilingual poems, those that require bilingual proficiency on the part of the reader, will still be "unmarked or expected in informal in-group communication among bilingual peers" (569). Therefore, according to Mendieta-Lombardo and Cintron, even poetry with a high degree of code-switching would be expected in a bilingual community, because it would reflect the members' manner of communicating. For monolingual speakers of English, however, this type of bilingual poetry would be highly marked and probably inaccessible to the reader.

While both types of Spanish/English poetry (highly marked and only slightly marked for monolingual English readers) commonly exist in the United States, authors who choose to switch between English and a language that is not as widely known as Spanish face an even greater chance of alienating their readers.

Code-Switching Between English and Languages Other Than Spanish

A bilingual author wishing to code-switch between Spanish and English can do so in a manner that is still relatively sure of reaching a broad audience. In addition to the bilingual audience, such as Mexican and other Latino Americans, the works are also intelligible to readers who may only have a limited knowledge of Spanish, and, as shown above, even those readers with little or no Spanish can be included in the audience if the author wishes to make provisions and use techniques to make the Spanish they include intelligible to everyone. Therefore, bilingual authors who choose to code-switch between Spanish and English can do so, at least on a limited basis, without fear of losing potential readers. Authors who are bilingual in English and another non–English language besides Spanish, such as English and Chinese or English and a Native American language, have a more difficult task if they wish to code-switch. They cannot rely on their U.S. readers to know even basic, simple vocabulary. As soon as an author inserts a word of Chinese without an explanation, for example, that portion of the work containing the Chinese expression becomes significantly marked and inaccessible for most U.S. readers. Consequently, the writers who wish to include their non–English languages in their writing mostly do so on a limited basis. They make the meaning of the non–English passages clear from context or provide a translation or an explanation of the marked passages.

As we shall see, even with a language that is not widely known in the U.S., the use of the author's heritage language in a work strengthens the tie between the author's work and the heritage culture, making that culture more accessible to the reader. Gish Jen in her novel *Typical American* frequently uses expressions from Chinese to enrich the cultural sense of the novel, and she provides explanations or direct translations to keep the monolingual English reader from becoming confused. In the following examples, the English translations follow directly after the Chinese:

"*Lazy*," says his father. "*Stupid. What do you do besides eat and sleep all day?*" The upright scholar, the ex-government official, calls him a *fan tong*—a rice barrel [Jen 4].

****

His father looks away. "*Opposites begin in one another*," he says. And, "*Yi dai qing qing, qi dai huai*— one generation pure, the next good for nothing [Jen 5].

Jen does not try, as Mora did, to smoothly integrate the translation into the text. She simply repeats the Chinese phrase in English. Whereas Mora has to assume that many of her readers would understand the Spanish and, therefore, has to work out a way to translate the Spanish into English without appearing too redundant, Jen can safely assume that most of her readers will not understand the Chinese and thus does not have to worry about redundancy. However, since the vast majority of her readers will not understand the Chinese at all, she uses it sparingly. Yet some inclusion of Chinese, even when it must be directly translated, gives the reader a sense of contact with the culture and of being privy to the family conversations.

To convey the sense that Chinese is being spoken even when the author is writing in English, Jen uses italics when her characters are supposed to be speaking in Chinese — even though the words on the page are in English. Thus, when two Chinese speakers are speaking to each other, and would normally be speaking in Chinese, the dialogue is set in italics. In this manner, her characters can even code-switch in their speech, as they naturally might, without the author switching from English:

Today Janis took me to this house with a winding walkway. *Really* darling! *However, it was very* overpriced, *they're going to have trouble selling it for anything near what they're asking. And yesterday I saw a* breakfast nook with built-in benches — [Jen 152].

With the italics, Jen gives the reader the impression that he or she is following along and understanding the conversation in Chinese. The switches from italicized to unitalicized words gives the sense that the characters are code-switching between Chinese and English. The language remains English, but the English is presented, at times, in a manner to make it intentionally different. The code-switching in the above example takes place according to a general use of code-switching. Words directly associated with U.S. culture, in this case domestic architecture and the housing market, words such as "winding walkway," "overpriced" and "breakfast nook with built-in-benches," are not italicized, indicating they are spoken in English. This simulated code-switching not only allows a more intimate glimpse into the life of the character, since the reader can understand the character's "Chinese" language, but also, the character's use of typical, upscale American English expressions when discussing real estate emphasizes her ambition to buy into the American Dream as a house owner.

Louise Erdrich also sparingly uses words from her heritage language, Chippewa, in her novel *Love Medicine*. Although she usually does not give a direct translation of the word, she discusses it enough so that the reader gets a sense of the meaning. Erdrich can do this without the discussion of the word seeming awkward or out of place, because in most cases, her characters are not that familiar themselves with the Chippewa language and often muse about the meanings of the words from the "old language." The passage below occurs when Marie undergoes a difficult labor in childbirth:

Each labor I had been through had its word, a helping word, one I could use like an instruction to get me through. I searched my mind, let it play in the language. Perhaps because of Rushes Bear or because of the thought of Fleur, the word that finally came wasn't English, but out of childhood, out of memory, an old word I had forgotten the use of, *Babaumawaebigowin.*

I knew it was a word that was spoken in a boat, but I could not think how, or when, or what it meant.... I fell asleep again, and woke in darkness, laboring strong. Now I clung on to their voices, all I had, as they spoke to me in low tones, as they told me when to hold my breath and when to let it go. I understood perfectly although they spoke only the old language. Once, someone used my word. *Babaumawaebigowin*, and I understood that I was to let my body be driven by the waves, like a boat to shore, like someone swimming toward a very small light. I followed directions and that way, sometime the next afternoon, my child was born [Erdrich 102–03].

A character's lack of familiarity with his or her own native language gives the author an opportunity to explain the non–English words to the reader, but sometimes the author prefers to leave the reader confused as a means of forcing the reader to share in the character's confusion. In *House Made of Dawn*, N. Scott Momaday uses his character's lack of familiarity with his own heritage language and purposely avoids giving translations for Native American words that occur in the novel. Momaday rarely inserts Native American words or phrases, but when he does, the reader is often left in the dark as to the meanings of the words. This is not surprising, since on at least one occasion, the main character, Abel, is as confused by the words as is the reader. Abel, cut off from his traditional life in the Jemez pueblo in New Mexico, finds he is unable to understand the words of his dying grandfather. His grandfather speaks in a state of delirium, but this is not the only reason that Abel cannot understand him. Abel returns to the pueblo after serving as a soldier in World War II and after suffering a harrowing relocation to Los Angeles that left his hands physically crushed from a beating and his whole body sick with alcoholism. Since Abel's grandfather, Francisco, is a man of tradition and speaks the old language, Abel can not understand his grandfather and feels the loneliness and despair of not only losing someone he loves, but also of being cut off from his own roots. While dying, the grandfather speaks in a jumble of Spanish and the Native American language of the Jemez pueblo:

But each day his voice had grown weaker, until now it was scarcely audible and the words fell together and made no sense: "*Abelito ... Kethá ahme ... Mariano ... frío ... se dió por ... mucho, mucho frío ... vencido ... aye, Porcingula ... que blanco, Abelito ... Diablo blanco ... Sawish ... Sawish ... y el hombre negro ... sí ... muchos hombres negros ... corriendo, corriendo ... frío ... rápidamente ... Abelito, Vidalito ... ayempah? Ayempah!*" [Momaday 195].

By not providing a translation or a context within which to understand these words, the reader shares Abel's frustration. Although individual words may make sense to the reader, especially the Spanish words, and the reader can recognize some of the words as names of characters in the novel, the overall meaning of the grandfather's attempt to communicate is lost. Since the reader, like Abel, cannot understand all of the grandfather's words, yet knows that the words have importance, the reader can, to some extent, share Abel's anxiety over the loss of language, the loss of communication, the loss of tradition, and the loss of his grandfather.

Momaday also uses Native American words at the very beginning of the novel (the first word in the prologue) and at the end (the very last word of the final section). These words, respectively, are *Dypaloh* and *Qtsedaba*. These are traditional words in the Jemez language used to frame an oral storytelling—*Dypaloh* indicating the story is beginning and *Qtsedaba* indicating the end. By framing the story with these words, Momaday inserts the novel into the conventions of oral storytelling. Although these words might be overlooked by all but the most careful readers, their placement at the very beginning and the very end provide a context within which a reader might discern their meanings.

As the length of this section on code-switching testifies, it is a complex and diverse way for an author to create a hybrid perspective within a work. The availability of two, and sometimes more, languages for expression adds a richness to the texture of the work beyond what the authors could achieve with one language. The use of the native or heritage language along with English demonstrates that there is more than one way to view a situation, more than one way to express a thought. Within code-switching, even if one language is only used to a limited extent, both languages carry importance. Code-switching is thus a significant technique through which a language that was once deterritorialized may become relocated and put forward as an acceptable partner with English within the literature of the United States.

Signifyin'

> Deep down in the jungle so they say
> There's a signifying motherfucker down the way,
> There hadn't been no disturbin' in the jungle for quite a bit,
> For up jumped the monkey in the tree one day and laughed,
> "I guess I'll start some shit" [Gates 55].

Near the beginning of this chapter, during the opening discussion of Deleuze and Guattari, it was mentioned how African Americans have been able to change the English language to reflect their cultural heritage, or in Deleuze's and Guattari's words, to use it for "strange and minor uses" (17). They parenthetically wrote: "This can be compared in another context to what Blacks in America today are able to do with the English language" (17). However, once a language begins to be used for "strange and minor uses," in the hands of a skilled writer, it can expand in purpose and become, as was seen with code-switching, an assertion of the language as a viable co-language with English (or in this case a co-variety with standard English) capable of providing a new and alternative perspective.

Signifying (or Signifyin'), a way of talking which alters the normal meaning of the English word, is an example of a type of speech originating in the African American community. While Signifying uses the English language, the alteration in the meanings and implications of the words gives the language a multiple perspective while not, technically, being multilingual. The meaning of an expression relies more on the gap between the conventional meaning of the word and the new meaning assigned to it than it does on the simple assignation of a new meaning.

Henry Louis Gates in *The Signifying Monkey: A Theory of African-American Literary Criticism* describes Signifying as "the (political, semantic) confrontation between two parallel discursive universes: the black American linguistic circle and the white" (Gates 45). Usually, in the English language, signification refers to the meaning that a word (or sign) is intended to convey. Its use in communication depends, usually, on its limiting the possible meanings that a word can carry in order to avoid confusion. However, Signifying in the black vernacular sense of the word (for which we will use a capital S) turns the purpose of signification upside down. Instead of limiting the associations and meanings a word can have, black Signifying proliferates the associations, creating plays on words, puns and other rhetorical word play. Although almost always humorous, there is a subversive nature to Signifying. The usual semantic orientation to a word is disrupted and the word itself is emptied, partially, of its accustomed meaning and refilled with a new one. However, the old meaning leaves its vestiges, and the new use of the word carries the new signification with echoes of the old still clinging to it. In this way, the word itself comes to contain a hybrid perspective, becoming what Mikhail Bakhtin terms double-voiced. "In such discourse there are two voices, two meanings and two expressions.... A potential dialogue is embedded in them, one as yet unfolded, a concentrated dialogue of two voices, two world views, two languages" (Bakhtin 324–25).

The adding of a new meaning to a word, particularly one that contrasts sharply with the old, is a political act as well as a linguistic one. Gates refers to Signifying as a way language can be "decolonized for the black's purposes" (50). Signifying rebels against the received meanings of words as handed down by the white, English-speaking culture, and with creativity and much humor, forms something new that is a reflection of black culture.

The opening pages of *Song of Solomon* by Toni Morrison show how naming places can be a subversive form of Signifying. The story tells how a street of the city, officially named Mains Avenue, came to be known as Doctor Street among the city's black inhabitants because the only black doctor in town lived on that street. People in the black community became so used to calling the street Doctor Street that they began to use it as their official address, causing problems with mail delivery and with locating people for the draft. To put an end to the confusion over the street's name, the town's legislators attempted to decree what the name of the street would be:

> They had notices posted in the stores, barbershops, and restaurants in that part of the city saying that the avenue running northerly and southerly from Shore Road fronting the lake to the junction of routes 6 and 2 leading to Pennsylvania, and also running parallel to and between Rutherford Avenue and Broadway, had always been and would always be known as Mains Avenue and not Doctor Street.
> It was a genuinely clarifying public notice because it gave Southside residents a way to keep their memories alive and please the city legislators as well. They called it Not Doctor Street, and were inclined to call the charity hospital at its northern end No Mercy Hospital since it was in 1931 ... before the first colored expectant mother was allowed to give birth inside its wards and not on its steps [Morrison 4–5].

As Gates discusses in *The Signifying Monkey*, the stories of Monkey, told in rhyming poetry, reach back into the times of slavery, are Afro-American, and probably originated with a monkey figure who accompanied the gods in Cuban mythology. The Signifying Monkey is a trickster figure, with the trickster's gift of gab, able to talk his way through any situation with word play and verbal gymnastics. Gates writes of the language in which the tales are told, "The poetry in which Monkey's antics unfold is a signifying system: in marked contrast to the supposed transparency of normal speech, the poetry of these tales turns upon the free play of language itself, upon the displacement of meanings" (53). The basic structure of the tales involves Monkey, a lion and an elephant. Monkey tells Lion that Elephant has insulted him. Monkey speaks in figurative language, but Lion can only understand the words literally. Misunderstanding, and outraged at the supposed insult, Lion goes to Elephant to demand an apology. Elephant then pounds Lion, who realizing the mistake he has made, in turn pounds Monkey. As Gates writes, "It is this relationship between the literal and the figurative, and the dire consequences of their confusion, which is the most striking repeated element of these tales" (55).

References to Signifying Monkey or to Signifying itself appear in hundreds of recordings of black music from the past century, including "Jazz Gillum, Count Basie, Oscar Peterson, the Big Three Trio, Oscar Brown, Jr., Little Willie Dixon, Snatch and the Poontangs, Otis Redding, Wilson Pickett,

Smokey Joe Whitfield, and Johnny Otis — among others" (Gates 51). Like jazz music itself, Signifying consists of tropes, of repetitions of rhetorical structures repeated with slight variations. Some of the common tropes include loud-talking, testifying, calling out, rapping, and playing the dozens.

Gates points out in his book that few scholars have managed to define Signifying in full. More often, they take one of the tropes of Signifying and mistake it for the whole. The dozens are often cited as an example of Signifying, and basically involve verbally insulting someone's relatives, particularly the mother, as a form of attack. Another common trope is louding or loud-talking. Loud-talking occurs when someone makes a comment to someone else about a third person, just loud enough for the third person to hear, but since the third person only hears the comment indirectly, he or she cannot respond and is limited to comments like, "What did you say?" to which the Signifying party can respond with an insult such as, "I wasn't talking to you!" But Signifying is much more than insults and attacks. It can be used to make someone feel good as well as bad, to express one's own feelings, or to make a point indirectly through humor. It is often the manner in which something is said even more than the substance of what is said that indicates Signifying. The following conversation among Milkman, Pilate, Hagar and Reba in Morrison's *Song of Solomon* shows the subtlety and humor involved in Signifying that might rise easily from a conversation. In this passage, the characters discuss Reba's luck at winning prizes. She has just won a diamond ring for being the half-millionth customer at the local Sears store:

> "What're you going to do with the ring?" Milkman asked her.
> "Wear it. Seldom I win something I like."
> "Everything she win, she give away," Hagar said.
> "To a man," said Pilate.
> "She don't never keep none of it...."
> "That's what she want to win — a man...."
> "Worse'n Santa Claus...."
> "Funny kind of luck ain't no luck at all...."
> "*He* comes just once a year..." [47].

Through humor (plays on the words "win" and "comes" and comparing Reba to Santa Claus both in the way she gives things away and in how rarely she "comes"), an important aspect about Reba emerges that is actually somewhat sad. Although she is lucky at winning prizes, it is clearly not prizes she wants but a man.

Signifying includes a host of elaborate word games and innuendoes, following intricate patterns and definite rules, which allow for a rich improvisation on the English language. It is yet another way in which ethnic writers, in this case African Americans, can lay claim to language, make it their own, and not be condemned to speaking in a manner that merely copies the dominant English. Although the words retain associations to their meanings in the white culture, Signifying creatively subverts the received meanings of the English language, creating a double-voiced language capable of expressing different views, emotions and meanings simultaneously. Deceptively simple on the surface, yet conceptually complex, Signifying is one of the ways that African American writers, through the use of double-voiced language, infuse a hybrid perspective into their works.

Metalanguage

Instances of metalanguage, characters or narrators discussing language itself, also provide a multilingual aspect to a narrative text. The characters in ethnic U.S. American literature are usually bilingual to some extent. Conscious of the connections between language and culture, they on occasion may examine the intricate differences between English and their heritage language and relate these differences to the broader contrasts they see between the two cultures. Also, explaining and describing their heritage language becomes a means by which the characters or narrators can explain aspects of their culture to their English-speaking audience.

Richard Rodriguez's vivid descriptions of the Spanish language in *Hunger of Memory: The Education of Richard Rodriguez* clearly illustrate how a text written in one language can give the flavor of another through discussions about language itself. Rodriguez begins the book with his childhood, describing the warmth of his family and the closeness he feels to them. He is a child that listens carefully to language and develops early a sense of language for close, private moments with the family (Spanish), and for formal, public moments outside the house (English). He speaks of his first language, Spanish, with poignant nostalgia:

> A family member would say something to me and I would feel myself specially recognized. My parents would say something to me and I would feel embraced by the sounds of their words. Those sounds said: *I am speaking with ease in Spanish. I am addressing you in words I never use with* los gringos. *I recognize you as someone special, close, like no one outside. You belong with us. In the family.*
> *(Ricardo.)* [Rodriguez 16].

****

> Tongues explored the edges of words, especially the fat vowels. And we happily sounded that military drum roll, the twirling roar of the Spanish *r*. Family language: my family's sounds. The voices of my parents and sisters and brother. Their voices insisting: *You belong here. We are family members. Related. Special to one another. Listen!* [Rodriguez 18].

But Richard Rodriguez is ambitious, and he soon realizes that the public language, English, is the key to success. His parents agree, and after a teacher visits them and suggests that they speak English at home, English becomes the home language, even though both parents, particularly the father, speak it poorly. Rodriguez moves further and further away from Spanish until he speaks it only with difficulty. He excels at school and wins scholarships with ease, but there is a price to pay.

> Embarrassed, my parents would regularly need to explain their children's inability to speak flowing Spanish during those years. My mother met the wrath of her brother, her only brother, when he came up from Mexico one summer with his family. He saw his nieces and nephews for the very first time. After listening to me, he looked away and said what a disgrace it was that I couldn't speak Spanish, '*su proprio idioma.*' He made that remark to my mother; I noticed, however, that he stared at my father [Rodriguez 29].

Rodriguez continues to speak English exclusively, goes to college and becomes a successful writer. He achieves his dreams for successful assimilation and establishes the public identity he desires. He has no doubt at the end of *Hunger of Memory* that he has chosen the correct path, no matter what else has been lost upon the way. But what has been lost is great: the connection with his parents, their language, and their culture. In the end of the book, there is a deep sense of sadness, and the reader wonders, even if Rodriguez does not, if the loss is too great. "I take it [a coat] to my father and place it on him. In that instant I feel the thinness of his arms. He turns. He asks if I am going home now too. It is, I realize, the only thing he has said to me all evening" (Rodriguez 195).

Hunger of Memory is about the loss of a language and about the other losses of culture and family cohesiveness that accompany it. It is a close study of the private, intimate language that Rodriguez knows as Spanish, and of its formal, public counterpart, English. To read Rodriguez's descriptions of Spanish is to become intimate with the language, even if the reader knows no Spanish at all. In this manner, Rodriguez is able to write a book almost entirely in English and yet keep the Spanish language continually present.

The Chinese American author Gish Jen often presents aspects of Chinese culture (as they are practiced and perpetuated by Chinese Americans) through direct explanations of Chinese cultural concepts, including Chinese terms. To illustrate a concept, she sometimes relates it to the Chinese language and provides her readers with a short language lesson. In the following passage, Jen describes what she sees as a Chinese cultural attitude of only being able to do so much, of not expecting too much of oneself. She relates this to a grammatical structure in Chinese, sometimes referred to in introductory Chinese classes as the resultative verb, which indicates whether an undertaken action had the expected results or not. Below, Ralph, the main character of *Typical American*, is chastised by his mother for not listening during his lessons:

> Finally, irked, she says what his tutor always says, "*You listen but don't hear!*" — distinguishing, the way the Chinese will, between effort and result. Verbs in English are simple. One listens. After all, why should a listening person not hear? What's taken for granted in English, though, is spelled out in Chinese; there's even a verb construction for this purpose. *Ting de jian* in Mandarin means, one listens and hears. *Ting bu jian* means, one listens but fails to hear. People hear what they can, see what they can, do what they can; that's the understanding. It's an old culture talking. Everywhere there are limits [Jen 4].

In this succinct manner, Gish Jen relates an aspect of Chinese culture and also lets us know something about Ralph, the main character of *Typical American*. Ralph will travel to the United States, but since he has already shown the tendency to listen but not hear, the reader has a foreshadowing of his misadventures to come. Because Ralph cannot let go of the influence of the "old culture," he excuses his limitations and does not push himself to achieve in the United States. Consequently, he falls prey to people who seek to use and dominate him.

The concept of change occurring between two opposites (*yin* and *yang*) in a waxing, waning fashion is central to the Chinese classic *Book of Changes*, and to the Chinese world view in general. Gish Jen uses the concept in *Typical American* in the chapter entitled "Chang-Kees" to indicate the Chang family's transformation from Chinese to U.S. American. Again the concept is presented as a mini language lesson: "In Mandarin, change is handily expressed: a quick *le* at the end of the sentence will do it, as in *tamen gaoxing le*— now they are happy. Everywhere there are limits, but the thin fattens, the cloudy clears. What's dry dampens. The barren bears" (123). Gish Jen uses aspects of the Chinese language to explain traditional Chinese cultural concepts. By this means, she enhances her text by adding an additional layer of Chinese linguistic meaning to her English descriptions of Chinese culture, giving her explanation a multilingual dimension. She also underscores the cultural changes the Changs experience by explaining, in both English and Chinese, how Chinese speakers express a change in a situation.

As we saw in the previous section on code-switching, similarly to Chinese American authors who wish to include the Chinese language in their works, Native American authors who want to incorporate their heritage languages, and yet still reach a non–Native American audience, must consider how to do so in a manner that will not frustrate Anglo-American readers. Few people living in the United States who are not Native American have any knowledge of a Native American language, and although a Native American may know the language of his or her own tribe, he or she may not necessarily know anything about other Native American languages. For these reasons, Native American authors tend to use Native American languages very sparingly and may also use discussions about language in their texts in place of using actual native-language words. Certain characters may be presented as speaking in a Native American language, for example, even if their exact words are not given. Also, comments may be made about the Native American language by a character or the narrator without specifics being given.

In *Love Medicine*, Louise Erdrich connects the speaking of a Native American language to characters that are still tied to tradition and that have lived a traditional life. Moses Pillager is one such character. When he was a baby, a coughing sickness devastated the community, killing many children. To save Moses' life, his mother devised a way to trick the spirits and pretended that Moses was already dead. She did the preparations for his funeral, laid out spirit food and put his clothes on him backwards. Everyone looked past him as if he were invisible, and no one was allowed to speak his real name. Moses survived the sickness, but as Lulu's uncle tells her, though Moses escaped the sickness, "the cure bent his mind" (75). Having been treated as one of the dead, Moses was never able to fit back into the society and, therefore, went to live alone on an island. Moses lives on the island in a traditional manner and continues to act as though dead, wearing his clothing backwards, walking backwards, and speaking only in the old language. When Lulu Lamartine goes to live with Moses on his island, he is not sure she is real and checks her reflection with a mirror. Lulu and Moses become lovers, and on the first night they spend together, Lulu remarks, "I woke to find him speaking in the old language, using words that few remember, forgotten, lost to people who live in town or dress in clothes. It was as though he had found his voice, and it purred around me in a whisper" (Erdrich 81).

When connected with tradition and with speakers who live in the traditional manner, the characters of *Love Medicine* look upon the old language with respect. However, when used by modern, non-traditional Native Americans for political purposes, the view toward the old language changes. As Lulu grows older in the novel, she becomes a political force within the community. Her son, Lyman, has become a businessman on the reservation and manages a tomahawk factory. Progressive, businesslike, and with a knack for earning money, Lyman has little use for traditional ways, especially when taken on by non-traditional people. He has the following conversation with his mother:

"The four-legged people. Once they helped us two-leggeds."
This was the way her AIM [American Indian Movement] bunch talked, as though they were translating their ideas from the original earth-based language. Of course, I knew very well they grew up speaking English. It drove me nuts [Erdrich 307].

As the above examples show, authors can give a sense of language and show the importance language plays in the lives of their characters without having to code-switch or to use much, if any, of the heritage language itself. Metalanguage, talking about language, is thus an effective way of adding a multilingual perspective to a work without losing the English-speaking audience.

Silence

The use of silence and the many ways in which silence can be integrated into a text are also forms of creating a hybrid perspective through language and through the absence of language. Language at its most basic level is made up of sounds and silences. Although we usually think of the sounds (or in writing, the written words) as carrying the meaning of an utterance, silence is meaningful as well. Without silences, words would run together and meaning would be lost. But beyond this simple word-separating function, silence can also carry meaning within a discourse and within the broader context in which the discourse takes place. Silences can occur for many reasons. A person may be physically unable to make sounds; may be psychologically unable to put together language in a way that makes sense to a listener; may be able to make sounds, but cannot speak the language in which the discourse is taking place; or, the person may speak in the same language, but for social or political reasons, is prevented from speaking; and finally, a speaker may speak, but no one listens.

Although it is rarely the case in ethnic U.S. American literature that a character remains silent because of a physical inability to make sound, this possibility is raised in Maxine Hong Kingston's partially autobiographical novel, *The Woman Warrior: Memoirs of a Girlhood Among Ghosts*. In this novel, Maxine, the protagonist, relates a story about her mother cutting her tongue when she was a baby.

> She pushed my tongue up and sliced the frenum. Or maybe she snipped it with a pair of nail scissors. I don't remember her doing it, only her telling me about it, but all during childhood I felt sorry for the baby whose mother waited with scissors or knife in hand for it to cry — and then, when its mouth was wide open like a baby bird's, cut. The Chinese say "a ready tongue is an evil" [Kingston 163–64].

In spite of the Chinese proverb warning about the evils of a ready tongue, Maxine's mother, who, incidentally, was also a doctor, wanted her daughter to have a tongue capable of producing any and all sounds necessary for any language. This is just one of many incidents in which Maxine's mother, Brave Orchid, acts contrary to the beliefs of traditional Chinese culture. Although she verbally supports the traditional views, including the view that values sons over daughters, Brave Orchid often acts contrary to tradition in order to indirectly let her daughter know that she has many opportunities in life. When Maxine asks her mother why she cut her tongue, Brave Orchid replies, "I cut it so that you would not be tongue-tied. Your tongue would be able to move in any language. You'll be able to speak languages that are completely different from one another. You'll be able to pronounce anything. Your frenum looked too tight to do those things, so I cut it" (Kingston 164).

In spite of her mother's good intentions and her cutting of the frenum to free Maxine's tongue, Maxine finds as she grows that she has difficulty talking. Her problem, however, is not physical, but psychological. When she begins school, Maxine finds that she lacks the confidence to speak out, and that speech is actually painful for her.

> When I went to kindergarten and had to speak English for the first time, I became silent. A dumbness — a shame — still cracks my voice in two, even when I want to say "hello" casually, or ask an easy question in front of the check-out counter, or ask directions of a bus driver.... A telephone call makes my throat bleed and takes up that day's courage [Kingston 165].
>
> ****
>
> It was when I found out I had to talk that school became a misery, that the silence became a misery. I did not speak and felt bad each time that I did not speak. I read aloud in first grade, though, and heard the barest whisper with little squeaks come out of my throat. "Louder," said the teacher, who scared the voice away again. The other Chinese girls did not talk either, so I knew the silence had to do with being a Chinese girl [Kingston 166].

As a child, Maxine disowns the Chinese side of her Chinese American self, particularly her difficulty in speaking, which she attributes to being Chinese. Her resentment of her own silence is brought clearly into the open when she sadistically torments another Chinese girl in the basement of their school.

> "If you're not stupid," I said to the quiet girl, "what's your name?" She shook her head, and some hair caught in the tears; wet black hair stuck to the side of the pink and white face. I reached up (she was taller than I) and took a strand of hair. I pulled it. "Well, then, let's honk your hair," I said. "Honk. Honk." Then I pulled the other side — "ho-o-n-nk" — a longer pull; I could see her little white ears, like white cutworms curled underneath the hair. "Talk!" I yelled into each cutworm [Kingston 177].

The girl represents everything Maxine hates about herself that she attributes to being Chinese. She hates the girl's appearance, including her straight, black hair and delicate neck, but most of all, she hates the girl's silence. She takes the girl's silence as weakness, as the literal personification of a person with no voice. Maxine knows the girl can talk, because she will read aloud when asked to by the teacher, but she is completely incapable of expressing any aspect of herself. She is a non-person in Maxine's view, and Maxine fears this has something to do with her as well, with being a Chinese female.

Maxine abuses the quiet girl physically, trying to force her to talk to end the torture, but the girl does not talk. Soon, Maxine is reduced to tears as she tries to bribe the girl and pleads desperately for her to talk. The girl, however, never talks, confirming Maxine's suspicions that Chinese girls are without will, without voice, without value. As Elaine H. Kim explains in *Asian American Literature: An Introduction to the Writings and Their Social Context*, Maxine is calling upon the woman warrior spirit within her. "She attacks her anti-self, an alter-ego, another Chinese American girl who represents the fragility and softness of the victim as opposed to the survivor" (205). After her attack on the Chinese girl, Maxine suffers a physical, and perhaps mental, breakdown. She is sick for eighteen months from a mysterious illness that is never named. During her illness, the life line in the palm of her hand breaks in two, indicating her need to resolve the split in herself and create an integrated Chinese American self that can function and survive in the U.S.

As mentioned in chapter three, in *Reading Asian American Literature: From Necessity to Extravagance*, Sau-ling Cynthia Wong devotes a chapter to a discussion of the racial shadow. The character of the quiet girl, whom Maxine tortures, like Pauline discussed in chapter three, is another example of the racial shadow. To briefly reiterate, Wong relates the racial shadow to the psychological process of projection. When a character has internalized racism against his or her own self and group, projection of those racist thoughts onto another can be a defense mechanism. The double, as Wong explains, results from the protagonist *disowning* parts of him- or herself and projecting those unfavored aspects onto another. The character may experience a split or fragmentation of the self, creating another version of the self. This alternate self, or double, may be presented by the author as a hallucination or as "a separate, autonomous character in the fictional world" (83). Either way, "the double is symptomatic of a crisis in self-acceptance and self-knowledge: part of the self, denied recognition by the conscious ego, emerges as an external figure exerting a hold over the protagonist that seems disproportionate to provocation or inexplicable by everyday logic" (82). The quiet girl is Maxine's racial shadow.

Maxine encounters the quiet girl in the schoolyard, after classes, and they descend downstairs to the isolated basement of the school. The time of day is twilight, sometimes in literature considered a liminal time. Wong describes the scene as "reminiscent of many classic tales of the doppelgänger [double self]. Twilight, that transition between day and night, signals that the protagonist is in between orders of reality, about to cross proscribed boundaries or receive an unusual visitant" (86). In this liminal space, the between space as described by Victor Turner and discussed in chapter three, Maxine is free to act out irrationally and even violently. The quiet girl does nothing overtly to provoke Maxine, but her very silence is what drives Maxine to hysteria. As Wong points out, "the violent outburst is motivated not by awareness of dissimilarity but by awareness of kinship" (88). Maxine fears being the quiet girl, never finding a voice, forever being locked into a silence from which she cannot vocalize her thoughts and desires. She fears that being Chinese might resign her to such a fate, since within her culture of Chinese Americans, she sees so much secrecy, so much that can never be expressed, so much that must be hidden from white society. Elaine Kim explains how Maxine's silence lies at the heart of her growing up in a Chinese American household. "Chinese Americans ... have been silenced by a combination of Chinese American influences. Besides their parents' refusal or inability to explain things to their children, there is the secrecy with which they must defend themselves against American laws that discriminate against them" (204). As Wong succinctly states, "The quiet girl represents that residue of racial difference which dooms Chinese Americans to a position of inferiority in a racist society" (89).

The problems Maxine faces in her silence go well beyond shyness or difficulty with language. Silence is the manifestation of her struggle with identity as a Chinese American. Maxine eventually comes to grips with the paradoxes that plague her in her younger years and eventually, like the swordswoman with words on her back, she finds her voice through writing.

The Chicano author Richard Rodriguez undergoes a similar experience to Maxine's when he first attends school and has to speak English. In *Hunger of Memory* he writes of the nuns at his Catholic school:

> Their voices would search me out, asking me questions. Each time I'd hear them, I'd look up in surprise to see a nun's face frowning at me. I'd mumble, not really meaning to answer. The nun would persist, "Richard, stand up. Don't look at the floor. Speak up. Speak to the entire class, not just to me!" But I couldn't believe that the English language was mine to use.... I continued to mumble. I resisted the teacher's demands.... Silent, waiting for the bell to sound, I remained dazed, diffident, afraid [Rodriguez 20].

But while Maxine finds her early school experiences debilitating, Richard sees them as a necessary time of discomfort that he had to go through in order to learn that he had a public voice. For Richard, the key to success in life as expressed in *Hunger of Memory* rests in being able to effectively present oneself publicly, regardless of the losses one may incur in one's private life as a result of losing the family language.

> One day in school, I raised my hand to volunteer an answer. I spoke out in a loud voice. And I did not think it remarkable when the entire class understood. That day, I moved very far from the disadvantaged child I had been only days earlier.

The belief, the calming assurance that I belonged in public, had at last taken hold [Rodriguez 22].

Richard's silence stemmed from his lack of confidence in speaking English, and when he learned the language well enough to easily express himself, the anxiety disappeared. However, Maxine's anxiety does not disappear even after she grows up. Her anxiety seems to be not just tied to language, but to her lack of confidence in herself and to her lack of a sense of self worth. She has been raised in a Chinese community that extols the value of boys and that disparages girls.

> When one of my parents or the emigrant villagers said, "Feeding girls is feeding cowbirds," I would thrash on the floor and scream so hard I couldn't talk. I couldn't stop.
> "What's the matter with her?"
> "I don't know. Bad, I guess. You know how girls are. 'There's no profit in raising girls. Better to raise geese than girls.'"
> "I would hit her if she were mine. But then there's no use wasting all that discipline on a girl. 'When you raise girls, you're raising children for strangers'" [Kingston 46].

Maxine's silence goes deeper than a problem with English. Her voice has been silenced for her by the disparagement of females she endures from the members of her community, including, at times, the opinions of her own parents. She is confused and does not know how to fit into the Chinese culture of her community, which at least on the surface seems to devalue females, and at the same time to fit into the broader U.S. American society as a whole, which demands that one speak with confidence in what Richard Rodriguez terms one's public voice. Eventually, Maxine does find her public voice, but through writing rather than speaking. Writing is a way for Maxine to find her voice privately, and then to share it publicly without the requirement of making loud enough sounds for others to hear.

To expand the understanding of how authors use silence in their texts, King-Kok Cheung, a Chinese American literary critic, has developed a theory of articulate silence in her book *Articulate Silences: Hisaye Yamamoto, Maxine Hong Kingston, Joy Kogawa*. Cheung argues that articulate silence is a technique particularly common in the works of Asian American women. Articulate silence is a means of indirectly telling a narrative, allowing dreams or the retelling of myths and legends to carry the important meanings of a literary work. King-Kok Cheung attempts to explain why women in particular use these devices to tell their stories. She argues that there are cultural differences in writing when Asian literature is compared to Western literature, and that there is an added gender difference as well. Asian women writers, unlike Western women or male Asian American writers, tend to write with silence in an attempt to express their opinions in a subtle manner that will not be immediately rejected by their readers — as a more direct approach might be. Silence can be the theme of a piece, as when the author writes about ways in which women are blocked from expressing themselves, or it can be the method. As a method of writing, the author who utilizes silence writes her story indirectly. Cheung specifically cites the works of Maxine Hong Kingston as utilizing this indirect form of telling her story through the use of traditional Chinese myths and legends. The legend of Fa Mu Lan, for example, shows how Maxine eventually reconciles the paradoxes of being both Chinese and U.S. American. Like Fa Mu Lan, who demonstrates how to be both a filial daughter and a courageous warrior, Maxine learns to broaden her mind enough to accept the contrasts of a multicultural existence. Kingston also uses the legend of Ts'ai Yen, a second-century Chinese poetess who was captured by barbarians, to show that when one cannot communicate the conventional way through language, an alternative form of communication, such as provided by music, might cross the language gap. Living for years among people who did not understand her language, the poetess Ts'ai Yen learned to make her emotions known through songs. Similarly, Maxine learns to use writing, including the retelling of ancient myths and legends, to express herself in a way that allows a hybrid perspective, the mythic and the ordinary, to add multiple layers of meaning that a direct telling would not contain.

Chinese American author Sigrid Nunez, who is actually Panamanian, Chinese and German, also writes about silence that stems from one's lack of cultural identity. In her book *A Feather on the Breath of God*, Nunez writes about her father, Chang. Chang is half Chinese and half Panamanian. His father was a Chinese merchant from Shanghai whose trade route for tobacco and tea took him back and forth between Shanghai and Colón, Panama. In each port he had a wife and two sons. Chang, born Carlos, was taken to Shanghai soon after his birth to be raised by the Chinese wife. At the age of ten, he was sent back to Panama again where he lived with his mother for a year until she died. Next he emigrated from Panama to the United States with his Uncle Mee, enrolled in school and went by the name of Charles. The confusion Chang experienced in deciding what name to use reflects his confusion over his ethnic identity:

> Then came the Second World War and he was drafted. It was while he was in the army that he finally became an American citizen. He was no longer calling himself Charles but Carlos again, and now, upon becoming a citizen, he dropped his father's family name and took his mother's. Why a man who thought of himself as Chinese, who had always lived among Chinese, who spoke little Spanish, and who had barely known his mother would have made such a decision in the middle of his life is one of many mysteries surrounding my father [Nunez 8].

While in the army in Germany during World War II, Chang meets and marries Sigrid's mother, Christa, who only speaks German. They return to live in the United States, but neither feels at home in the United States. Christa learns to speak English well, although with a German accent, but Chang never seems to improve. When his three daughters are born, Chang and his family can only communicate haltingly as they have no real language in common. Chang's cultural differences and difficulty with English infuriate his German wife, and their lives are filled with quarreling:

> She had no patience with my father's quirks. The involuntary twitching of a muscle meant that someone had given him the evil eye. Drinking a glass of boiled water while it was still hot cured the flu. He saved back issues of *Reader's Digest* and silver dollars from certain years, believing that one day they'd be worth a lot of money. What sort of backward creature had she married? His English drove her mad. Whenever he didn't catch something that was said to him (and this happened all the time), instead of saying "What?" he said "Who?" "Who? Who?" she screeched back at him. "What are you, an owl?" [Nunez 12–13].

As a result, Chang remains silent most of the time and lives out his life in isolation. Sigrid remembers a day when she was young, however, when she was at Coney Island with her parents and they ran into four Chinese men who seemed to be friends of her father's. She remembers that day, and the surprise she feels, because that is the only time she hears her father speak Chinese, and the only time that she has an indication that he might have some friends. At home, Chang rarely speaks, and when he does, he answers inappropriately, never quite knowing what is going on.

The Nunez family is poor and lives in the housing projects in spite of the fact that Chang works several jobs in the effort to support them. Although he lives in the same house, he stays separate from Christa and his daughters. For a time, he and Sigrid eat dinner late together because Sigrid is taking dancing lessons, but they eat in silence.

> As I recall, the person sitting across the kitchen table from me was like a figure in a glass case. That was not the face of someone thinking, feeling, or even daydreaming. It was the clay face, still waiting to receive the breath of life....
> After dinner, he stayed at the kitchen table, smoking and finishing his beer. He never joined the rest of us in the living room in front of the television. He sat alone at the table, staring at the wall. He hardly noticed if someone came into the kitchen for something. His inobservance was the family's biggest joke [Nunez 20–21].

Even when Chang dies, he still is estranged from his family and is unable to communicate. "Though I was not there to hear it, I am told that he cursed my mother and accused her of never having cared. By the end of the week, when he spoke it was only in Chinese" (Nunez 25).

With the possible exception of some acquaintances in Chinatown, acquaintances unknown to his family, no one seems to know Chang, including Chang himself. His cultural and linguistic background is confused to the point where he has no definite cultural traits and no language in which he can fully express himself. Although Chinese is his first language, it is abruptly cut off when he is ten and replaced by Spanish, then English, then German, and finally back to English, a language he is required to use in the United States but which he never really learns. Since Chang lives during a time when languages other than English are even less viable for communicating in the U.S. than they are now, neither his Spanish nor his Chinese have a chance to develop. The lack of ability to communicate not only isolates Chang, but also molds his entire personality. According to his wives' relatives, he was kind and generous in his youth, giving them money and gifts of coffee and food from the military base. But somewhere between Shanghai, Panama, Germany and the United States, Chang becomes lost and loses the self that he can show to the world. He becomes a silent man, completely unknown to those who should be the closest to him.

Whether through the inclusion of words from the character's or narrator's heritage language, through explanations of language, or even through the lack of words, silence, ethnic writers in the United States have explored a myriad of ways to introduce multilingual techniques of writing into their texts. Multilingualism adds dimension to the works, changing perspectives with the changes in language, adding a multiplicity to the work and drawing the reader into a closer understanding of the character's multifaceted culture. The multilingual aspects allow the authors of these works to reclaim their languages, and the languages themselves, when used within the U.S. American context, become less deterritorialized, less out of place, and begin to become part of U.S. American language. With the reclamation of language comes the reclamation of social power. As Pérez-Torres states in *Movements in Chicano Poetry*:

> The Chicana[/o] transforms the positions of power implicit in the choice of linguistic expression. Language becomes a marker of displacement and reclamation, a marker of self-identity and self-empowerment. It is also a way of manifesting history with every word. The presence of Spanish is a presence through history of discrimination and exploitation. Every Spanish word represents a refusal to capitulate to English ethnocentricity [227].

Works that use multilingual techniques make it abundantly clear that some residents of the U.S. speak languages other than English, and that these languages are capable of a full range of expression and can depict circumstances and feelings of multicultural life that are uniquely U.S. American.

To welcome the use of other languages besides English in U.S. literature does not reduce the status of English, as some fear. Werner Sollors in the introduction to *Multilingual America* writes about the advantages of making a move from an "English only" to an "English plus" approach to U.S. American literature (1–13).* In this piece, he emphasizes the acceptance of other languages in the United States as a necessary impetus for social change for minority-language people. Sollors asks the question:

> Would not a focus on "English plus other languages" mean a further strengthening of English as the public language and a clearer understanding of language rights of minorities (and thus be likely to reduce social conflicts), bringing about a higher degree of literacy in English as well as more bilingual and multilingual fluency for everybody...? [3].

The answer to Sollors' question must be "yes." The alternative, "English only," as we saw poignantly with Chang in Sigrid Nunez's *A Feather on the Breath of God*, is to force people to stifle their native and heritage languages, to leave part of themselves unexpressed, and in short, to condemn them to silence. But as we have seen in this chapter, ethnic minority authors in the United States are not about to remain silent. They will write their literature, and when they choose to, they will use non–English languages to do it.

---

*"English plus" is a slogan used by the National Education Association.

Conclusion:
Hybrid Perspectives and the Demarginalization of Ethnic Literature in the United States

In a chapter entitled "The Accent of 'Loss': Cultural Crossings as Context in Julia Alvarez's *How the Garcia Girls Lost Their Accents*," David T. Mitchell discusses how the presence of multiple narrators in the postcolonial novel allows for differing and often conflicting points of view towards the same events. The inclusion of different narrators, several from first-person viewpoints as well as from third, allows the novel to reflect "the shifting and multiple nature of postcolonial identity itself" (168).

Although most of the novels discussed in this book are not considered postcolonial, the characters we have explored exhibit multiple identities similar to postcolonial characters. They share a similar multiplicity of language, culture and identity with postcolonial characters and differ from them primarily in that many ethnic groups in the United States have immigrated in, some by choice, instead of being the victims of colonization within their home countries. Others, however, were originally brought unwillingly to the United States (many African Americans) or were incorporated into its boundaries against their wishes, as in the case of Native Americans and some Mexican Americans whose ancestors found themselves involuntarily living within U.S. borders. These latter characters are, technically, still under the influence of colonization and therefore are not postcolonial. Because of these differences, the characters discussed in this work are outside a strict delineation of postcolonialism, but their struggles with multiple identities and with preserving their heritage culture in the face of an overwhelming, dominant majority have much in common with those of postcolonial literature. In both postcolonial and ethnic U.S. literature, hybrid perspectives pervade the fictional characters' everyday lives.

An author's use of multiple narrators (what Mitchell terms multipleperspectivity) serves to break apart the more usual one-voice, authoritative tone of narration, and as a result, "multipleperspectivity succeeds in breaking the binary between narrator and narrated and paves the way for the interruptive force of hybrid postcolonial forms" (168). The breaking of binary relationships upsets the hierarchies inherent within these binary structures — hierarchies built upon unequal relationships such as dominant to subdominant, and majority to minority. In other words, once one binary assumption is cracked, such as the relationship of narrator to what is narrated, the potential is there for others to fall, such as inferior to superior, and the destruction of assumed binary relationships can work, eventually, to invert unequal social hierarchies.

Hybrid perspectives that undermine the status quo, however, are not only limited to a multiplicity of narrators (Mitchell's multipleperspectivity). We have seen how this subversive, equalizing force also works through an author's use of other strategies that introduce a hybrid perspective: magical realism, differing perspectives on geographical space, multiple subjectivity, humor and multilingualism. This inclusion of hybrid perspectives from various sources breaks down the binary relationships by diffusing the novel's point of view, and by allowing contrary stances to simultaneously occupy the same narrative space. Through this use of hybrid perspectives, ethnic literature has moved away from a minority status and has gained access into the mainstream of U.S. American literature.

To see how contemporary ethnic literature has moved away from its earlier, minority-literature characteristics, we will once again look at the characteristics of a minority literature as defined by Gilles Deleuze and Félix Guattari in *Kafka: Toward a Minor Literature*. In the preceding chapter on multilingualism in ethnic U.S. literature, we looked at the first characteristic that defines minority literature as a literature in which "language is affected with a high coefficient of deterritorialization" (Deleuze and Guattari 16). The expression "deterritorialization" indicates that the literature is composed in a language that is constructed by a minority group within a major language, and thus the deterritorialized language is separated both from the geographical place of origin of the author (the author's heritage homeland) and from the majority language of the author's current habitation. Deleuze and Guattari use the Jewish literature of Warsaw and Prague as an example, a situation in which the German language used by the Jewish minority was a deterritorialized language. The condition of writing in a deterritorialized language, Deleuze and Guattari maintain, turned the Jewish minority's literature "into something impossible — the impossibility of not writing, the impossibility of writing in

German, the impossibility of writing otherwise" (16). Because of the conditions of oppression and misery, it was impossible for the Jews in Prague not to write, but writing in German would not reach the Czech-speaking majority, and besides, German was the language of the German oppressors occupying Prague. (As Deleuze and Guattari explain, the non–Jewish Germans in Prague were also a deterritorialized population within Czechoslovakia.) Writing in Czech was also not possible, according to Deleuze and Guattari, because even for those who knew Czech well enough, to write in Czech only increased the pain of displacement felt by the Jews in Czechoslovakia. This "impossibility" of literature for the minority group, therefore, characterizes a minority literature for Deleuze and Guattari, a literature that must necessarily exist, to the extent that it does exist, on the margins of the society in which it is written.

Ethnic literature in the United States, however, finds a solution to this dilemma of "impossibility" due partly to the increase in ethnic pride that was launched in the 1960s and partly to the increased globalization of the world's societies. An ethnic author writing exclusively in his or her heritage language need no longer only depend on members of his or her own ethnic group in the U.S. for an audience, but can also write for audiences overseas. For languages such as Spanish, a sizeable audience exists within the U.S. made up of both native speakers of Spanish and those who have learned the language in school or from their acquaintances. However, ethnic writers in the U.S. overcame the "impossibility" of writing primarily through the development of a multiple form, the use of hybrid perspectives, as a strategy to incorporate more than one culture into ethnic literary works.

Authors such as Gloria Anzaldúa, for example, have forsaken the either-or binary of whether to write in their heritage language or in English by combining two or more languages within their works. These bilingual works represent more than a switching between one language and another; they are an amalgam of the languages that work together within U.S. society, particularly in the borderland regions, to create a heteroglossic discourse. Heteroglossia, according to Bakhtin, characterizes the discourse of all societies to greater or lesser extents, and in the U.S., it broadens to encompass not only varieties of social registers and regional dialects, but may also include completely different languages.

The breaking of the binary relationship between dominant and subdominant languages, and the coexistence of two or more languages within the literary discourse, dissolves the hierarchal relationship between the languages and asserts the author's heritage language as possessing importance. Even if the author only inserts small portions of his or her heritage language, as does Gish Jen, the heritage language is highlighted, thrown into relief, and represented as a language existing alongside of English. Obviously, literature in the author's heritage language or in combinations with English is not only possible (no longer "impossible"), but flourishing. The common occurrence of texts containing two or more languages, and their acceptance by the general reading audience in the United States, moves these texts from a minority status into the mainstream of U.S. literature.

The second of the three characteristics of minority literatures "is that everything in them is political" (Deleuze and Guattari 17). Deleuze and Guattari contrast minor with major literature, claiming major literature deals with individual concerns "familial, marital, and so on," and the social setting of a major work serves as a "mere environment or background" (17). In minor literature, according to Deleuze and Guattari, there may be individual concerns, but they are only important in how they exemplify the overriding political concerns of the group. "The individual concern thus becomes all the more necessary, indispensable, magnified, because a whole other story is vibrating within it" (17). This is indeed the case in some works of ethnic literature in the United States, but certainly not in all. Leslie Marmon Silko's *Almanac of the Dead* would be an example of a work with an all-encompassing political concern — the necessity and inevitability of Native Americans to reclaim their land. Each episode, each character links into the eventual overturn of the current, corrupt society depicted in the novel, a society created by the European invaders, and points to the march of indigenous people up from the south, a movement which will eventually result in the return of the land to the Native Americans. Ana Castillo's *So Far from God*, although it deals with the concerns and interrelationships of a Mexican American family, links most of the family members to some institution within the dominant society that eventually brings about the character's demise. The novel lampoons the medical profession for "misdiagnosing" La Loca's death at the age of three. It ridicules the church through La Loca's unwillingness to have anything to do with the priest or the church after her resurrection. La Loca's sister, Esperanza, dies while reporting on the Gulf War, and Fe, another sister, succumbs to a terrible cancer because of her faith in the industrial complex of the United States, which knowingly allows her to work with carcinogenic chemicals. La Loca herself dies from AIDS. In these novels and many others, political issues form the central core of the work, and the novels develop around them.

However, in ethnic literature of the United States, works that do not focus overtly on a political message are increasingly prevalent. Some, such as Rudolfo Anaya's *Bless Me, Ultima*, set in New Mexico, make virtually no reference at all to the presence of non–Mexican Americans. Other works such as Amy Tan's *The Joy Luck Club*, Leslie Marmon Silko's "Yellow Woman," Maxine Hong Kingston's *The Woman Warrior*, and many of Sandra Cisneros' short stories might have the social milieu as a distant backdrop, but the driving concerns of the characters revolve around family, marital and love relationships. A character such as Maxine in *The Woman Warrior* might be struggling to reconcile a duality in her identity, resulting from growing up Chinese American, but the struggle is presented as more personal than political and is eventually resolved by her turning toward a strength within herself—a strength she discovers through her mother's stories rather than through any type of overt social or political activism. It is true that the works that do not focus on an overt political message may nevertheless have a political impact incorporated into the form of the novel. Indeed, the inclusion of any of the hybrid perspectives we have discussed carries a political message, one that asserts the languages and worldviews of the authors' ethnic groups. But to claim that everything in these works is political, indifferent to individual or family concerns beyond politics, is simply not the case.

While this second characteristic of a minor literature, an exclusively political content, applies to a number of works by ethnic authors in the U.S., the fact that there are many exceptions as well contradicts the second characteristic. As stated by Deleuze and Guattari, the preoccupation with politics provides no room whatsoever for non-political concerns, concerns that, contrary to expectation, form the center of many ethnic U.S. works. These non-political issues are often personal, human concerns that serve to integrate ethnic literature into U.S. literature in general and thereby contribute to the spread of its appeal to readers who are not members of the author's ethnic group.

The third characteristic of a minor literature as it is defined by Deleuze and Guattari claims that a minor literature is collective rather than individual:

> In it [minor literature] everything takes on a collective value. Indeed, precisely because talent isn't abundant in a minor literature, there are no possibilities for an individuated enunciation that would belong to this or that "master" and that could be separated from a collective enunciation [Deleuze and Guattari 17].

Since the "collective" nature of a minor literature, according to Deleuze and Guattari's words above, is premised on a lack of talent, a lack of authors from within the minority group, there can be no question that this characteristic does not apply to ethnic literature in the United States. There is a plethora of ethnic writing in the U.S., and even a cursory glance at bookstore and library shelves, or at anthologies of U.S. literature, will bear evidence that no such lack in either talent or abundance exists. Still, the notion that ethnic literature is a collective literature, standing for the concerns of the group rather than for the individual author, bears closer attention.

Just as some works of ethnic literature center on political concerns, some also seek to speak for the experiences of the ethnic group as a whole. Often the works that are overtly political and those that enunciate the concerns of the collective group are one and the same. Some ethnic authors feel an obligation to speak out about politics and to represent their group. These works are characterized not only by their attachment to a specific ethnic identity, but also by their concern with identity politics. The writers who believe ethnic works should represent the ethnic group, when commenting about the role of an ethnic author, profess the need for a strong ethnic literature as a resistance to the white, dominant culture in the United States.

In the introduction to *An Other Tongue*, Alfred Arteaga clearly states the dichotomy he sees existing between the self and an "other." He writes, "The self and other conceived at each site of different histories, different local cultures, are conceived by different processes of subjectification, engendered by different displacements of power.... U.S. Anglo-American nationalists define their nation to the exclusion of my people" (3). Not only is there an insurmountable separation between the ethnic groups, according to Arteaga, but a definite hierarchy is in place that keeps Mexican Americans and other ethnic groups at the bottom of the social-economic order. Also in *An Other Tongue*, in a chapter with the same title, Arteaga expresses his view that Mexican Americans are colonized subjects, caught in a situation where the colonist "never goes home" (17). In such an environment, aspects of the dominant culture gradually erode the subdominant culture. Arteaga views this erosion as particularly insidious in the area of language, not only because the colonized gradually lose their use of their native language, but because the dominant language and forms of discourse are used to implicate an inferior status for the colonized peoples. Arteaga writes, "The colonized subject becomes the (sub)altern Other prescribed by the dominant discourse in the act of articulating that discourse"(17). Recognizing the subversive power of language, Arteaga proposes that Chicano discourse can and should resist Anglo hegemony, and that the heteroglossia in Chicano/a writing is a form of resistance. "The mere presence of Chicano discourse resists Anglo American suppression of heteroglossia, much as the background noise of menials jars a social gathering" (14). While Arteaga's view of the inequality that characterizes relationships between ethnic minority groups and the dominant white group in the United States is not in dispute here, his underlying belief that it is the role of the ethnic author to politically resist such domination does raise some concerns regarding an author's freedom for creative expression, a freedom which Arteaga seems to deny to ethnic authors who do not wish to take up the cause. Arteaga thus presents a clear case of an author and critic who strongly promotes the political purpose of ethnic literature as both a collective representation of and a means of preserving the culture of the ethnic group.

Similar in tone to Arteaga, Sheng-mei Ma's *Immigrant Subjectivities in*

Asian American and Asian Diaspora Literatures categorizes Asian Americans as a separate, oppressed group within U.S. American culture: "But even after having been naturalized as U.S. citizens, they remain alienated due to, primarily, their non–Caucasian physical traits" (11). On the one hand, Ma expresses resentment for the separation of Asian Americans from mainstream U.S. culture; on the other hand, he warns against the dangers of mainstreaming and thereby losing a sense of Asian cultural heritage. In Ma's view, Asian Americans are separated not only from Anglo Americans, but also from recent Asian immigrants. He criticizes writers such as Maxine Hong Kingston and Frank Chin for adopting Anglo American views of Asian immigrants and for perpetuating negative stereotypes, all, he claims, in an effort to gain acceptance from the dominant Anglo culture. Ma writes the following about Chinese Americans:

> Simply put, Chinese Americans frequently take on the white gaze at their nonwhite object. Depicted as born and brought up in the United States, many Chinese American characters in fiction internalize ... the Orientalist cultural assumptions, which obliterate the differences between Chinese and themselves. Considering themselves, thus, inferior or nonmainstream, many seek to assimilate by adopting the white gaze and by projecting onto China and Chinese immigrants Orientalist — often racist — stereotypes. By so doing, they separate themselves from what they deem to be the *true* Other, China and Chinese immigrants, creating the impression that they could identify with mainstream America. Therefore, a large number of texts in Chinese American discourse Orientalize China, its immigrants to the United States, and ultimately American-born Chinese. This divorcing of oneself from one's ethnicity bespeaks a disguised self-hatred [25].

In this vein, Ma even goes so far as to suggest that Maxine Hong Kingston's marriage to an Anglo and the use of his last name are means to gain acceptance by mainstream U.S. readers. He also claims that Kingston's feminist theme in *The Woman Warrior* is meant merely to increase the popularity of her work. For Ma, the purpose of Asian American literature is to enhance the political identity of Asian Americans as a people with an Asian heritage who are, nevertheless, entitled to full membership in U.S. society. Literature by Asian Americans which casts any negative light on Asia or its immigrants to the United States, must, in Ma's view, be reflecting a form of self-hatred and/or an overeagerness to assimilate to the dominant Anglo American culture.

Although authors and literary critics such as Arteaga and Ma have strong and definite ideas about the obligations of ethnic authors to accurately represent their ethnic groups and their group's political issues with a collective voice, some notable authors have shied away from limiting their works to these ends and have rejected the notion of being ethnic representatives. As early as 1975, N. Scott Momaday was asked in an interview with Wm. T. Morgan, Jr., if he viewed himself as a spokesperson for Native Americans; Momaday unequivocally answers "no."* He stated that assuming such a role would be presumptuous and that in his writing he seeks above all to express his own individual views and concerns. Leslie Marmon Silko similarly rejected the notion of a "Native American" perspective in a 1977 interview with Dexter Fisher, and she expressed her views on ethnicity and what she saw as the necessarily individual perspective of the writer. Silko denied that there is such a thing as a "Laguna point of view" that she represents; there is only her point of view as it has developed against the background of the Laguna culture in which she was raised.† Rudolfo Anaya, talking with David Johnson and David Apodaca in 1979, expressed similar views concerning the necessary connection between artistic creativity and the individuality of the writer. Anaya went so far as to say that the creativity of the artist is compromised if the community dictates to the artist the concerns that he or she must portray.‡ And in 1980,

---

*Momaday's full response is as follows: "No, and it's something I don't think about very often. I don't identify with any group of writers, and I don't think of myself as being a spokesman for the Indian people. That would be presumptuous, it seems to me. I don't ... when I write I find it a very private kind of thing, and I like to keep it that way. You know, I would be uncomfortable I think if I were trying to express the views of other people. When I write I write out of my own experience, and out of my own ideas of that experience, and I'm not concerned to write the history of a people except as that history bears upon me directly. When I was writing *The Way to Rainy Mountain*, for example, I was dealing with something that belongs to the Indian world, and the Kiowa people as a whole, but I wasn't concerned with that so much as I was concerned with the fact that it meant this to me — this is how I as a person felt about it. And I want my writing to reflect myself in certain ways — that is my first concern" (Morgan 50).

†Below is the text of Silko's answer to Fisher:

F: Is there such a thing as a "Native American" perspective? Or would you say there's a tribal perspective?

S: As far as perspective goes, there's mine. Leslie Marmon. And insofar as I've grown up here and learned things here and loved people from here, the perspective I have involves very definitely Laguna and Laguna people and Laguna culture. What I write about and what I'm concerned about are relationships. To that I bring so many personal things that have been affected by where I come from, but I don't think one should oversimplify and say this is a Laguna point of view. It's my point of view, coming from a certain background and place [Fisher 25–26].

‡Rudolfo Anaya's words to Johnson follow:

Johnson: Is this part of how you see your role as a writer? That is, rediscovering that ... body of belief for the Chicano?

Anaya: Not for the Chicano. For myself.

Johnson: Is there a larger role for these works in terms of a people or a region? Or isn't this part of your consideration?

Anaya: I don't know how much of a consideration it can be when you're writing, when you're creating any work of art. I don't think that most artists think in terms of the overall, the world view. It flows from within, it flows from the individual, and it flows into whatever particular work of art you are into.

Johnson: But outside the actual process of creating the work, aren't you somehow asked by the community to be something more? As the author of *Bless Me, Ultima*, doesn't the movement itself make demands, ask you to play a *role as a writer*, not just as a creator?

Anaya: It's true that the Chicano literary movement of the '60s and '70s has looked at its writers, and the artists in the plastic and visual arts, to begin to give a picture, or to present the sense of the overview. What are we as a people? I don't think the artist should get caught up in that. I think any kind of description or dictation to the artist as a creative person will ruin his creative impulse [Johnson and Apodaca 36–37].

Maxine Hong Kingston also answered questions about being a representative for Chinese Americans in an interview with Arturo Islas and Marilyn Yalom.* Interestingly, in the interview with Islas and Yalom, Kingston equated the problem of ethnic writers being placed in the position of "spokesperson" as related to the number of works available by the authors of a particular ethnic group. This point of scarcity of works contributing to the collective nature of a minor literature was also emphasized by Deleuze and Guattari. In more recent years, Kingston has reiterated this connection between a lack of works and the authors of those works being seen as representative of their ethnic groups. She also claims that the problem of collective enunciation in ethnic works is disappearing as more and more Chinese American authors become published. In a 1989 interview with Paul Skenazy, Kingston said:

> I think the problem [of one author being seen as representative of a whole culture] has to do with not having enough books. If there were lots of books about us then every book wouldn't have to carry the burden of being representative. Then everyone would see that since there's such a variety in the way that we write, there must be a variety in our people. The situation is really correcting itself in a miraculous way this very year.... [Several newly published Chinese and Asian American books are mentioned.] Chinese Americans must really be at a center of some well of creative energy. So this problem of each one of us causing a civil war every time we publish a book — maybe that will not happen any more [Skenazy 156].

Again, in 1991, Kingston addressed this same issue of representation and collectivity of voice in an interview with Donna Perry. By the time of this interview, however, the expectation that Kingston wrote books that were representative of her race was not the only problem. She also mentioned a growing number of critical voices that feel she *was* trying to represent the ethnic group as a whole, and resented it:

> This is the same thing that I have heard so many black writers say that they have to take the whole responsibility of race. Then at the same time, there are people of our own community, other Chinese Americans, who will say, "Well, how dare you speak for us? Who voted for you? How can you make fun of us?" [Perry 182–83].

---

*Maxine Hong Kingston's exchange with Islas follows:
Islas: As the author of two highly successful books that spring from your personal ethnic background—*The Woman Warrior* and *China Men*—do you see yourself as representative of the Chinese American community?
Kingston: That is a very difficult problem because there is an expectation among readers and critics that I should represent the race. And then there are the white people who pick up the work and say, "She must be just like the rest of them." I don't like hearing non–Chinese people say to a Chinese person, "Well now I know about you because I have read Maxine Hong Kingston's books." Each artist has a unique voice. Many readers don't understand that. The problem of how "representative" one is will only be solved when we have many more Chinese American writers. Then readers will see how diverse our people are [Islas 21].

Thus, in relation to the third characteristic of a minor literature as expressed by Deleuze and Guattari, the collective assemblage of enunciation, we have seen how ethnic literature in the United States has moved away from being a minor literature as it has increased from few books to many, and from a representative mission to a rejection of representative goals. The collective/representative mission is rejected first by the authors, who stress the necessity of an individual voice for their own creativity, and then by the readers, who also reject and even resent the notion that an ethnic author speaks for their group with a collective voice. This strong emphasis on individualism by ethnic writers for their own artistic freedom and by ethnic readers who do not want someone to speak for them gives clear evidence that demonstrates the influence of U.S. culture on U.S. ethnic literature in terms of the primacy it places on individualism. Because of this strong commitment to individualism and rejection of collectivism on the parts of some ethnic writers, it seems that much of ethnic literature in the United States does not fit Deleuze and Guattari's third characteristic.

Counteracting each of the three characteristics for a minor literature, the U.S. ethnic authors' abilities to create multiple perspectives within their works have moved the works away from this marginal classification. In terms of language, we have seen how authors have incorporated their own heritage languages into their works, thus breaking down the division and hierarchical relationship of dominant to subdominant language. In terms of politics, we have seen how authors can present a political backdrop to their works, yet deal with personal, nonpolitical issues within the same literary space. And finally, we have seen how the works of ethnic authors in the United States can draw upon their cultural backgrounds, make their cultures part of their works, yet still retain an individual, creative voice. In addition to these areas singled out by Deleuze and Guattari, we have also seen how hybrid perspectives occur in other dimensions of literary works, such as perceptions of the ordinary and the magical as part of one reality; differing yet simultaneous perceptions of the meanings of landscapes and man-made spaces; multiple subjects within a complex, multicultural identity; and the flexibility and ironic meanings and double uses of humor. Even the classifications of ethnicity themselves have become doubled, blurred, allowing characters to slip from one ethnic designation to another. Indeed, the very form of these works, as well as the content in some, resists the notion that there is only one viewpoint and that the only acceptable viewpoint is that determined by the dominant group. The breaking down of preconceived viewpoints, based on only one way of viewing a narrative, has worked to move ethnic literature in the United States away from the margins and more toward the center of U.S. literature by undermining the very concept of a dominant viewpoint expressed within a dominant literature. Through the use of hybrid perspectives, ethnic authors have done much to invert our ethnic stereotypes and our unequal social hierarchies. With the use of hybrid perspectives, the dominant culture's language, customs, and worldview are not able to shut out those of the minority groups. And it is in this respect, refusing to accept only one dominant view and allowing the voices of minorities to be heard, that ethnic literature not only makes a significant literary contribution to the U.S., but also narrows the gaps between the ideals and the realities of democracy in the United States.

Works Cited

Aldama, Frederick Luis. *Postethnic Narrative Criticism: Magicorealism in Oscar "Zeta" Acosta, Ana Castillo, Julie Dash, Hanif Kureishi, and Salman Rushdie.* Austin: University of Texas Press, 2003.
Alexie, Sherman. *The Lone Ranger and Tonto Fistfight in Heaven.* New York: HarperPerennial, 1994.
Allen, Paula Gunn. "Iyani: It Goes This Way." *The Remembered Earth: An Anthology of Contemporary Native American Literature,* edited by Geary Hobson. 191–193. Albuquerque: Red Earth Press, 1979.
———. *The Sacred Hoop: Recovering the Feminine in American Indian Traditions.* Boston: Beacon Press, 1986.
Anaya, Rudolfo. *Bless Me, Ultima.* New York: Warner Books, 1994.
———. "The Silence of the Llano: Notes from the Author." *Literature of the Southwest.* Spec. issue of *MELUS* 11, no. 4 (1984): 47–57.
Andrews, Jennifer. "In the Belly of a Laughing God: Reading Humor and Irony in the Poetry of Joy Harjo." *American Indian Quarterly* 24, no. 2 (spring 2000): 200–218.
Anzaldúa, Gloria. *Borderlands / La Frontera: The New Mestiza.* San Francisco: Aunt Lute Books, 1987.
Arnold, Ellen L., ed. *Conversations with Leslie Marmon Silko.* Jackson: University Press of Mississippi, 2000.
Arteaga, Alfred. *Chicano Poetics: Heterotexts and Hybridities.* Cambridge: Cambridge University Press, 1997.
———, ed. *An Other Tongue: Nation and Ethnicity in the Linguistic Borderlands.* Durham: Duke University Press, 1994.
Bakhtin, Mikhail M. *The Dialogic Imagination: Four Essays by M. M. Bakhtin.* University of Texas Press Slavic Series, no. 1. Trans. Caryl Emerson and Michael Holquist. Ed. Michael Holquist. Austin: University of Texas Press, 1981.
Ballinger, Franchot. *Living Sideways: Tricksters in American Indian Oral Traditions.* Norman: University of Oklahoma Press, 1998.
Bhabha, Homi K. *The Location of Culture.* New York: Routledge, 1994.
Borges, Jorge Luis. "The Garden of Forking Paths." *Labyrinths: Selected Stories and Other Writings,* edited by Donald A. Yates and James E. Irby. 19–29. New York: New Directions, 1964.
Boskin, Joseph. *Rebellious Laughter: People's Humor in American Culture.* Syracuse: Syracuse University Press, 1997.
Bowers, Maggie Ann. *Magic(al) Realism: The New Critical Idiom.* New York: Routledge, 2004.
Brady, Mary Pat. "The Contrapuntal Geographies of *Woman Hollering Creek and Other Stories.*" *American Literature* 71, no. 1 (1999): 117–150.
Broncano, Manuel. "Landscapes of the Magical: Cather's and Anaya's Explorations of the South-

west." *Willa Cather and the American Southwest*, edited by John N. Swift and Joseph R. Urgo. 124–135. Lincoln: University of Nebraska Press, 2002.

Browder, Laura. *Slippery Characters: Ethnic Impersonators and American Identities.* Chapel Hill: University of North Carolina Press, 2000.

Bruce-Novoa, Juan. *Chicano Poetry: A Response to Chaos*. Austin: University of Texas Press, 1982.

Burciaga, Jose Antonio. *Spilling the Beans*. Santa Barbara: Joshua Odell, 1995.

Cabeza de Vaca, Álvar Núñez. *Naufragios y Comentarios*. 1555. México, DF: Editorial Porrúa, S. A., 1988.

Cao, Xue-qin. *The Story of the Stone (Hong lou meng)*. Trans. David Hawkes. 1792. Middlesex, Eng.: Penguin Books, 1973.

Carpentier, Alejo. "On the Marvelous Real in America." *Magical Realism: Theory, History, Community*, edited by Lois Parkinson Zamora and Wendy B. Faris. 75–88. 1949. Durham: Duke University Press, 1995.

Castillo, Ana. *So Far from God*. New York: Plume, 1994.

Cederstrom, Lorelei. "Myth and Ceremony in Contemporary North American Native Fiction." *The Canadian Journal of Native Studies* 2, no. 2 (1982): 285–301.

Cervantes, Lorna Dee. "Barco de refugiados/Refugee Ship." *Emplumada*, edited by Lorna Dee Cervantes. Pitt Poetry Series. 40–41. Pittsburgh: University of Pittsburgh Press, 1981.

Cheung, King-Kok. *Articulate Silences: Hisaye Yamamoto, Maxine Hong Kingston, Joy Kogawa*. Ithaca: Cornell University Press, 1993.

Cisneros, Sandra. *Woman Hollering Creek and Other Stories*. New York: Vintage Contemporaries, 1992.

Clements, William M. "The Way to Individuation in Anaya's Bless Me, Ultima." *Midwest Quarterly: A Journal of Contemporary Thought* 23, no. 2 (winter 1982): 131–143.

Colón, Cristóbal. *Textos y documentos completos*. Edición de Consuelo Varela, Nuevas Cartas: Edición de Juan Gil. Madrid: Alianza Editorial, 1982.

Coltelli, Laura. "Leslie Marmon Silko." *Conversations with Leslie Marmon Silko*, edited by Ellen L. Arnold. 52–68. Jackson: University Press of Mississippi, 2000.

Comer, Krista. *Landscapes of the New West: Gender and Geography in Contemporary Women's Writing*. Chapel Hill: University of North Carolina Press, 1999.

Coulombe, Joseph L. "The Approximate Size of His Favorite Humor: Sherman Alexie's Comic Connections and Disconnections in *The Lone Ranger and Tonto Fistfight in Heaven*." *American Indian Quarterly* 26, no. 1 (winter 2002): 94–115.

Deleuze, Gilles, and Félix Guattari. *Kafka: Toward a Minor Literature*. Trans. Dana Polan. Theory and History of Literature, vol. 30. Minneapolis: University of Minnesota Press, 1986.

Deloria, Philip J. *Playing Indian*. New Haven: Yale University Press, 1998.

D'Haen, Theo L. "Magic Realism and Postmodernism: Decentering Privileged Centers." *Magical Realism: Theory, History, Community*, edited by Lois Parkinson Zamora and Wendy B. Faris. 191–208. Durham: Duke University Press, 1995.

Domina, Lynn. "'The Way I Heard It': Autobiography. Tricksters, and Leslie Marmon Silko's Storyteller." *SAIL* 19, no. 3 (fall 2007): 45–67.

Doty, William G. "Native American Tricksters: Literary Figures of Community Transformers." *Trickster Lives: Culture and Myth in American Fiction*, edited by Jeanne Campbell Reesman. 1–15. Athens: University of Georgia Press, 2001.

Erdrich, Louise. *The Bingo Palace*. New York: Perennial, 1994.

———. *The Last Report on the Miracles at Little No Horse*. New York: Perennial, 2001.

———. *Love Medicine*. New and Expanded Version. New York: HarperFlamingo, 1998.

———. *Tracks*. New York: Perennial, 1989.

Escandón, María Amparo. *Esperanza's Box of Saints*. New York: Simon & Schuster, 1999.

"Ethnic, Ethnicity." *Random House Webster's College Dictionary*. 2nd ed. 1997.

"Ethnic, Ethnicity." *Webster's New Collegiate Dictionary*. 1977.

Fantini, Alvino E. "Social Cues and Language Choice: Case Study of a Bilingual Child," *Bilin-*

gualism in the Southwest, 2nd ed., rev., edited by Paul R. Turner. 87–110. Tucson: University of Arizona Press, 1982.

Faris, Wendy B. "Scheherazade's Children: Magical Realism and Postmodern Fiction." *Magical Realism: Theory, History, Community*, edited by Lois Parkinson Zamora and Wendy B. Faris. 163–190. Durham: Duke University Press, 1995.

Fisher, Dexter. "Stories and Their Tellers — A Conversation with Leslie Marmon Silko." *Conversations with Leslie Marmon Silko*, edited by Ellen L. Arnold. 22–28. Jackson: University Press of Mississippi, 2000.

Fishkin, Shelley Fisher. "Interview with Maxine Hong Kingston." *Conversations with Maxine Hong Kingston*, edited by Paul Skenazy and Tera Martin. 159–167. Jackson: University Press of Mississippi, 1998.

Flax, Jane. "Multiples: On the Contemporary Politics of Subjectivity." *Disputed Subjects: Essays on Psychoanalysis, Politics, and Philosophy*, edited by Jane Flax. 92–110. New York: Routledge, 1993.

Flores, Angel. "Magical Realism in Spanish American Fiction." *Magical Realism: Theory, History, Community*, edited by Lois Parkinson Zamora and Wendy B. Faris. 109–117. Durham: Duke University Press, 1995.

Foreman, P. Gabrielle. "Past-On Stories: History and the Magically Real, Morrison and Allende on Call." *Magical Realism: Theory, History, Community*, edited by Lois Parkinson Zamora and Wendy B. Faris. 285–303. Durham: Duke University Press, 1995.

Frankenberg, Ruth, ed. *Displacing Whiteness: Essays in Social and Cultural Criticism*. Durham: Duke University Press, 1997.

García, Reyes. "Sense of Place in Ceremony." *The Ethnic-Novel: Appalachian, Chicano, Chinese and Native American*. Spec. issue of *MELUS* 10, no. 4 (1983): 37–48.

García Márquez, Gabriel. *One Hundred Years of Solitude*. Trans. Gregory Rabassa. New York: HarperPerennial, 1998.

Gates, Henry Louis. *The Signifying Monkey: A Theory of African-American Literary Criticism*. New York: Oxford University Press, 1989.

Gilbert, Joanne R. *Performing Marginality: Humor, Gender, and Cultural Critique*. Detroit: Wayne State University Press, 2004.

Glazer, Nathan, and Daniel Patrick Moynihan. *Beyond the Melting Pot: The Negroes, Puerto Ricans, Jews, Italians, and Irish of New York City*. Cambridge: MIT Press, 1963.

Graulich, Melody, ed. *"Yellow Woman": Leslie Marmon Silko*. New Brunswick: Rutgers University Press, 1993.

Greenblatt, Stephen. *Marvelous Possessions: The Wonder of the New World*. Chicago: University of Chicago Press, 1991.

Gross, Lawrence W. "The Trickster and World Maintenance: An Anishinaabe Reading of Louise Erdrich's *Tracks*." *SAIL* 17, no. 3 (fall 2005): 48–66.

Guenther, Irene. "Magic Realism, New Objectivity, and the Arts During the Weimar Republic." *Magical Realism: Theory, History, Community*, edited by Lois Parkinson Zamora and Wendy B. Faris. 33–73. Durham: Duke University Press, 1995.

Gutwirth, Claudia. "'Stop Making Sense': Trickster Variations in the Fiction of Louise Erdrich." *Trickster Lives: Culture and Myth in American Fiction*, edited by Jeanne Campbell Reesman. 148–167. Athens: University of Georgia Press, 2001.

Hawley, Steven. "Making Metaphor Happen: Space, Time and Trickster Sign." *Arizona Quarterly* 64, no. 2 (summer 2008): 95–122.

Hom, Marlon K. *Songs of Gold Mountain: Cantonese Rhymes from San Francisco Chinatown*. Berkeley: University of California Press, 1987.

Hsia, C. T. *The Classic Chinese Novel: A Critical Introduction*. New York: Columbia University Press, 1968.

Hwang, David Henry. *F.O.B.* and *The House of Sleeping Beauties*. New York: Dramatists Play Service, 1983.

Ife, B. W., ed. and trans. *Christopher Columbus: Journal of the First Voyage (Diario del primer viaje) 1492*. Warminster, Eng.: Aris & Phillips, 1990.

Islas, Arturo, with Marilyn Yalom. "Interview with Maxine Hong Kingston." *Conversations with Maxine Hong Kingston*, edited by Paul Skenazy and Tera Martin. 21–32. Jackson: University Press of Mississippi, 1998.
Jen, Gish. *Mona in the Promised Land*. New York: Vintage Contemporaries, 1997.
_____. *Typical American*. New York: Plume, 1992.
Jin, Ha (Jin Xue Fei). *The Writer as Migrant*. Chicago: University of Chicago Press, 2008.
Johnson, David, and David Apodaca. "Myth and the Writer: A Conversation with Rudolfo Anaya." *Conversations with Rudolfo Anaya*, edited by Bruce Dick and Silvio Sirias. 29–48. Jackson: University Press of Mississippi, 1998.
Karem, Jeff. "Keeping the Native on the Reservation: The Struggle for Leslie Marmon Silko's Ceremony." *American Indian Culture and Research Journal* 25, no 4 (2001): 21–34.
Kim, Elaine H. *Asian American Literature: An Introduction to the Writings and Their Social Context*. Philadelphia: Temple University Press, 1982.
Kingston, Maxine Hong. *China Men*. New York: Vintage International, 1989.
_____. *Hawai'i One Summer*. Honolulu: University of Hawai'i Press, 1998.
_____. *Tripmaster Monkey: His Fake Book*. New York: Vintage International, 1990.
_____. *The Woman Warrior: Memoirs of a Girlhood Among Ghosts*. New York: Vintage International, 1989.
Kocks, Dorothee E. *Dream a Little: Land and Social Justice in Modern America*. Berkeley: University of California Press, 2000.
Leal, Luis. "Magical Realism in Spanish American Literature." 1967. *Magical Realism: Theory, History, Community*, edited by Lois Parkinson Zamora and Wendy B. Faris. 119–124. Durham: Duke University Press, 1995.
Lee, A. Robert. *Multicultural American Literature: Comparative Black, Native, Latino/a and Asian American Fictions*. Jackson: University Press of Mississippi, 2003.
Lee, Gus. *China Boy*. New York: Penguin Books, 1991.
Leveen, Lois. "Only When I Laugh: Textual Dynamics of Ethnic Humor." *MELUS* 21, no. 4 (winter 1996): 29–55.
Lim, Shirley Geok-lin. "Immigration and Diaspora." *An Interethnic Companion to Asian American Literature*, edited by King-Kok Cheung. 289–311. Cambridge: Cambridge University Press, 1997.
Lo, Kuan-chung. *Three Kingdoms: China's Epic Drama: Ca. 1330–ca. 1400*. Trans. and ed. Moss Roberts. New York: Pantheon, 1976.
Lopez, Barry. *Giving Birth to Thunder, Sleeping with His Daughter: Coyote Builds North America*. New York: Avon Books, 1977.
Lowe, John. "Monkey Kings and Mojo: Postmodern Ethnic Humor in Kingston, Reed, and Vizenor." *MELUS* 21, no. 4 (winter 1996): 103–126.
Lu, Hsun. *Selected Stories of Lu Hsun*. Trans. Yang Hsien-yi and Gladys Yang. Peking: Foreign Languages Press, 1972.
Ma, Sheng-mei. *Immigrant Subjectivities in Asian American and Asian Diaspora Literatures*. Albany: State University of New York Press, 1998.
Mackin, Jonna. "Split Infinities: The Comedy of Performative Identity in Maxine Hong Kingston's *Tripmaster Monkey*." *Contemporary Literature* 46 no. 3 (autumn 2005): 511–534.
Malcolm, Cheryl Alexander. "Going for the Knockout: Confronting Whiteness in Gus Lee's *China Boy*." *MELUS* 29, no. 3/4 (autumn/winter 2004): 413–426.
McAllister, Mick. "Homeward Bound: Wilderness and Frontier in American Indian Literature." *The Frontier Experience and the American Dream: Essays on American Literature*, edited by David Mogen, Mark Busby, and Paul Bryant. 149–158. College Station: Texas A&M University Press, 1989.
Mendieta-Lombardo, Eva, and Zaida A. Cintron. "Marked and Unmarked Choices of Code Switching in Bilingual Poetry." *Hispania* (Sept. 1995): 565–572.
Momaday, N. Scott. *House Made of Dawn*. 1968. New York: Harper & Row, 1989.
_____. *The Names: A Memoir*. New York: Harper & Row, 1976.

Mora, Pat. *House of Houses*. Boston: Beacon Press, 1997.
Morrison, Toni. *Beloved*. New York: Plume, 1988.
———. *Song of Solomon*. New York: Plume, 1987.
Myers-Scotton, Carol. *Duelling Languages: Grammatical Structure in Codeswitching*. Oxford: Clarendon, 1993.
Narcisi, Lara. "Wittman's Transitions: Multivocality and the Play of *Tripmaster Monkey*." *MELUS* 30, no. 3 (fall 2005): 95–111.
Nelson, Robert M. *Place and Vision: The Function of Landscape in Native American Fiction*. New York: Peter Lang, 1993.
Nieh, Hua-ling. *Mulberry and Peach: Two Women of China*. Trans. Jane Parish Yang with Linda Lappin. Boston: Beacon Press, 1988.
———. *Sang ching yu tau hong*. Hong Kong: You Lian, 1976.
Nunez, Sigrid. *A Feather on the Breath of God*. New York: HarperPerennial, 1996.
Orr, Lisa. "Theorizing the Earth: Feminist Approaches to Nature and Leslie Marmon Silko's Ceremony." *American Indian Culture and Research Journal* 18, no. 2 (1994): 145–157.
Patell, Cyrus R. K. "The Violence of Hybridity in Silko and Alexie." *Journal of American Studies of Turkey* 6 (1997): 3–9.
Peñalosa, Fernando. *Chicano Sociolinguistics: A Brief Introduction*. Rowley, MA: Newbury House, 1980.
Pérez-Torres, Rafael. *Movements in Chicano Poetry: Against Myths, Against Margins*. Cambridge Studies in American Literature and Culture, no. 88. New York: Cambridge University Press, 1995.
Powell, Timothy B., ed. *Beyond the Binary: Reconstructing Cultural Identity in a Multicultural Context*. New Brunswick: Rutgers University Press, 1999.
Purves, Alan C., ed. *Tapestry: A Multicultural Anthology*. Englewood Cliffs, NJ: Globe Book, 1993.
"The Questions on the Form — 2010 Census." *United States Census Bureau 2010*. http://2010.census.gov/2010 census/how/interactive-form.php (accessed 19 March 2010).
Radway, Janice. "What's in a Name?: Presidential Address to the American Studies Association, 20 November, 1998." *American Quarterly* 51, no. 1 (Mar 1999): 1–32.
Rappoport, Leon. *Punchlines: The Case for Racial, Ethnic, and Gender Humor*. Westport, CN: Praeger, 2005.
Rebolledo, Tey Diana. "Walking the Thin Line: Humor in Chicana Literature." *Beyond Stereotypes: The Critical Analysis of Chicana Literature*, edited by María Herrera-Sobek. 91–107. Binghamton, New York: Bilingual Press, 1985.
Reesman, Jeanne Campbell, ed. *Trickster Lives: Culture and Myth in American Fiction*. Athens: University of Georgia Press, 2001.
Rodriguez, Richard. *Days of Obligation: An Argument with My Mexican Father*. New York: Penguin Books, 1993.
———. *Hunger of Memory: The Education of Richard Rodriguez*. New York: Bantam Books, 1983.
Roh, Franz. "Magical Realism: Post-Expressionism." *Magical Realism: Theory, History, Community*, edited by Lois Parkinson Zamora and Wendy B. Faris. 15–31. 1925. Durham: Duke University Press, 1995.
Ruoff, A. LaVonne. "Ritual and Renewal: Keres Traditions in Leslie Silko's 'Yellow Woman.'" *"Yellow Woman": Leslie Marmon Silko*, edited and with an introduction by Melody Graulich. 69–81. New Brunswick, NJ: Rutgers University Press, 1993.
Rutherford, Jonathan. "The Third Space: Interview with Homi Bhabha." *Identity: Community, Culture, Difference*, edited by Jonathan Rutherford. 207–221. London: Lawrence & Wishart, 1990.
Saeta, Elsa. "A *MELUS* Interview: Ana Castillo." *MELUS* 22, no. 3 (1997): 133–149.
Sanchez, Rosaura. *Chicano Discourse: Socio-historic Perspectives*. Rowley, MA: Newbury House, 1983.
Scheninger, Lee. "Writing Nature: Silko and Native Americans as Nature Writers." *MELUS* 18, no. 2 (summer 1993): 47–60.

Siebert, Gayle Ruth. "Frontiering Tayo's Interior Landscapes: A Vizenorian Exploration of the Fragmented Self." *The Image of the Frontier in Literature, the Media, and Society: Selected Papers from the 1997 Conference of the Society for the Interdisciplinary Study of Social Imagery, March 13–15, 1997, Colorado Springs, Colorado*, edited by Will Wright and Steven Kaplan. 198–204. Pueblo: The Society for the Interdisciplinary Study of Social Imagery, University of Southern Colorado, 1997.

Shih, Nai-an. *Water Margin*. Trans. J. H. Jackson. Cambridge, MA: C & T, 1976.

Silko, Leslie Marmon. *Almanac of the Dead*. New York: Penguin Books, 1991.

———. *Ceremony*. New York: Penguin Books, 1986.

———. "Yellow Woman." *"Yellow Woman": Leslie Marmon Silko*, edited by with an introduction by Melody Graulich. 31–43. New Brunswick, NJ: Rutgers University Press, 1993.

Simpkins, Scott. "Sources of Magic Realism / Supplements to Realism in Contemporary Latin American Literature." *Magical Realism: Theory, History, Community*, edited by Lois Parkinson Zamora and Wendy B. Faris. 145–159. Durham: Duke University Press, 1995.

Skenazy, Paul, and Tera Martin, eds. *Conversations with Maxine Hong Kingston*. Jackson: University Press of Mississippi, 1998.

Smith, Jeanne Rosier. *Writing Tricksters: Mythic Gambols in American Ethnic Literature*. Berkeley: University of California Press, 1997.

Smith, Patricia Clark, with Paula Gunn Allen. "Earthly Relations, Carnal Knowledge: Southwestern American Indian Women Writers and Landscape." *The Desert Is No Lady: Southwestern Landscapes in Women's Writing and Art*, edited by Vera Norwood and Janice Monk. 174–196. New Haven: Yale University Press, 1987.

So, Christine. "Delivering the Punch Line: Racial Combat as Comedy in Gus Lee's *China Boy*." *MELUS* 21, no. 4 (winter 1996): 141–155.

Sollors, Werner. *Beyond Ethnicity: Consent and Descent in American Culture*. New York: Oxford University Press, 1986.

———, ed. *Multilingual America: Transnationalism, Ethnicity, and the Languages of American Literature*. New York: New York University Press, 1998.

Tan, Amy. *The Hundred Secret Senses*. New York: Ivy Books, 1995.

Tan, Amy. *The Joy Luck Club*. New York: Ivy Books, 1989.

Tarter, James. "Locating the Uranium Mine: Place, Multiethnicity, and Environmental Justice in Leslie Marmon Silko's Ceremony." *The Greening of Literary Scholarship: Literature, Theory, and the Environment*, edited by Steven Rosendale. 97–110. Iowa City: University of Iowa Press, 2002.

Todorov, Tzvetan. *The Fantastic: A Structural Approach to a Literary Genre*. Trans. Richard Howard. Cleveland: The Press of Case Western Reserve University, 1973.

Toelken, Barre. Foreword. *Giving Birth to Thunder, Sleeping with his Daughter: Coyote Builds North America*, by Barry Lopez. xi–xiv. New York: Avon Books, 1977.

Tu, Wei-ming, ed. *The Living Tree: The Changing Meaning of Being Chinese Today*. Stanford, CA: Stanford University Press, 1994.

Turner, Victor. "Myth and Symbol." *The International Encyclopedia of Social Sciences*. 576–582. New York: Macmillan, 1968.

Vizenor, Gerald. *Griever: An American Monkey King in China*. Minneapolis: University of Minnesota Press, 1987.

Walker, Nancy A. *A Very Serious Thing: Women's Humor and American Culture*. Minneapolis: University of Minnesota Press, 1988.

Walter, Roland. *Magical Realism in Contemporary Chicano Fiction*. Frankfurt am Main: Vervuert Verlag, 1993.

Wang, L. Ling-chi. "Roots and the Changing Identity of the Chinese in the United States." *The Living Tree: The Changing Meaning of Being Chinese Today*, edited by Tu Wei-ming. 185–212. Stanford, CA: Stanford University Press, 1994.

Wilson, Rawdon. "The Metamorphoses of Fictional Space: Magical Realism." *Magical Realism: Theory, History, Community*, edited by Lois Parkinson Zamora and Wendy B. Faris. 209–233. Durham: Duke University Press, 1995.

Wong, Sau-ling Cynthia. *Reading Asian American Literature: From Necessity to Extravagance*. Princeton: Princeton University Press, 1993.
Wu, Ch'eng-en. *Monkey*. Trans. Arthur Waley. New York: Grove Press, 1958.
———. *Journey to the West*. Trans. and ed. Anthony C. Yu. Chicago: University of Chicago Press, 1977.
Yak, Laura K. "Racial and Ethnic Classifications Used in Census 2000 and Beyond." *United States Census Bureau, Population Division*. http://www.census.gov/ftp/pub/population/www/socdemo/race/racefactcb.html (accessed 12 April 2000).
Yan, Zhen. *Bai xue hong chen* (*White Snow, Red Dust: An Episode in the Maple Country*). Brampton, Ont.: Canada Mirror Books, 1996.
Yin, Xiao-huang. *Chinese American Literature Since the 1850s*. Urbana: University of Illinois Press, 2000.
Yu, Li-hua. *You jian zong lu, you jian zong lu*. Taibei: Hwang Guan, 1967.
Zamora, Lois Parkinson, and Wendy B. Faris, eds. *Magical Realism: Theory, History, Community*. Durham: Duke University Press, 1995.

Index

"The Accent of 'Loss': Cultural Crossings as Context in Julia Alvarez's *How the Garcia Girls Lost Their Accents*" 184
accommodation 82, 83–84, 86
Alamo 47
Aldama, Frederick Luis 22, 40
Alexie, Sherman 115, 122–123, 125–126
Alice in Wonderland 34
alienation 82, 84–85
Allen, Paula Gunn 51, 52, 53, 55, 58
Almanac of the Dead 187
American Dream 139, 140, 142, 145, 165
Anaya, Rudolfo 14, 68, 86*fn*, 187, 191
Die andere seite (*The Other Side*) 25
Andrews, Jennifer 115, 118
Anzaldúa, Gloria 14, 18, 47, 80, 87–89, 94, 95, 148, 158–159, 160–161, 186
Apodaca, David 71, 191
"The Approximate Size of His Favorite Humor: Sherman Alexie's Comic Connections and Disconnections in *The Lone Ranger and Tonto Fistfight in Heaven*" 126
"The Approximate Size of My Favorite Tumor" 125–126
Aristophanes 124
Arteaga, Alfred 158, 189, 190
Articulate Silences: Hisaye Yamamoto, Maxine Hong Kingston, Joy Kogawa 179–180
Asian American Literature: An Introduction to the Writings and Their Social Context 93, 95, 177, 178
assimilation 1, 79, 81, 82, 83, 86, 89–90, 92, 95–96, 172

Bai xue hong chen (*White Snow, Red Dust: An Episode in the Maple Country*) 82, 152–153
Bakhtin, Mikhail 17, 116, 124, 147, 168, 186
Ballinger, Franchot 97–98
Beckmann, Max 25

Beloved 39, 41, 86*fn*
Beyond Ethnicity: Consent and Descent in American Culture 4, 6
Beyond Stereotypes: The Critical Analysis of Chicana Literature 124
Beyond the Binary: Reconstructing Cultural Identity in a Multicultural Context 7
Beyond the Melting Pot 5
Bhabha, Homi 9, 10, 57
The Bingo Palace 106–107
Bless Me, Ultima 14, 68–71, 86*fn*, 187, 191*fn*
Bonetti, Kay 94*fn*
Bontempelli, Massimo 26
Book of Changes (*I Ching*) 135*fn*–136*fn*, 173
borderlands 47–48, 65, 148, 158, 160, 186
Borderlands/La Frontera: The New Mestiza 18, 47, 80, 87–89, 148, 158–159, 160–161
borderline subjectivity 86
Borges, Jorge Luis 13, 28, 32
borrowing (linguistic) 148
Boskin, Joseph 116, 117*fn*
Bowers, Maggie Ann 24
Brady, Mary Pat 127–128
Broncano, Manuel 71
Browder, Laura 5
Bruce-Novoa, Juan 159
bruja 69
Bunker, Chang and Eng (conjoined twins) 102–103
Burciaga, José Antonio 119, 127

Cabeza de Vaca, Álvar Núñez 28–29
Carpentier, Alejo 13, 22*fn*, 26, 28
Carter, Dan T. 6
Carter, Forrest 6
Castillo, Ana 34–36, 40, 83, 125, 129, 187
Cederstrom, Lorelei 52
Census Bureau 8
Ceremony 13, 14, 41–44, 48–57, 62
Cervantes, Lorna Dee 161

203

Chanady, Amaryll 22*fn*
Chang and Eng (conjoined twins) 102–103
Chavez, Cesar 127
Cheung, King-Kok 18, 179, 180
Chicana 87
Chicano 87, 191
Chicano Discourse 156
Chicano Poetics 158
Chicano Poetry: A Response to Chaos 159–160
Chicano Sociolinguistics 154
chicken pull 63, 63*fn*–64*fn*
Chief Buffalo Child Long Lance 5
Chin, Frank 190
China Boy 143–144
China Men 74, 138–139, 192
Chinatown 75–76, 76*fn*
Chinese American Literature Since the 1850s 149
Chinese Exclusionary Act 81–82
Chirico, Giorgio de 28
Cintron, Zaida A. 163
Cisneros, Sandra 127, 187
civil rights 2, 5
Clements, William 70
Coatlique (Aztec goddess) 14, 88–89, 95
code-switching 17, 148, 154–167
Coltelli, Laura 124
Columbus, Christopher 27, 28
Comer, Krista 10, 47, 48, 52, 74
consent and descent 4
"The Contrapuntal Geographies of *Woman Hollering Creek and Other Stories*" 127–128
Contreras, Francisco 28
Conversations with Maxine Hong Kingston 73*fn*
Coulombe, Joseph L. 126
Coyote 120–124, 135
Culture Clash (comedy group) 119
curandera 69

Dachau 25
Days of Obligation: An Argument with My Mexican Father 89–92
Deleuze, Gilles 12, 16, 19, 146, 167–168, 185–187, 188, 192, 193
defamiliarization 29–30
"Delivering the Punch Line: Racial Combat as Comedy in Gus Lee's *China Boy*" 143–144
Deloria, Philip 126
deterritorialization 146, 147, 167, 182, 185–186
D'Haen, Theo L. 32–33
The Dialogic Imagination 17, 116, 124, 147

"Discourse in the Novel" 147
Displacing Whiteness 6
Disrupted Subjects 85
diversity 9
Dix, Otto 25
Domina, Lynn 110
Doty, William G. 99
the dozens (Signifyin') 170
Dream a Little: Land and Social Justice in Modern America 46
Duelling Languages: Grammatical Structure in Codeswitching 148

"Earthly Relations, Carnal Knowledge: Southwestern American Indian Women Writers and Landscape" 51, 58
Eaton, Edith (Sui Sin Far) 102
Eaton, Winnifred (Miss Watanna) 102
The Education of Little Tree 6
"*Entartete*" *Kunst* ("*Degenerate*" *Art*) 25
Equal Opportunity Program (Affirmative Action) 7
Erdrich, Louise 15, 18, 41, 80, 103, 106, 108, 165, 174
Ernst, Max 25
Escandón, María Amparo 36–38, 131
Esperanza's Box of Saints 36–38, 41, 131–134
ethnic (definition) 2–3
ethnic pride 82, 84
ethnicity: defintion 3; and race 6
ex-votos 127–129

Fa Mu Lan (legendary Chinese woman warrior) 14–15, 92, 94–95, 96, 99, 180
The Fantastic: A Structural Approach to a Literary Genre 24*fn*
fantasy 23, 24, 29, 44
Fantini, Alvino E. 155
Faris, Wendy 13, 22, 22*fn*, 32, 33, 34, 38–39, 40, 41
A Feather on the Breath of God 19, 86*fn*, 180–182, 183
Fisher, Dexter 125, 191
Fishkin, Shelley Fisher 164
Fitts, Dudley 28
Flax, Jane 85
Flores, Angel 22*fn*, 28
F.O.B. 83, 92, 95–96
Foreman, P. Gabrielle 23
Frankenberg, Ruth 6
"Frontiering Tayo's *Interior Landscapes*" 49

Garcia, Reyes 56
García Márquez, Gabriel 13, 31–32
"The Garden of Forking Paths" 30, 32
Gates, Henry Louis 18, 167–168

Gilbert, Joanne R. 115, 117
Giving Birth to Thunder, Sleeping with his Daughter: Coyote Builds North America 120, 121–122, 123
Glazer, Nathan 5
"Going for the Knockout: Confronting Whiteness in Gus Lee's *China Boy*" 144
Greenblatt, Stephen 27–28
Griever 125
Gross, Lawrence W. 108
Grosz, George 25
Guattari, Félix 12, 16, 19, 146, 167–168, 185–187, 188, 192, 193
Guenther, Irene 25
Gutwirth, Claudia 104, 107
Gwan Gung (legendary Chinese warrior) 92, 95

Hafen, P. Jane 62, 65
Hawai'i One Summer 74
Hawley, Steven 97
heritage culture 11
heritage language 11
heteroglossia 17, 147, 186, 189
heterotext 158
Hom, Marlon K. 76*fn*
House Made of Dawn 14, 61–68, 84, 86, 86*fn*, 166–167
House of Houses 18, 38, 41, 162–163
Hsu, Cho-yun 81
Hsüan-tsang (7th century Buddhist monk) 100
humor: 114–145; and American Dream 139–145; and mitigating tragedy 124–134; and overturning the status quo 114–124; and religion 127–129, 131–134
The Hundred Secret Senses 39–40
Hunger of Memory: The Education of Richard Rodriguez 18, 89, 91, 171–172, 178–179
Hwang, David Henry 83, 92, 95

I Ching (Book of Changes) 135*fn*–136*fn*, 173
identity: 1, 15; chicano 127; and language 153, 155, 159, 160–161, 180, 182; multicultural 80–113, 180–182, 188; and place 45, 47, 48, 49, 52, 57, 66, 67, 68, 71, 73, 74, 77, 78–79; politics 189; postcolonial 184; public 172, 178–179
Identity: Community, Culture, Difference 9
Immigrant Subjectivities in Asian American and Asian Diaspora Literatures 189–190
"Immigration and Diaspora" 142
Immigration and Nationality Act 2, 82
"In the Belly of a Laughing God: Reading Humor and Irony in the Poetry of Joy Harjo" 115

An Interethnic Companion to Asian American Literature 142
interlingualism 160
The International Encyclopedia of Social Sciences 98–99
Islas, Arturo 73*fn*, 136, 137, 192
"Iyani: It Goes this Way" 52

Jen, Gish 16, 18, 139, 141*fn*, 142, 144, 164–165, 172–173, 186
Jin, Ha (Jin Xue Fei) 149
Johnson, David 71, 191
Johnson, Lyndon 2
The Journey to the West 15, 99–100, 101
The Joy Luck Club 187
Jünger, Ernst 26

Kafka, Franz 28, 29, 146, 153
Kafka: Toward a Minor Literature 12, 16, 146, 167–168, 185–187
Kaiser, Georg 26
Karem, Jeff 50
"Keeping the Native on the Reservation" 50
Keres Indians 58
Kim, Elaine 93, 95, 177, 178
Kingston, Maxine Hong 1, 14, 15, 18, 71, 72, 73, 78, 79, 80, 86*fn*, 92, 94*fn*, 100, 100*fn*, 101, 135, 136, 138, 175–179, 180, 187, 190, 192
Kocks, Dorothee E. 46
Kubin, Alfred 25

Landmarks of Healing: A Study of House Made of Dawn 62
"Landscapes of the Magical" 71
Landscapes of the New West 10, 47, 52, 74
"The Language of Betrayal" 149
The Last Report on the Miracles of Little No Horse 108
Leal, Luis 22*fn*, 29
Lee, A. Robert 45
Lee, Gus 143, 144
Leveen, Lois 117, 119, 145
Lim, Shirley Geok-Lin 142
liminal (liminality) 98–99, 113, 177–178
"Little Miracles, Kept Promises" 127–129, 134
Living Sideways: Tricksters in American Indian Oral Traditions 97–98
The Living Tree: The Changing Meaning of Being Chinese Today 82
"Locating the Uranium Mine" 52
The Lone Ranger and Tonto Fistfight in Heaven 115–116, 122–123, 125–126
Long, Sylvester 5
longhair 63

Lopez, Barry 120–121, 122
Love Medicine 15, 18, 41, 80, 103–106, 107, 165–166, 174
Lowe, John 125, 136
Lu, Hsun 150–151

Ma, Sheng-mei 189–190
Mackin, Jonna 103
"A Madman's Diary" 150–151
"Magic Realism, New Objectivity, and the Arts During the Weimar Republic" 25
magical realism 12, 13, 21–44, 80
Magical Realism: Theory, History, Community 22, 22*fn*, 33–34
"Magical Realism and Postmodernism: Decentering Privileged Centers" 32–33
Magical Realism in Contemporary Chicano Fiction 25
"Magical Realism in Spanish American Fiction" 22*fn*, 28
"Magical Realism in Spanish American Literature" 22*fn*, 29
"Making Metaphor Happen: Space, Time and Trickster Sign" 97
Malcolm, Cheryl Alexander 144
Mallea, Eduardo 28
"Marked and Unmarked Choices of Code Switching in Bilingual Poetry" 163
marvelous 27–28
Marvelous Possessions: The Wonder of the New World 27
marvelous real 28
mascots 126
melting pot 4–5
Mendieta-Lombardo, Eva 163
mestiza 87, 89
mestizaje 28, 87
mestizo 87, 91, 158
metalanguage 18, 148, 171–175
"Metamorphoses of Fictional Space: Magical Realism" 23, 46
Metamorphosis 29
Mexican American War 48
Miller, Arthur 78
minor literature 12, 16, 146, 185, 188, 193
Mitchell, David T. 184–185
Momaday, N. Scott 14, 61, 62, 63, 84, 85, 86, 86*fn*, 166, 167, 190–191
Mona in the Promised Land 16, 143, 144
The Monkey King 15, 99–103, 125, 135–136
"Monkey Kings and Mojo: Postmodern Ethnic Humor in Kingston, Reed and Vizenor" 136
Mora, Pat 18, 38, 41, 162–163, 164
Morgan, Wm. T., Jr. 190–191

Morrison, Toni 39, 86*fn*, 169, 170
mosaic (multicultural) 5
Movements in Chicano Poetry 161–162, 182
Moynihan, Daniel Patrick 5
Mulberry and Peach: Two Women of China (Sang ching yu tau hong) 17, 86*fn*, 149–150
Multilingual America: Transnationalism, Ethnicity, and the Languages of American Literature 150*fn*, 182–183
Multicultural American Litrature 45
multiple subjectivity 85–86, 86–113
multipleperspectivity 185
"Multiples: On the Contemporary Politics of Subjectivity" 85
Myers-Scotton, Carol 148*fn*
myth 98
"Myth and Ceremony in Contemporary North American Native Fiction" 52–53
"Myth and Symbol" 98–99

N. Scott Momaday: The Cultural and Literary Background 63
The Names 62, 62*fn*, 63*fn*
Nanabozho (Chippewa trickster) 15, 103–107
Narcisi, Lara 78, 102, 136
"Native American Tricksters: Literary Figuras of Community Transformers" 99
Nee, Phil 119
Nelson, Robert 46, 51*fn*–52*fn*, 52, 53, 64, 66, 67
Nieh, Hua-ling 17, 86*fn*, 149
Nunez, Sigrid 19, 86*fn*, 180–182, 183

"On the Marvelous Real in America" 13, 22*fn*, 26
One Hundred Years of Solitude 31–32
O'Neill, Eugene 78
Onís, Frederico de 32
"Only When I Laugh: Textual Dynamics of Ethnic Humor" 117
Orr, Lisa 53
An Other Tongue 189
Outka, Paul 72, 73

pachucos 160
Palm Trees Again, Palm Trees Again (You jian zong lu, you jian zong lu) 86*fn*
"Pan-Indianism and Tribal Sovereignties in *House Made of Dawn* and *The Names*" 62, 65
"Past-On Stories: History and the Magically Real, Morrison and Allende on Call" 23
Patell, Cyrus 56
Peñalosa, Fernando 154

Pérez-Torres, Rafael 161, 182
Performing Marginality 115
Perry, Donna 192
Pinder, Wilhelm 25
Place and Vision: The Function of Landscape in Native American Fiction 46, 51*fn*–52*fn*, 52, 53, 64, 66, 67
Playing Indian 126
pocho (Chicano code-switching) 154
Post-Expressionism 24, 25
Post-Expressionism, Magical Realism 24, 26
postcolonial 184–185
Postethnic Narrative Criticism 22, 40
postmodernism 32–33, 34
Powell, Timothy 7
Proust, Marcel 28
"Publish or Perish: Food, Hunger, and Self-Construction in Maxine Hong Kingston's *The Woman Warrior*" 72
Punchlines: The Case for Racial, Ethnic and Gender Humor 118–119

racial shadow 112–113, 177–178
Radway, Janice 2*fn*
Rappoport, Leon 118
Reading Asian American Literature: From Necessity to Extravagance 95, 112–113, 138, 177–178
real maravilloso (marvelous real) 28
Realism 24
Rebellious Laughter: People's Humor in American Culture 116–117, 117*fn*
Rebolledo, Tey Diana 124
"Redefining Chinese American Literature from a LOWINUS Perspective: Two Recent Examples" 150*fn*
"A Reflection on Marginality" 81
"Refugee Ship" 161
"Rethinking American Culture: Maxine Hong Kingston's Cross-Cultural *Tripmaster Monkey*" 77
Revista de Occidente (journal) 26
rites of passage 98
"Ritual and Renewal: Keres Traditions in Leslie Silko's 'Yellow Woman'" 58
Rodriguez, Richard 15, 18, 89–92, 94, 171–172, 178–179
Roh, Franz 13, 24–25, 26
Roland, Walter 25
"Roots and Changing Identity" 82
Ruoff, A. LaVonne 58
Russian Formalists 29
Rutherford, Jonathan 9

The Sacred Hoop 51, 53, 55
Saeta, Elsa 125

salad bowl (multicultural model) 5
Sanchez, Rosaura 155, 156, 157
Sang ching yu tau hong (Mulberry and Peach) 17, 86*fn*, 149–150
Scarberry-García, Susan 62
"Scheherazade's Children: Magical Realism and Post-modern Fiction" 13, 34
Scheninger, Lee 57
Schubnell, Matthias 63
September 11, 2001 5
Shakespeare 124
Shan, Te-hsing 150*fn*
Siebert, Gayle Ruth 49
signifiers 9
Signifying (Signifyin') 18, 148, 167–171
Signifying Monkey 169
The Signifying Monkey: A Theory of African-American Literary Criticism 168
silence 18, 148, 175–182; articulate silence 179–180
Silko, Leslie Marmon 13, 41, 48, 49, 51, 52, 57, 58, 61, 67, 96, 110, 124, 125, 187, 191
Simpkins, Scott 29, 32
Skenazy, Paul 78, 192
Slippery Characters: Ethnic Impersonators and American Identities 5
Smith, Jeanne Rosier 10, 77, 104
Smith, Patricia Clarkson 51, 58
So, Christine 143–144
So Far from God 34–36, 40, 83, 129–131, 134, 187
"Social Cues and Language Choice: Case Study of a Bilingual Child" 155
sojourner 82–83
Sollors, Werner 4, 6, 150*fn*, 182–183
Song of Solomon 169, 170
Songs of Gold Mountain: Cantonese Rhymes from San Francisco Chinatown 76*fn*
"Sources of Magic Realism / Supplements to Realism in Contemporary Latin American Literature" 29
Spilling the Beans 119–120, 127
"Split Infinities: The Comedy of Performative Identity in Maxine Hong Kingston's *Tripmaster Monkey*" 103
"'Stop Making Sense': Trickster Variations in the Fiction of Louise Erdrich" 104
Storyteller 110
Sui Sin Far (Edith Eaton) 102

Tan, Amy 39–40, 187
Tarter, James 52
tejanos (native Texans) 47
"The Territorialization of the Imaginary in Latin America: Self-Affirmation and Resistance to Metropolitan Paradigms" 22*fn*

"Theorizing the Earth" 53
The Three Kingdoms 76, 102
Todorov, Tzvetan 24*fn*
Toelken, Barre 121, 123
Tracks 80, 107–110
Treaty of Guadalupe-Hidalgo 48, 81
"The Trickster and World Maintenance: An Anishinaabe Reading of Louise Erdrich's *Tracks*" 108
tricksters 10, 14, 15, 80, 97–113, 169
Tripmaster Monkey: His Fake Book 15, 74–78, 100–103, 135–136
Ts'ai, Yen (2nd cent. Chinese poet) 180
Tu, Wei-ming 82
Turner, Victor 98–99, 178
Typical American 18, 139, 164, 173

van Gennep, Arnold 98
A Very Serious Thing: Women's Humor and American Culture 114
"The Violence of Hybridity in Silko and Alexie" 56
Virgin of Guadalupe 15, 89, 90–91, 92, 127, 128, 160–161
Vizenor, Gerald 125

Walker, Nancy 114
"Walking the Thin Line: Humor in Chicana Literature" 124
Wang, L. Ling-chi 82
Warhol, Andy 30
The Water Margin 77, 102
"'The Way I Heard It': Autobiography, Tricksters and Leslie Marmon Silko's *Storyteller*" 110

"The Way to Individuation in Anaya's *Bless Me, Ultima*" 70
The Way to Rainy Mountain 191*fn*
White Snow, Red Dust: An Episode in the Maple Country (*Bai xue hong chen*) 82, 152–153
Wilson, Rawdon 23, 46
"Wittman's Transitions: Multivocality and the Play of *Tripmaster Monkey*" 78, 102, 136
Woman Hollering Creek and Other Stories 127–129
The Woman Warrior: Memoirs of a Girlhood Among Ghosts 1, 15, 18, 71–74, 79, 86*fn*, 92–95, 136–138, 175–179, 180, 187, 188, 190, 192
Wong, Sau-ling Cynthia 95, 112–113, 138, 177–178
The Writer as Migrant 149
"Writing Nature: Silko and Native Americans as Nature Writers" 57
Writing Tricksters: Mythic Gambols in American Ethnic Literature 10, 104
Wu, Ch'eng-en 99–100

Yalom, Marilyn 73*fn*, 136–137, 192
Yan, Zhen 82, 152
"Yellow Woman" 14, 57–61, 67, 96–97, 187
Yin, Xiao-huang 149
You jian zong lu, you jian zong lu (*Palm Trees Again, Palm Trees Again*) 86*fn*
Yu, Anthony C. 101
Yu, Li-hua 86*fn*

Zamora, Lois Parkinson 22, 22*fn*, 33

www.ingramcontent.com/pod-product-compliance
Lightning Source LLC
Chambersburg PA
CBHW032056300426
44116CB00007B/772